COURTLINESS AND LITERATURE
IN MEDIEVAL ENGLAND

David Burnley

COURTLINESS AND LITERATURE IN MEDIEVAL ENGLAND

LONGMAN
LONDON AND NEW YORK

Addison Wesley Longman
Edinburgh Gate, Harlow,
Essex CM20 2JE, England
and Associated Companies throughout the world.

Published in the United States of America
by Addison Wesley Longman Inc., New York.

© Addison Wesley Longman Limited 1998

First published 1998

ISBN 0 582 29216 6 PPR
ISBN 0 582 29215 8 CSD

British Library Cataloguing-in-Publication Data
A catalogue record of this book is available from the
British Library

Library of Congress Cataloging-in-Publication Data
Burnley, J.D.
    Courtliness and literature in medieval England / David Burnley.
        p.   cm. -- (Longman medieval and Renaissance library)
    Includes bibliographical references (p.   ) and index.
    ISBN 0-582-29216-6 (CSD). -- ISBN 0-582-29215-8 (PPR)
    1. English literature--Middle English, 1100–1500--History and criticism. 2. Great
Britain--Court and courtiers--History. 3. Literature and society--England--History.
4. Civilization, Medieval, in literature. 5. Courts and courtiers in literature.
6. Courtly love in literature. 7. Courtesy in literature. 8. Chivalry in literature.
I. Title. II. Series.
PR275.C65B87   1997
820.9'353--dc21   97-8831
                                                                    CIP

Set by 7 in 10.5/12pt Bembo
Produced by Longman Singapore Publishers (Pte) Ltd.
Printed in Singapore

Contents

FOR EMMA

Abbreviations

AN	Anglo-Norman
ANTS	Anglo Norman Text Society
BD	*Book of the Duchess* (Chaucer)
BLE	*Book of London English* (ed. Chambers and Daunt)
CA	*Confessio Amantis* (Gower)
CFMA	Classiques françaises du moyen âge
CT	*The Canterbury Tales*
EETS ES	Early English Text Society Extra Series
EETS OS	Early English Text Society Original Series
GP	*General Prologue (The Canterbury Tales)*
HF	*House of Fame*
KnT	*Knight's Tale*
LGW	*Legend of Good Women* (Chaucer)
MchT	*Merchant's Tale*
ME	Middle English
MED	*Middle English Dictionary*
MLProl	*Man of Law's Prologue*
MO	*Mirour de l'Omme*
ns	new series
OED	*Oxford English Dictionary*
ParsT	*Parson's Tale*
PL	*Patrologia Latina* (ed. Migne)
RS	Rolls Series
RTC	*Le Roman de Toute Chevalerie*
RvT	*Reeve's Tale*
SATF	Société des anciens textes français
ShT	*Shipman's Tale*
SNT	*Second Nun's Tale*
ST	*Summa Theologiae*
TC	*Troilus and Criseyde* (Chaucer)
WBProl	*Wife of Bath's Prologue*
WBT	*Wife of Bath's Tale*

Preface

Felix qui potuit rerum cognoscere causas.

(Virgil, *Georgics* 2, 1, 490)

The motto ('Lucky is he who has been able to understand the causes of things') which the University of Sheffield chose to place beneath its arms, probably with scientific explanations in mind, has a peculiar appropriateness to this book, and especially to this preface to it. This is an extended essay which seeks to explain some features of human behaviour both as it is depicted in medieval texts and as it is still experienced in everyday life. Especially, it tries to bridge the gap between our modern experience and medieval idealism when the latter seems inexplicable to the former. But the sentiment is appropriate also in another way, for medieval books often began with a rehearsal of the causes why the work came into being. These causes were multiple and need not be discussed here, but like earlier books, and indeed like most phenomena, this essay too has multiple causes. It originated many years ago when I was a postgraduate at the University of Durham studying Anglo-Norman and Middle English romance; the conceptions of appropriate behaviour encountered in those early romances subsequently proved useful as a foundation for understanding the values of later medieval literature. It should be emphasized, however, that this was not an introduction to dispassionate social history; the perspective is too biased and the coverage of society too incomplete. The medieval literature of England is a mirror not of how people really behaved, but more of how a section of society felt they *ought to* behave, and certainly of how they wished to be viewed by their contemporaries. A certain stability in their outlook is preserved throughout which makes this a topic worthy of investigation. All aspects of approved behaviour are reflected in it, from politeness in speech and

helpfulness in demeanour to skills in hunting, in chess or even in
versifying. We can identify with many of these values and activities.
Walter Map tells the story of how Henry I's chamberlain had got
into the habit of drinking up the glass of wine provided as a
nightcap for the king, but often left unfinished. When Henry rose
in the night and found his wine gone, instead of making a fuss, he
henceforward ordered two glasses to be provided. Map approves
this wisdom and tact as an example of courtliness, and we can easily
concur. Other circumstances are more difficult to recognize. Not
least among the pastimes of a leisured society was the discussion of
its own behaviour, and often of what we now call 'relationships'.
There has been a lengthy tradition – now fortunately modified – of
discussing the medieval and early Renaissance experience of 'courtly
love' as if it were simply an adult game played by rules like chess or
backgammon. These rules have often seemed bizarre, and the behaviour of the participants in the game has seemed unbelievable to
modern readers. A further cause of this book is the desire to place
the important theme of love in medieval English literature into a
context which may help to explain the manner in which love is
presented in these medieval works. But the overwhelming cause of
the entire book is the desire to help to mediate the self-reflexive
picture of medieval society in England to a modern world where its
values are becoming more and more difficult to understand.
Understanding, of course, need not mean approval. Medieval attitudes
to hunting, women, or to the under-privileged are not congruent
with those widespread today. Yet there may be something to learn
simply from observing an alternative configuration of social values,
and the past has as much right to our understanding as exotic
modern societies. Indeed, our own past may cast some light upon
the structures of the modern society in which we live, and occasionally I may have prompted speculation along these lines, perhaps
in terms of modern business or military ethics which reflect
medieval perspectives, but in general I have tried to represent the
medieval world in its own terms without evaluative comparison
with more recent perspectives and attitudes. Such comparison has
been left implicit.

The method which I have adopted in reconstructing the values
of the medieval period is an eclectic one. It is essentially one of
calling to witness relevant passages from texts written in Middle
English or Anglo-Norman, and sometimes supported by Latin sources.

The process of interpretation is focused by the informal lexical analysis of words which seem to be of key importance to the concepts with which I am concerned. However, my purpose has been to present the result of interpretation in as accessible a manner as possible, so that there is very little discussion or justification of the lexicological procedures involved. Because I wanted to make the medieval sources speak for themselves, making the associations between words available to the reader, I have generally quoted texts in the original languages; but I have always provided translations into modern English. For similar reasons, I have not sought to overload my pages with footnotes, but incorporated much of the essential documentation into the text. Although no chapters reproduce them exactly, some of the material has appeared in more fully documented form in articles published in *The Review of English Studies, Modern Language Review, Studia Neophilologica, Speculum,* and elsewhere. I have, however, tried to record in the bibliography a reference to all titles and authors to which I am knowingly indebted, and I apologize for any omissions.

The historical span which this book covers is approximately four hundred and fifty years from the Norman Conquest until the end of the fifteenth century. It considers courtliness as essentially a medieval French inheritance, and does not follow its reflexes into the Renaissance or trace its antecedents in Old English. The former period's concern with courtesy and nurture is familiar from translations of Italian works and their reflection in the English works of Surrey, Spenser, and (often ironically) Shakespeare; but courtliness is not often associated with Old English. Nevertheless, although it was not so prominent a feature of literature in earlier times, recent authors, such as Jaeger and Scaglione, have drawn our attention to the development of courtliness in a Germanic background. The highest levels of Old English secular society focused on the community of the hall, so that the protocols of social interaction there were inevitably of importance, and although expressed in different terms, courtly behaviour certainly existed in Anglo-Saxon times. In some scenes in *Beowulf,* in the assertion of a woman's role expressed in the *Maxims,* and in the 'allegiance scene' in *The Wanderer* we are given glimpses of it. This last has been noted by scholars. Interestingly, a second scene in which the exile sees in his mind's eye his erstwhile hall-companions and greets them *gliwstafum* has not usually been perceived equally as a memory of court custom.

The form *gliwstaf* is normally translated 'cries of joy', but a supplement to Ælfric's *Glossary* (*Volume of Vocabularies*, ed. Wright) gives for *wynsum gliw* the Latin *facetiae*, a word which was associated with *facundia* and *urbanitas* in later Latin, and which is rendered *curtesie* and *gaberie* in Old French. Is it not possible that the exile, prefiguring the later custom advocated in the *Roman de la Rose*, eloquently greets his familiar visions with the polished phrases of courtly address, but receives no cordial reply? Whatever the answer to this question, it is important to acknowledge that post-Conquest courtesy did not emerge *ex vacuo* any more than it evaporated at the dawn of the Renaissance. Ideals which determine humans' behaviour towards one another are the persistent and inevitable consequence of living in an ordered society. They are ever-present, but their chameleon nature sometimes hides this obvious fact from the observer. This book seeks not only to delineate some of those ideals, but to trace some of the changes which took place during that part of the story which we call the middle ages, when courtliness and French cultural values were nearly synonymous in England.

The topic, even within its chronological limits, is a rich one, and cannot be exhaustively treated in a book of this kind. I have been content with tracing some of the themes which surface and submerge, separate and re-combine during the four hundred and fifty years of the later middle ages. Among these are the emergence of courtly values from the background of the feudal hall, the values of heroic literature, and monastic culture, the confrontation between transcendental Christian values and the secular and aesthetic ones of *curtesie*, and the accommodation reached between the two perspectives. But the ideals of courtliness faced modification from a different perspective: the philosophical tradition which challenged the assumption that nobility was an inheritance, locating it in the virtue of the individual, which was matched by the social and economic concerns of a more pastorally oriented clergy, whose criticism of courtliness was based on more pragmatic grounds. The earliest French texts acknowledged the possibility of courtly peasants and burgesses, but these only became influential with the development of a wealthy bourgeoisie, who found the philosophical and pastoral perspectives congenial to their concerns, and courtly values were adopted to suit the city council rather than the king's *curia*. The conception of a world in which status depended on good citizenship and reputation, and advancement on individual merit and politeness, was emerging in the late medieval period, and that in which glory depended on the combination of circumstances of birth and a capacity for action began its long decline.

The preparation of this book has been long, and interrupted by other activities, so it is more than usually difficult to specify acknowledgements in the conventional way. I have learned a great deal from colleagues both home and abroad, in conferences and in conversation, from my fellow-teachers in Sheffield and from the students I have taught. It is simplest and fairest to record my appreciation of fellow medievalists everywhere, who have been without exception *curteis and servysable*. Deserting anonymity, I should make special mention of my family, and of my wife Helen, who has always found the resources to treat my occasional neglect of family duties with tact and humour.

JDB
University of Sheffield
September 1996

Chapter 1

Prologue

The prudent man must understand how appalling it will be when all this world shall stand devoid of prosperity, as now variously throughout this earth, walls stand blown by the wind, covered in frost, the ramparts ruined.

(*The Wanderer*, ed. Dunning and Bliss, 74–7)

The days have been slipping away, and all the glories of the earthly kingdom; there are now neither kings, emperors, nor gold-givers as once there were.

(*The Seafarer*, 80–3)

The Old English poets considering the approach of the millennium preferred to look back gloomily on the glories of the past and reflect on what they saw as a history of decline. The future seemed all too finite. For, as the world approached its thousandth year since the birth of Christ, many in Christendom felt justified in a belief that time had almost reached its end and that Doomsday might dawn on the morrow. Past experience encouraged apprehension. Christendom had passed through two centuries of violent disruption: internally, at the hands of rapacious Christians, and from without under the onslaught of Vikings, Moors, and Magyars.[1] Yet, in fact, the worst was already over. Even as Olaf Tryggvason promoted the evangelization of the Viking world, the Church in France brought together Christian magnates to swear compacts of peace in Le Puy (975), Charroux, near Poitiers (989), Limoges (1000), Beauvais (1023), Toulonges near Perpignan (1041), and Narbonne (1054).[2] In Spain the days of Moorish domination were past their peak. Indeed, on the continent of Europe, the eleventh century can be seen as ushering in a new period of prosperity and security, fostered by the increasing moral authority of the Church and upheld by the organized military and political power of major landowners under the feudal system. But it held special tribulations for the population of England, who still had to endure conquest by

Normans and Scandinavians, and they faced the doomsday of the assessment and expropriation of their land by a foreign conqueror. If the eleventh century was a watershed for western civilization in general, in England it was so in double measure, for in addition to the changes which took place in the whole of Europe at this time, England also underwent the nearly complete substitution of its ruling class, and many of the cultural values which they had esteemed and upheld, at the hands of Duke William of Normandy. An account of the events leading to the Norman Conquest, and its success at Hastings, is contained in the embroidery which Bishop Odo, William's half-brother, commissioned for his cathedral at Bayeux not many years afterwards. The account given was probably worked by English seamstresses, but it is designed to present the Norman point of view, and its version of events should be handled circumspectly.[3] But its reporting of the events of political history concerns us less than its iconography, and in particular certain of the scenes which its designer apparently considered important to his overall conception. They are scenes whose importance as images was also recognized by literary authors writing in and just after this time of cultural transition.

The first of these key images is a group of three connected scenes occurring nearly a third of the way through the tapestry. They lack the exuberance of many of the accompanying battle scenes, but their importance to the point of view being pressed by the overall design cannot be over-emphasized. In the first of these Harold has been shipwrecked on the French coast, is rescued, and taken to meet William; in the second, he has joined him in a successful campaign against one of his enemies, Conon of Britanny. Harold and William are seen standing on the battlefield facing one another, the former holding a pennant. William reaches out, and with his left hand places a helmet on Harold's head. Above them is the explanation in Latin *hic Willelm dedit Haroldo arma* 'here William gave arms to Harold'. This is immediately followed by a representation of their journey to Bayeux, where the final scene of this little group takes place. In it William is shown enthroned in majesty, his sword lying across his shoulder, while before him Harold stands with his hands resting on two reliquaries. The Latin gloss reads *ubi Harold sacramentum fecit Willelmo duci* 'Where Harold made an oath to Duke William'. The arms-giving and the subsequent oath thus form part of a strategy by which the designer of the tapestry asserted Harold's debt to William, and in particular in these scenes expressed that debt as one of a special kind of loyalty:

that loyalty owed by a vassal to his lord, or by a knight to him who grants him arms.

The concepts of vassalage and knighthood are unlikely to have held the same compulsion for Harold as they did for William, for although both Anglo-Saxon and Norman culture had together inherited from the Germanic past a regard for the obligations existing between lord and man, the institution of knighthood had developed only on the Continent, where it had become closely entangled with that more institutionalized kind of vassalage to which eighteenth-century political commentators later gave the name, 'the feudal system'.[4] The interdependence of feudal obligations and knighthood is connoted in the close juxtaposition of the oath of fealty and the grant of arms in the imagery of the Bayeux tapestry. It is apparent also in the post-Conquest history of the English language itself, for the Norman word for a mounted retainer, *chivalers*, was not adopted by the English, who instead preferred their native words *ridere* and *cniht*. The difference in etymologies illustrates a difference in perception. In French, the earliest connotations of the word *chivalers* must have been those of a mounted warrior, fighting on horseback (*a cheval*) in a way unknown to the Anglo-Saxons, whose battles were infantry engagements even at the time of Hastings. The English word *ridere* testifies to a similar perception, but when they called such warriors *cnihtas*, the English were using a word whose earlier meaning had been 'retainer' or 'servant', thus ignoring the role of cavalrymen to emphasize rather a subservient position within the feudal hierarchy. Clearly, in this early period, the conception of knighthood did not necessarily carry the associations of chivalric idealism and elevated status which had been developed by the fifteenth century. Although economic forces linked chivalric status to land-holding, and thus enhanced status, the system of feudal obligations and knighthood are in principle separable; and since both play such an important role in the literary representation of the society out of which courtliness grew, it will be worth setting aside a page or two to orientate ourselves in the details of each in turn.

The system of mutual obligations and loyalties, which functioned so effectively to impose peace and order in England after the Conquest, was descended from Carolingian vassalage and from ceremonies of fealty and homage comparable to those mentioned in earlier Anglo-Saxon literature. A similar affective dimension to that evoked in Old English poetry is suggested also within the feudal relationship by the use of the word *amor* to refer to fealty. But too

much should not be read into this, since the word could be interpreted to mean little more than that two men bound by an oath
would refrain from making war on each other.[5] Within this modest
requirement, the oath of fealty was seen as binding, and could only
be honourably revoked by a public act of *défiance* (Lat. *diffidatio*).
The binding nature of Harold's oath is made more apparent in the
Bayeux tapestry by the way in which it is sworn on the relics of
the saints, and, thus, sponsored by the Church. By encouraging
such sacred oaths, the Church united the social order imposed on
earth by feudal commitments with the celestial order guaranteed by
God, so that fealty became a matter not simply of personal honour
but of religious duty.

The feudal relationship differed from early vassalage also in the
fact that fealty carried with it the presumption of special obligations
legally imposed on both parties. Lord and vassal now owed each
other particular 'services' (*servitium*) as a consequence of fealty. The
vassal's service to his lord took two forms: that associated with
military and practical matters, known as 'aid' or 'help' (*auxilium*),
and that associated with the peaceful management of his affairs,
known as 'counsel' (*consilium*). Although *auxilium* was romantically
supposed to imply personal aid in prosecuting wars, it could also be
commuted to cash payments to be used for such military purposes,
or for important social occasions such as the knighting of the lord's
eldest son, the marriage of his eldest daughter, or the ransom of the
lord himself. It could imply no more than armed attendance on one
of the lord's excursions through his domains, providing in effect an
armed escort, often with little more than ceremonial function. It
may even mean providing such a company to attend the lord on
pilgrimage. *Consilium* was an obligation to make oneself available for
consultation when required, to offer advice and guidance in
political or administrative decisions. The discharge of this obligation
of *consilium* is, in fact, the remote ancestor of the modern
parliament.[6] In return for such services, the lord offered his vassal
protection and maintenance. The former may be as military aid,
calling upon the services perhaps of his other vassals, or it may be
legal protection by defending his dependant in a court of law;
maintenance was provided ideally by that grant of land, known as a
'fief' or *feudum* (from which the word 'feudalism' was derived).
The vassal, under the protection of his lord, was expected to
maintain himself from the proceeds of this fief, with a sufficient
number of men to fulfil his obligation of *auxilium*. Important lords
and kings, whose possessions were large and whose political affairs

were complicated, or those who wished to impress by the magnificence of their way of life, could provide maintenance not simply by the grant of land but by the direct provision of board and lodging to those retainers who were required to be in close attendance. Although far-flung feudal retainers might be called to a *parlement* in their lord's hall in fulfilment of their duty of *consilium*, it was the permanent residents there, the members of his *familia*, or household, who formed a social milieu which, in larger examples, we call his 'court'.

The personnel actually present in an early medieval court would, of course, vary according to whether the household was that of a king or of a lesser nobleman. Literary sources portray a social spectrum extending from scullions to seneschals, but except for comic purposes, life in the kitchen is of little consequence in literature. The exception to this is when the hero's adventures lead him from the elevated circles in which he properly belongs to take up covert employment in the kitchen, as in various versions of the Havelok story or indeed in Chaucer's *Knight's Tale*. But literature is normally concerned with the military elite. Among these, certain distinctions can usefully be made, the most fundamental being that between those who owe service as the result of an act of fealty, and those, even of quite elevated status, who owe it in exchange for a salary. The latter in Anglo-Norman sources are *retenuz* or *soudeier* (the latter word is derived from the Latin coin *solidus*, 'shilling' with which he was paid, and is the origin of our modern word 'soldier'). These men, retained and paid by their lord for their services, are often mentioned with a hint of disdain in idealizing literary sources. Although salaried soldiers were certainly quite common, honour was considered to lie within the bounds of feudal loyalty and was not to be earned from wages. Among those attached to the household by ties of loyalty, Latin sources distinguish between the *juvenes* and *seniores*.[7] Although the words certainly have connotations of relative age, the former is often used to refer simply to those who have not yet attained knighthood or any position of responsibility, whereas the latter have the status of proved and valued members of the court community. The *juvenes*, who may in fact be no younger than many of the *seniores*, occupy a position of precarious prosperity, dependent entirely on their lord's favour, since they have not established possession of a fief, hold no office, and may not have attained knighthood. Among them may be numbered that group whom vernacular literary sources habitually call *ligers bacheliers* 'light bachelors', so contrasting their irresponsible existence with that of their betters, the *chivalers* and office-holders such as the *seneschals* (in Middle English, *steward*), who administered justice and managed the household, or the *mareschal*, who originally deputized for the lord as leader of his army.[8] These last were men at the summit of their career in feudal service, a position which is suggested, perhaps, by the name *honur*, which was given to the large fief to which they would retire at the end of their service at a royal court. At the foot of this career ladder are those youths, often the sons of vassals, who are attached to the court, and who are known as *valez* in Anglo-Norman sources, but in Middle English as *squiers* or *pages*. They are present in the court both to carry out certain domestic duties and also to learn the customs of the court and the military skills which they will need when they are armed as knights. They are often found in the care of an experienced man as tutor or *mestre*. Such young men, brought up and advanced within a household, are considered to owe loyalty and affection beyond that of ordinary fealty, and they are distinguished as *nourris*: that is, people nurtured (ME, *ynorisshed*) by the generosity of the lord himself. Betrayal by such an intimate member of the *familia* is naturally regarded as particularly heinous. In the late fourteenth century, Chaucer alludes to the special threat represented by the *famulier foo* (*CT, MchT,* 1784).

The estate of knighthood, towards which the young *valez* aspired, was, by the twelfth century, the most prestigious degree in feudal society. Its origin, however, is fraught with some controversy.[9] It has been argued that the beginnings were with the late Roman cavalryman, and that the adoption of the stirrup during the eighth century transformed the role and status of the mounted warrior. The horse, from being merely a convenient mode of transport, became an essential instrument of battlefield strategy. It was now possible to wield sword and lance from the saddle with deadly effect upon foot soldiers and less risk to oneself.[10] With their rapid deployment and overwhelming force, mounted warriors could then become a powerful new weapon in the century before the millennium. The details of this picture have been contested, at least for the earliest period,[11] but it cannot be denied that cavalry tactics could decisively change the course of battles, as they were to do at Hastings. Consequently, growing acknowledgement of the effectiveness of the mounted warrior − the *chivalers* − enhanced his value by comparison with that of ordinary infantry. Maintaining the horse and equipment of such warriors was costly. Nevertheless, possession of these advantages could quickly repay (in terms of success in battle and plunder) the investment made, and there are early records of great sums being paid for horse and armour. In later times, an economic incentive remained, even in times of peace, when fortunes could still be made from winnings in tournaments. By their efficiency and by their wealth, mounted warriors therefore established for themselves an elite position, and this *de facto* separation from the common herd soon found symbolic expression in the ceremonies associated with the attainment of knighthood. These, of course, were intimately connected with the hierarchy of feudal society. The young *bacheliers* in the household of his lord could hope eventually to be dubbed by him. In later times this ceremony of *adoubement* was attended by religious observances, the young knight keeping vigil before his arms placed on the altar on the night before the event, and a priest officiating at the grant of arms, as well as delivering the symbolic blow to which the word *adoubement* originally referred. But until the end of the twelfth century the business was largely secular, and when the lord symbolically girded on the sword of the new knight, both were well aware of the economic investment which had been made by supplying the arms. If an oath of fealty had not previously been made, it was a natural consequence of the bestowal of arms. Thus, whether Harold was actually knighted by William in the scene represented in the Bayeux tapestry, or merely commended by the presentation of arms, the sequence of events depicted follows a pattern which naturally leads on to an oath of fealty: dubbing, arming, and the fealty to a lord are tightly interwoven concepts.

The newly dubbed knight, then, occupied a position in his society which was defined by a matrix of relationships. Above all, by the loyalty which he owed his lord. But there were two other major axes on which his loyalty might be plotted, relics of the position of the Germanic warrior of the past: these were those of companionage and lineage. The former represents a special bond of loyalty and friendship between two or more equals, and may have various significances. The twelfth-century knight calls *cumpainz* (oblique form *cumpagnons*) those with whom he serves as fellow vassals in the hall of the same lord. Indeed, the etymology of the word – which is from a phrase meaning 'to share bread' – endorses this sense, but the word is also used in an extended sense between those who have sworn brotherhood. In addition, companionage may also exist between men related by blood, and here it is superimposed upon the ties of lineage, that loyalty which is owed by convention to the clan.

This network of loyalties which was the measure of the early medieval knight can be summed up in a common adjective used in
praise of the hero in epics and early romances alike: he repeatedly
attracts the epithet *li leals*. This does not necessarily imply loyalty to
any particular person, or on any special matter, but describes a
personality in whom integrity and loyalty are fundamental assets. In
the *Chanson de Roland*, which although written in France survives
complete only in an Anglo-Norman copy, the villain Ganelon is
assailed by the narrator with the epithets *li fels* (oblique case: *felon*)
'vile, treacherous (man)', *li parjurez* 'foresworn (man)'. The nature
of his villainy, which is asserted by these words, is that he has
betrayed those expectations of faith proper to a good knight and
vassal. Other insults offered in the poem, *bricun, culvert, de put aire*,
allude to the moral or social despicableness of his entire lineage.

If multi-faceted loyalty is one of the outstanding virtues esteemed in the *Chanson de Roland*, and breach of it the major vice,
the second outstanding virtue, as G.F. Jones has demonstrated, is
effectiveness.[12] Heroes are repeatedly called *proz*, and less often
vaillanz. The former word is derived from the Latin *prod est*, 'it is
profitable'; the latter means something very similar, 'worthy,
efficacious'. These approbatory epithets reflect virtues respected by
the small elite military group to which the knight belonged. By
comparison with later romantic conceptions of knighthood they are
of a strikingly unspiritual and secular kind, and this is emphasized
by the way in which the phrase *bon hum* 'good man' is repeatedly
used as an estimate simply of military prowess rather than of moral
character.[13] This amorality is apparent also in the way in which the
expression of efficacy in battle, perceived as a virtue, is sometimes
made in quite surprising terms, as when Roland himself is called
pesme e fiers, 'fierce and proud' or when *estultie* 'recklessness' and
legerie 'lightness, frivolity' are accepted as worthy characteristics in
such a context. The connotations of the latter two are usually with
rashness and folly, and the etymon of *pesme* is Latin *pessimus* 'worst'.
The word *fiers* and its noun *fierte* have been the subject of much
attention from Old French scholars, who have revealed two
important components of meaning – those of ferocity and of
pride.[14] Now, in the context of Christian humility and pacifism, all
these epithets may be taken to imply a totally reprehensible
character; but in the context of a military ethic maintained among a
small elitist group, where their violent consequences are turned
outwards against a common enemy, they can be regarded as
valuable assets. The dilemma posed by such figures in peacetime

society has found literary expression in figures from Heremod to Coriolanus, but such qualms do not at present concern us. It is from the moral imperatives of pride in arms and self-esteem, and from the unreflective and impulsive nature of his actions, that the knight draws that military effectiveness which makes him admired by his companions and valued by his lord.

The world he inhabits is not dominated by concepts of sin and consequent feelings of individual guilt and remorse in the one instance or quiet self-satisfaction in the other. Rather it is a world in which public reputation is paramount: the heroic life is a sequence of enterprises which must result either in public and triumphant success, and accompanying *joie*, or equally public and humiliating débâcle, and *doel*. The latter word, often inadequately translated as 'sorrow', carries with it powerful connotations of chagrin and frustration, just as *joie* carries those of unconcealed triumph. The life of the early medieval knight, like that of Germanic heroes before him, is compelled by the need to gain – along with the material advantage which is the outward sign of success – the praise and esteem, *los* and *pris*, of those whose opinion he values.[15]

The medieval knight is embedded in a society whose attention is directed towards him and constantly seeking to evaluate him. The recognition of his worth is therefore a controlling motive, and indeed the recognition of worth, designated by various words in various times and circumstances, is a major theme of medieval social commentary, as it is of this book. That such esteem is best gained by military success is the most enduring feature of the mythology of knighthood. Yet, even in earliest epic, it is implicitly acknowledged in the use of the words *proz* and *vaillanz* that the other virtues could play an equally practical role in achieving objectives. A man may be described as *proz* or *vaillanz* not simply for the force of his right arm, but also for his skills in debate and negotiation in the hall; after all, feudal obligations called the vassal to *consilium* as well as *auxilium*. Although medieval sources emphasize the importance to the knight of both chivalry and courtesy, these latter accomplishments which accompany adroitness in the company of the hall, and the esteem which is attached to it, are of much greater importance to the subject of this book than the military skills which were associated with *auxilium* and chivalry.

In the *Chanson de Roland* the interplay between the qualities effective for each of these functions not only initiates the action, when Ganelon's resentment at being chosen for a dangerous diplomatic mission (for which Roland is considered too impulsive) matures into his treachery; but also such interplay between civil and heroic virtues is ever-present in the poem at a thematic level. We shall return to this towards the end of this chapter, but first, in order to see some of what has already been described put to artistic use, we must return to the initial scene mentioned in the Bayeux tapestry. This scene occurs close to the beginning of the story, where Harold's ship goes aground in France and he is met by a party of Guy de Ponthieu's men. Harold and his companions are escorted to Guy's castle of Beaurain. It is not clear what Guy's men were doing at the time of the encounter, except that they evidently form an armed guard for their leader, who does not seem to resemble Guy himself as he is later portrayed at his castle. On the return to Beaurain, however, the leader of the Normans and Harold both carry hawks, and a pair of hounds bring up the rear of the procession. It is not unlikely, therefore, that the designer of these scenes imagined Harold to have been apprehended by one of Guy's household out hawking with a band of retainers. The significance of these deductions will become apparent in a moment, but we must first travel back in time beyond the Conquest to the year 1000, where this chapter began.

At about the millennium, an unknown Anglo-Saxon monk living in the Southern part of England copied down an epic re-working, itself some generations old, of a story from the traditional history of the Germanic peoples. The action was set in Dark Age Scandinavia, and it contains a scene in which its hero, Beowulf, an outstanding young warrior of the Geat people, crosses from his home in Southern Sweden with his band of followers to come to the aid of King Hrothgar of Denmark. As his boat comes to shore, its arrival is sighted from the cliff-top by one of Hrothgar's thanes, whose duty it is to keep constant watch against sudden and unexpected arrivals from the sea. As the Geats come ashore, the narrative perspective changes to that of the watchman, who is greatly impressed by the band he sees before him, and especially by its leader. Eager to discover who they are, he addresses them:

>   Næfre ic māran geseah
> eorla ofer eorþan,   þonne is ēower sum,
> secg on searwum;   nis þæt seldguma,
>   wǣpnum geweorðad,   næfne him his wlite lēoge,
> ænlic ansyn.

(247–51)

I have never seen a greater among men on earth than one of you, a
warrior in his armour; that is no serving man glorified by weapons,
unless his appearance belies him.

When he has satisfied himself of their lineage and purpose, the coast-
guard conducts the band to Hrothgar's hall, where they are formally
introduced and their worth re-appraised:

Hȳ on wiggetāwum   wyrðe þinceað
eorla geæhtlan;   hūru se aldor dēah,
sē þǣm heaðorincum   hider wisade.

(368–70)

They in their war-gear seem worthy of the esteem of warriors; indeed,
the leader was very competent who led those fighters here.

The lineage of the hero is repeated, and King Hrothgar declares his
familiarity with Beowulf's family background; at which he and his
companions are welcomed into the royal household.

More than a hundred and fifty years after these events were written down, and after that cultural revolution whose origins are recorded
in the Bayeux tapestry, a clerk associated with the court of Henry
II, one *mestre* Thomas, wrote in Anglo-Norman what he claimed to
be a sequel to his earlier successful story of Aalof. If we are to
believe him, his *Romance of Horn* is in fact the only remaining part
of a trilogy based on the traditional history of England. It tells how
Horn first lost his kingdom as the result of a pagan invasion in
which the king, his father, was killed. Then, after a series of
adventures in exile, during which he avenges himself on the pagans
and acquires a wife and military glory, he returns to repossess his
lost inheritance. The story pattern of Thomas's work, then, is that
of romance, but his system of values is epic and clerical. Early in
the work, the young Horn, accompanied by a band of equally
youthful companions, dispossessed and set adrift in a small boat, is
cast up on a strange shore. The band is found by King Hunlaf's
seneschal, Herlant, who immediately recognizes the nobility of the
castaways shining through their misfortunes, and wonders about
their allegiance:

ki sunt cil valletun?
Unc ne vi gencesors par ma salvatïun.
Joe savrai ki il sunt, de quel avoeisun.
Bien semble k'(e)il seient fiz de gentil baron.

(146–9)

Who are those young men? God save me, I never saw nobler. I will know who they are, of what allegiance. They certainly seem to be the sons of noblemen.

They are conducted to the king, who demands Horn's name and family:

> 'Di va! cum as [tu] nun? ki furent ti parent?
> Di mei la verité,   ne t'esmaier neënt
> Tu avras mes en mei   mult bon apuiëment'.

(240–2)

Say now, what is your name? Who were your kinsfolk? Tell me the truth, and don't be afraid; you will henceforth have secure protection from me.

Hunlaf receives a full and detailed account of Horn's lineage, after which he accepts Horn and his band into his care, later remarking that he knew his father.

These two accounts of a landing in a foreign land belong to different historical periods and are not directly connected in any way, but nevertheless there are striking parallels between them, and some significant differences. Apart from the narrative events themselves, in both the Anglo-Saxon and the Anglo-Norman stories we have a picture of a heroic band of young men whose nobility is self-evident to the observer. The composition of the group reflects a social organization in which loyalty is owed by a band of companions to a leader, who is himself outstanding from his men:

> Li plus jofnes de tuz   en est li plus senez:
> Cil vus nomera bien   trestuz ses parentez.
> El païs, dunt il sunt,   ert il lor avuez,
> Pur taunt est, çoe m'est vis,   tut li meuz enparlez
> E si est li plus genz   e li meuz figurez

(227–31)

The youngest of them all is the most intelligent: he will cite for you his entire lineage. In their own land, he was their acknowledged lord, for he seems to me quite the most eloquent, just as he is the noblest, and the most handsome.

In both accounts, too, lineage is of extreme importance. Nobility may be apparent from face and demeanour, but it is lineage which furnishes the credentials of unknown new arrivals, assuring their hosts of their good faith. It is for this reason that both poems show the hero being formally questioned about his family background and allegiance.

Alongside these similarities, which are the product of loyalties to lineage and lordship, coupled with political alliances and poor communications, there are also striking differences between the stories in terms of detailed handling. In *Beowulf* the landing is spotted by one whose whole duty seems to be to keep watch against enemy attack. His esteem for Beowulf and his men arises from his estimate of their warlike potential. But in *Horn*, Herlant encounters his visitors in the context of peacetime recreation. He is out hawking with a party of knights, his companions in the service of Hunlaf, when he comes across the castaways by chance. His admiration for Horn arises not so much from the latter's warlike appearance as from his apparent nobility. His leadership is assumed from the fact that he is obviously intelligent (*senez*) and eloquent (*enparlers*), two peacetime accomplishments which are developed as a balance to military prowess as the poem unfolds. In different roles, as protector and protégé, Beowulf and Horn are accepted into the household of their respective hosts, where both experience some of the benefits of court hospitality and the ceremony of court behaviour. In the Anglo-Saxon poem formal speeches are made in the hall, brief accounts are given of musical entertainment, allusions are found to amusements such as horse-racing and hunting. The Anglo-Norman author follows in greater detail the career of his hero in the household of Hunlaf. Horn is placed in the care of Herlant as *mestre*, and he is trained in all the arts of peace and war:

> N'est estrument suz ciel, dunt sacet hom mortal,
> Dunt ne past tute gent dan Horn, l'enperïal;
> De bois e de rivere refait il autretal;
> D'eskermir en tuz sens n'est a li communal
> Nul ki vest'el païs u burel u cendal.
> Nul me siet [en]vers lui bien mener un cheval,
> Nul si porter escu od bucle de cristal
> . . .
> Li enfaunt sunt norri e mut sunt bien gardé,
> Mut par sunt tuit corteis e mut bien doctriné.
>
> (375–88)

There is no musical instrument known to man on which the noble Horn did not surpass all. It was the same with hunting and hawking. No one, high or low, in the land matches him in any way at sword play. Compared with him no one knows how to handle a horse well, nor bear a shield with crystal boss. . . . The children are educated and very well looked after. All are most courtly and well-taught.

His accomplishments commend him to all, and his rise in Hunlaf's service is rapid from the moment that he is appointed cup-bearer. This appointment brings him to the attention of the king's daughter, Rigmel, which will eventually prove his downfall and the occasion of a second banishment; but not before he successfully attains knighthood. In the *Romance of Horn* the practicalities of the grant of arms, the deep significance of the event, and the interconnection of knighthood with feudal ties all emerge clearly when Hunlaf's kingdom is suddenly threatened by a powerful force of Saracens. No one except Horn has the spirit to meet them, so that the young man must quickly be supplied with arms and knighted. The king equips him with his own armour, preserved since his youth, and girds on the sword with his own hands. This symbolic action is then repeated by Horn for each of his own band of retainers, on the grounds that he is their lord. The giving of arms, as was assumed by the designer of the Bayeux tapestry, carries with it the obligations of vassalage.

The events and ceremonies of the royal household form a back-cloth to the heroic action in *Beowulf*, but they are much more prominent in *Horn*, where the education of the hero in the accomplishments of the court, and the demonstration of his aptitude, are an important theme throughout. Connected with this, we may notice a further difference between the two poems in their treatment of one of the customs of the hall: this is that by which the warriors assembled on the ale benches in Anglo-Saxon poetry and proverb are served wine or ale by a woman (*Maxims*, I, 84–92). In *Beowulf*, Hrothgar's wife, Wealtheow, serves wine to her husband and addresses the warriors with good counsel and a plea for Beowulf's future protection for her sons. Wealtheow has a gravity and at the same time an awareness of vulnerability which awakens both our respect and sympathy. Thomas's treatment of this custom is quite different. For him, it is exotic and of antiquarian interest. In a flowering of baroque imagination he gives Rigmel thirty maidens as helpers as they go round the hall. Instead of serving as the occasion of sober advice and foreboding, the custom is developed as the recognition scene between parted lovers. Horn, having returned secretly from exile, makes his presence known by punning play on the drinking horn he has been offered, and by the surreptitious return of a ring slipped into the vessel. This simple event encapsulates for us how times have changed. The castaways on the shore, instead of being met by a guard, are met by a party out hawking; their subsequent life in the hall, instead of being assailed by a half-human monster, is an education in the proprieties of that society, only later followed by a demonstration of military prowess. The role of women in the hall is no longer that of dispensers of wine and wisdom, but rather the objects of romantic desire. The Bayeux tapestry account of the interception of Harold, with its armed hawking party, seems balanced neatly between the two worlds, and so serves as a useful symbol of a society in which the military, epic values of the past still survived, but were increasingly counter-balanced by the esteem accorded to peaceful accomplishments.

As a further demonstration of the emergence of courtly values around the millennium, we may consider the handling by various authors of another incident in the legendary history of Britain, part of the story of Hengest and Horsa. The tale first emerges in the ninth-century Latin of an Anglo-Welsh writer who has long been known as Nennius.[16] He tells how Vortigern came to lose his kingdom to the Jutes. Hengest invites Vortigern to a feast, and following Anglo-Saxon custom, has his daughter serve wine to the guests:

> . . . puellam iussit ministrare illis vinum et siceram et inebriati sunt et saturati sunt nimis. Illis autem bibentibus, intravit Satanus in corde Guorthigirni, ut amaret puellam, et postulavit eam a patre suo per interpretem suum et dixit: 'omne quod postulas a me impetrabis, licet dimidium regni mei'.
>
> (ed. Faral, *Légende Arthurienne*, p. 29)

> He ordered the girl to serve wine and drinks to them and they were satiated and extremely drunk. When they were drinking, Satan entered Vortigern's heart so that he fell in love with the girl and, through his interpreter, he asked her father to give her to him, and said: 'Anything you ask from me you may have; even half of my kingdom'.

Although it is stated that Vortigern loved the girl, this is hardly a love story. It is rather an exemplary tale of passion and folly, and its just deserts. Such love as can be found here arises from drink and the devil in Vortigern's heart. Here we have an ascetic clerical view of what is plainly regarded as a disgraceful episode. However, later versions of this scandalous event in early English history begin to elaborate it in a different way. Geoffrey of Monmouth, writing in 1137, presents a much more detailed picture:

Ut ergo regiis epulis refectus fuit, egressa est puella de thalamo aureum ciphum plenum uino ferens. Accedens deinde proprius regi flexis genibus dixit: 'Lauerd king, Waesseil!' At ille, uisa facie puelle, ammiratus est tantum eius decorem et incaluit. Denique interrogauit interpretem suum quid dixerat puella et quid ei respondere debeat. Cui interpres dixit: 'Uocauit te dominum regem et uocabulo salutationis honorauit. Quod autem respondere debes, est "Drincheil"'. Respondens deinde Uortegirnus 'Drincheil' iussit puellam potare cepitque ciphum de manu ipsius et osculatus est eam et potauit. Ab illo die usque in hodiernum mansit consuetudo illa in Britannia quia in conuiuiis qui potat ad alium dicit 'Waesseil'. Qui uero post illum recepit potum, respondet 'Drincheil'. Uortegirnus autem diuerso genere potus inhebriatus intrante Sathana in corde suo amauit puellam et postulauit eam a patre suo. Intrauerat, inquam, Sathanas in corde suo quia, cum Christianus esset, cum pagana coire desiderabat.

(*Historia Regum Britannie*, ed. Wright, p. 67)

While he was being entertained at a royal banquet, the girl came out of an inner room carrying a golden goblet full of wine. She walked up to the King, curtsied low and said: 'Laverd King, wasseil!' When he saw the girl's face, Vortigern was greatly struck by her beauty and was filled with desire for her. He asked his interpreter what it was that the girl had said and what he ought to reply to her. 'She called you Lord King', answered the interpreter, 'and did you honour by drinking your health. What you should reply is "drincheil".' Vortigern immediately said the words 'drincheil' and ordered the girl to drink. Then he took the goblet from her hand, kissed her and drank in his turn. From that day to this the tradition has endured in Britain that the one who drinks first at a banquet says 'wasseil' to his partner and he who takes the drink next replies 'drincheil'. Vortigern was tipsy from the mixture of drinks which he had consumed. Satan entered his heart, so that he fell in love with the girl, and asked her father to give her to him. I say that Satan entered his heart because, despite the fact that he was a Christian, he was determined to make love with this pagan woman.

(trans. Thorpe)

The changes made in the story are many and circumstantial. The entry of the girl with the golden chalice is a striking image, which seizes the attention of the reader as effectively as it did that of Vortigern. The event is situated in the context of elegant social ceremony, and the beauty of the girl is emphasized, so that there are perfectly understandable circumstances for Vortigern's attraction to her. Thus, psychological realism displaces an explanation based upon diabolic suggestion, and indeed this inherited material is largely explained away in terms of the undesirability of a match between a Christian and an unbeliever. In this version, the skills of the narrator are deployed to evoke understandable sexual attraction, condemnable by its circumstances, but not presented as primary evidence of culpable moral breakdown.

Two decades later, a Norman clerk, Wace, employing both the sources we have already seen, retold the story in the vernacular at greater length still. Wace follows the direction given by Geoffrey of Monmouth, taking a further step towards dramatic presentation and psychological realism:

> Dunc est fors de la chambre eissue
> Ronwen, mult bele, e bien vestue;
> Pleine cupe de vin porta.
> Devant le rei s'agenuilla,
> Mult humlement li enclina
> E a sa lei le salua:
> 'Laverd King, Wesheil!' tant li dist;
> Li reis demanda e enquist,
> Ki le language ne saveit,
> Que la meschine li diseit.
> Keredic respundi premiers,
> Brez ert, si ert bons latimiers,
> Ço fu li premiers des Bretuns
> Ki sout le language as Saissuns:
> 'Ronwen', dist il, 't'a salué,
> E seinnur rei t'ad apelé.
> Custume est, sire, en lur païs
> Quant ami beivent entre amis,
> Que cil dit Wesheil qui deit beivre
> E Drincheheil ki deit receivre;
> Dunc beit cil tut u la meitied
> E pur joie e pur amistied.
> Al hanap receivre a bailler
> Est custume d'entrebaisier'.
> Li reis, si cum cil li aprist
> Dist 'Drincheil' e si sorrist.
> Ronwen but e puis li bailla,
> E en baillant, le rei baisa.
> Par cele gent premierement
> Prist l'un us e cumencement
> De dire en cel païs Wesheil
> E de respundre Drincheheil,
> E de beivre plein u demi
> E d'entrebaiser lui e li.

(6947–80)

Then Ronwen, most beautiful and elegantly dressed, came out from the chamber bearing a cup filled with wine. She knelt before the king, bowing to him with great respect, and greeted him according to her custom: 'Lauerd King, Wesheil', thus she said to him. The king, who did not know the language, asked and enquired what the maiden was saying to him. Keredic replied first; he was a Briton, and was a good interpreter. He was the first among the Britons who knew the Saxon language. 'Ronwen', he said, 'has greeted you and called you Lord King. It is the custom, sire, in their country when friends drink together that the one who is about to drink, says "Wesheil", and the one who is about to receive says "Drincheil". Then the former drinks all or half for pleasure and for friendship. At the giving and receiving of the cup, it is the custom to exchange a kiss'. The king, just as he taught him, said 'Drincheil' and smiled. Ronwen drank and then gave it to him, and, as she gave it, kissed the king. It was from them that the custom of saying *Wesheil* and replying *Drinceheil* first originated in this country, and of drinking whole or half, and of him and her exchanging kisses.

Although this is followed by a rhetorical exclamation against the promptings of the Devil, it is apparent that the Devil's role is now little more than a conventional reflection on the way of the world. Wace has peopled the anecdote with named individuals: Keredic, whose name comes from Nennius, is now revealed to be an outstanding translator, and an informed commentator on Anglo-Saxon custom; the girl, named Ronwen throughout, and rather more fully realized, now takes the initiative in the matter of the kiss, but is acquitted of any impropriety by explaining it as part of established custom. The idea of sharing the cup as a symbol of *amistied* 'friendship' between men and women is a further inspiration of Wace's, who emphasizes the romantic implications of this custom by his significant choice of masculine and feminine pronouns *lui* and *li* in the final line. By these deft alterations he creates a scene in which we can well appreciate the effect upon Vortigern. The Devil is no longer needed as motivation, since psychological motivation springs naturally from the situation.

The moment has come to attempt a summary of what emerges from all these episodes, extending in time between the ninth century and the close of the twelfth. The overwhelming impression is one of change within continuity. The fundamental framework of loyalties to lord, companions, and lineage, and their importance as the guarantors of a man's good faith remain unchanged wherever they appear. Yet, by looking at scenes which mirror one another, but are chronologically separated, evolution in values becomes evident. From the dispensers of wine and good counsel in *Beowulf*, or the inciters of disastrous lust in Nennius, women in Wace or *Horn* are now the objects of love and desire interpreted in recognizably human terms. From the armed and menaced societies of *Beowulf*, where the virtues of the hero are those of the warrior, much greater emphasis falls upon the skills of peacetime – intelligence is emphasized alongside prowess. The recreations of peacetime now accompany continued readiness for war. Society centres on the household, finds leisure to cultivate greater refinement and ceremony, and its growing self-awareness encourages implicit contrasts with customs elsewhere. In the interest shown by Geoffrey of Monmouth and Wace in the origins of contemporary behaviour, however faintly, we can see the beginnings of that self-regard from which social theory grows. We are on the threshold of courtly society.[17]

The image of a threshold, placed at about the year 1000, has a certain general validity, and in England the Conquest of 1066 offers an alternative division, but we have also seen that such images should not be pressed too hard. Wise speeches in the hall, the pastimes of peace, the ceremonies of court life also punctuate *Beowulf*. The development is a matter of emphasis rather than a sharp division, a development in the way that those circles possessing the skills of literacy looked upon their world.

The epic *Chanson de Roland*, as well as lengthy battle scenes, contains a number of scenes in which Charlemagne calls upon his vassals under the obligation of *consilium* as well as that of *auxilium*. These council scenes, dealing with questions of terms of peace or the administration of justice, give opportunities for the display of talents other than those of simple violence and impulsiveness. Although, from its epic viewpoint subtlety and treachery may be related, and the poet is inclined to view non-combatant qualities with suspicion, nevertheless, council scenes play an important role, and none more than that in which the traitor, Ganelon, according to feudal justice, is brought to trial by his peers. In such circumstances, where there is no independent judiciary, a man's lord is his judge, so that the line between vengeance and justice can be an exceedingly fine one. The intention, however, is the pursuit of equity, and this can be sought in two ways: by handing the matter over to the judgement of God, or by an attempt at rationally argued judgement reached within the council. The first is that which corresponds to the heroic self-conceptions of the knightly class: a single combat in which God grants victory to the right. Although, in fact, substitutes often filled the roles, the confrontation was considered to take place between the accuser and the accused, and the winner was declared to be justified; success guaranteed *dreit*. To what extent medieval people regarded this procedure as an infallible test of right is debatable, for there is often a deep ambiguity between the metaphysical conception and the purely pragmatic purpose of trial by combat. Whatever the result, it could be given validity by claiming a *judicium dei*, yet in literary sources the procedure is often treated with a marked pragmatism, and there is no reference to the role of divine justice. Indeed, no specific criticism is offered when trials by combat are overtly rigged, as in the story of *Amis and Amiloun*. The judicial combat in the *Chanson de Roland*, that suggested by chivalric representatives in Chaucer's *Parliament of Fowls*, and that actually carried out in the *Knight's Tale* all have in common that they are simply means to solve a deadlock in argument, and they make no explicit reference to the reliability of the decision reached.

The second means of seeking justice is by means of argument and the decision of fellow vassals. It naturally requires very different virtues from those of single combat or the battlefield: wisdom, perspicuity, and eloquence. It may also require poise, and a kind of courage. In Marie de France's *Lanval*, the Queen, who is seeking vengeance on the hero, is pictured as a background presence constantly harassing the King to pressure his barons into reaching an acceptable verdict on Lanval. In such circumstances the pursuit of justice requires in the counsellors a range of skills which counterbalance those of the battlefield and which begin to be seen as essential to the complete man: self-possession, insight, tact, and eloquence. It is in the context of such council scenes, and specifically in application to the manner of speech, that we first encounter the word *curteis* in vernacular literature. It is said of Pinabel, Ganelon's defender in the trial scene, that 'Ben set parler e dreite reisun rendre' (3784), and shortly afterwards we are told that those of the Auvergne are the most *curteis* as everyone falls silent for Pinabel to speak (3796). A few lines later, Geoffrey of Anjou *curteisement* speaks to the emperor, putting the crucial plea for the prosecution that shared service to Charlemagne should have protected Roland from Ganelon's vengeance despite his formal and public *défiance* of Roland earlier. Indeed, Geoffrey's assertion that feudal loyalty should take precedence over personal quarrels carries the day. The precise meaning of *curteis* in these early uses in the

Chanson de Roland is not easy to define (Roland speaks *curteisement* to his companions in battle (1164)), but what all have in common is reference to the skills of peace, and especially those of speech and debate. We may also imagine that on at least two occasions there may be some association with the sympathy and understanding expressed in the speech which follows. In any case, such uses of the word corroborate what we have seen throughout this chapter, the emergence of courtliness from the skills of *consilium* and the social experiences of life in the feudal hall.

NOTES

1. Bloch, *Feudal Society*, I, pp. 1–38.
2. Duby, *Chivalrous Society*, pp. 123–333; Contamine, *War in the Middle Ages*, pp. 270–8.
3. Wormald, 'Style and Design', pp. 25–36; Wilson, *The Bayeux Tapestry*, pp. 204–12.
4. The derivative 'feudalism' is of nineteenth-century origin, but the phrase 'feudal system' was first used by Adam Smith in his *The Wealth of Nations* (1776). The adjective 'feudal' had been common in legal usage in the seventeenth century.
5. Ganshof, *Feudalism*, pp. 84–5.
6. Sayles, *The Medieval Foundations of England*, pp. 450–1.
7. Duby, *Chivalrous Society*, pp. 112–22.
8. The names of ranks changed the scope of their reference considerably during the medieval period. The Anglo-Norman *seneschal* was the lord's deputy, primarily responsible for the running of the household, whereas the *mareschal* was responsible for military leadership. In Middle English, by the early fourteenth century, the latter had taken over the household duties, and was an office equivalent to a steward. For details of the population of the later medieval court, see Green, *Poets and Princepleasers*, pp.13–70.
9. Hunt, 'Emergence of the Knight', pp. 93–114.
10. White Jr, *Medieval Technology and Social Change*, pp. 14–38.
11. Bachrach, 'Charles Martel, Mounted Shock Combat', pp. 47–75.
12. Jones, *Ethos of the Song of Roland*, pp. 20–2.
13. Nevertheless, the Chandos Herald preserves some of these old heroic values in the late fourteenth century, when he places *loialtee* as the supreme chivalric virtue, and understands the phrase *bon chivaler* to connote skill in arms (Mathew, 'Ideals of Knighthood', p. 358).
14. Pensom, 'Lexical Field of "Fiers" ', pp. 49–66; Burnley, 'Roman de Horn', pp. 385–97.
15. Peristany's distinction between 'guilt cultures' and 'shame cultures' has been applied to the criticism of the *Chanson de Roland* by G.F. Jones (Jones, *Ethos*, pp. 97–100), to Malory and Chaucer by Derek Brewer (Brewer, *Malory*, pp. 23–35) and to *Sir Gawain and the Green Knight* by John Burrow (Burrow,

Essays on Medieval Literature, pp. 117–31). The last, in particular, contains useful further references.

16. On the very doubtful validity of this ascription, see ' "Nennius" and the *Historia Brittonum*' in Dumville, *Histories*, Item X (first published in *Studia Celtica* 10/11 (1975/76), 78–95).

17. The *Roman de Toute Chevalerie* (2347–51) identifies Athens as the place of origin both of *curtesie* and the seven arts.

Chapter 2

The Emergence of Courtliness

To take the year 1000 as the threshold of courtliness is an attractive simplification encouraged by C.S. Lewis's famous remark that the changes which marked the emergence of courtly love occurred 'quite suddenly' at the end of the eleventh century.[1] But such a statement would require a great deal of qualification. Certainly, important social and ideological developments took place in the centuries following the millennium, but we should not exaggerate the watershed. The esteem for heroic military virtues underwent modifications, but they were joined rather than replaced by courtly values, and, in England, they persisted to some degree throughout the middle ages. In the early fourteenth century, the romance of *Richard Coer de Lion* is an attempt to create a *chanson de geste* in English, and the later alliterative *Morte Arthur* also preserves many of the older heroic values. The impression of suddenness in the emergence of courtly values is in part due to the paucity of sources in the crucial centuries, and it should not be forgotten that some aspects of formal behaviour in a courtly environment, although not heavily emphasized, are already to be found in Anglo-Saxon poetry. As we have seen, *Beowulf* describes a royal court with appropriate formal behaviour between its members, male and female, and the polite reception of visitors. Although the word 'court' is not Old English in origin, the word *hired* was used to translate Latin *familia* 'household', and continued in use in declining frequency throughout the medieval period, although it becomes rare after the thirteenth century and ceased to be productive in compounds. Politeness, then, was valued in the household in the first millennium, and courtly custom was observed. Refinement was cultivated too in a monastic environment, but the eleventh and twelfth centuries saw far greater opportunities than ever before to practise and elaborate such interests outside the protective walls of the monastery.

In seeking to understand the nature of the changes which took place in social values, we can begin with linguistic history, and a brief account of the early history of the medieval word *curtesie* and its related forms, for this casts valuable light upon the emergence of the ideal of courtliness. In form, the Middle English word *curt, cort* is borrowed from a similar French word which in turn is derived from the Latin *cohort-em*, which had both locative and social senses already in Latin. It could be used to refer to an enclosure, but also a group of people (in military contexts, a band of troops). In early French and English this equivocation between place and people continued. An essential aspect of courtliness, which has already been suggested in the previous chapter, is this association with the court or household of an important lord. The word *curt* appears in this sense in the *Chanson de Roland* (231) and in English, by the mid-twelfth century, in the *Peterborough Chronicle*. Here, its senses include not only the institution of the household with its company of retainers, but also the formal assembly in which vassals are called together for purposes of consultation. A decade earlier than this, Geoffrey Gaimar's Anglo-Norman *Estoire des Engleis* contains the adjective *curteis* used substantivally to refer to a member of such a household:

> De sa belté par la cuntree
> Esteit mult grant la renomee
> E quant [iloc] tanz en parloent,
> Cil de la curt i repeiroent
> E li curteis qui la veneient
> De sa belted mult bien diseient

(3609–14)

The fame of her beauty was very great throughout the land, and because it was much discussed [there], members of the court made their way there, and the courtiers who came there spoke very highly of her beauty.

Gaimar appreciates beauty and already associates such appreciation with courtliness. He has also been shown to exhibit an awareness of the values of *noblesce*, *barnage*, *richesce*, and *largetetz* (6495–512), representing the court of Henry I in purely idealizing terms, and he offers a precociously courtly treatment of the love of King Edgar and Elfthrida (3595–932), an affair which William of Malmesbury relates as a sombre scandal.[2] But elsewhere in his poem, the abstract qualities implied by the use of the adjective *curteis* are more to do with the worth of the courtier as determined by his effectiveness in battle (5500) or by his obvious prosperity

(5844). In the first case it appears to be synonymous with *proz* and in the second with *riche*. This is surprising to the modern reader, because, in the later medieval period, with which we are more familiar, military prowess was not considered fundamental to courtliness. What is especially notable about these early references is the close association which then existed between the noun *curt* and the derived adjective *curteis*. The latter essentially implied association with the court; but the precise virtues desirable in a man of the court were still, to a considerable extent, unsettled and a matter of individual opinion. Gaimar emphasized wealth and prowess; the author of the *Chanson de Roland*, however, already associated these virtues with gentleness of manner and articulateness in counsel.

Within two decades of Gaimar's work, the English court was able to read in Wace's *Brut* a greatly expanded conception of *curteisie* which found in it a whole range of gifts and accomplishments. Describing the legendary hero Bran, Wace remarks:

> Brennes parlout corteisement
> Si ert de grant afaitement;
> De bois saveit e de riviere
> E deduz de mainte maniere,
> Gent cors aveit e bel visage;
> Bien semblout home de parage.
>
> (2659–64)

Bran spoke like a courtier and was well-informed and accomplished at hunting and hawking and many sorts of recreation. He was elegant and had a handsome appearance. It was plain that he was a man of rank.[3]

These accomplishments serve the courtier in good stead, because, since he could speak well and offer good service – we are informed – he married richly and became a duke: one early example of a plot-line common in romance, where courtly accomplishments often serve as the cause of spectacular advancement. Military effectiveness is emphatically not scorned, but in romances from the end of the twelfth century an equal value is placed upon those other qualities of refinement which might distinguish the courtier, making him a pleasant companion or a useful functionary. The increasing estimation of peacetime values perhaps lies behind Wace's phrasing in his description of England as the flower of 'curtesie e d'enur' where:

Plus erent curteis e vaillant
Neïs li povre païsant
Que chevalier en altres regnes
E altresi erent les femes.

(10499–502)

Even the poor peasants were more *curteis* and worthy than knights in other kingdoms, and so also were the women.

The adjective *vaillant* is particularly interesting here. Until the last phrase, the reader is predisposed to assume that *vaillant* implies a military quality in contrast to the pacific virtues suggested by *curteis*, but the revelation that women too may possess this quality precludes any military significance. Implicit in this quotation is the assumption that courtliness might rather be expected in knights than in peasants or women, but the worth of all can be sought in moral and behavioural terms rather than in mere chivalric efficacy.

Although *curteisie* is clearly associated in the above quotation with milder virtues, it is quite uncertain from the context what these might have been. However, it is apparent that Wace, like the author of the *Chanson de Roland*, connected *curteisie* with skill in the art of speech, which he regarded very highly. Not only did Bran make his fortune through eloquence, but people came to Arthur's court 'to hear his courtesies' (10332).[4] The association seems, however, to be one dependent upon context and cannot be considered as the established sense of the word *curteis*. Describing the two daughters of King Ebronc, Wace remarks that one was eloquent and the other more 'corteise', and knew better how to live lavishly (*demener richeise*, 1566–8). In this context *curteisie* seems to be more particularly associated with riches and magnificence, and a contrast is drawn with eloquence. But the juxtaposition with eloquence is important, and although differences may be distinguishable in the aspects of courtliness displayed by different individuals, both wealth and eloquence are to be treated as common attributes of courtliness. The repeated association with eloquence is by no means fortuitous, and it has a very long history indeed. Although the word-form *curt* is derived from Latin *cohortem* and medieval Latin *curtis*, which have the senses both of 'troop, company' and also 'enclosure, yard', from very early times this word-form adopted some of the senses associated with the Latin word *curia*. In Classical Latin the word *curia* referred to an administrative division among the Roman people, but also to the meeting-place of the representatives of this division. Its significance

was then further shifted to refer to the Roman Senate, and later to
the Imperial Court, whose officials became known as *curiales*. In the
medieval period these associations with the court as an administrative centre, where decisions would be taken after debate, continued
when the word *curia* was used first of the Papal Court and then of
the courts of various national rulers. Medieval Latin exhibits in the
meaning of the words *curialis*, *curialiter*, and *curialitas* a similar
development to that we have traced in early Anglo-Norman sources,
but the evidence begins a little earlier. In Anglo-Latin *curialis* has
the meaning 'courtier' by 1065, and *curialiter* is recorded with the
meaning 'in the ways of the court; in courtly style' before 1140.
Senses connected with the particular manifestations of courtly
refinement follow this within a generation. From these earliest uses,
and throughout the medieval period, *curialitas* is associated with the
words *facetia*, *eloquentia*, *urbanitas*, *concilium*, *benignitas*, and contrasted
with *rusticitas*. This is not the place to investigate in full the
significance of such terms, but *urbanitas*, *facetia* and their opposite
rusticitas have a continuous history descending through monastic
culture from Roman times into the middle ages. The *dulcedo* which
Venantius Fortunàtus attributed to cultivated people in the early
medieval period was simply *urbanitas* by another name.[5] *Urbanitas*
(from Latin *urbs* 'a city') was an ideal of refinement and
sophistication associated with the city-dweller and man of affairs.[6]
As such, it contrasted in Latin usage with the *rusticitas* (from *rus* 'the
country'), the rougher manners and simplicity, of country peasants.
One of the principal characteristics of the urbane man was presumed
to be the accomplishment and wit of his speech, denoted by the
words *facetia* and *eloquentia*. In a society in which educated men
were familiar with two or three languages, it is not surprising to
find that these associations with administrative experience and with
eloquence were transferred from Latin into French and thence into
English in those situations where they seemed appropriate.

From the earliest formulations of the ideals of courtliness onwards, these ideals may be found entering into various associations
and oppositions. Courtliness is associated with the particular virtues,
gifts, or accomplishments desirable in the courtier, which, as they
are identified and tacitly agreed, become incorporated as part of the
broader conception. This conception is opposed, either antithet-
ically (to qualities regarded as inimical to the reputation of the
courtier) or complementarily (to qualities of equal esteem but
different nature). Although the precise nature of the virtues or vices
of a courtier may undergo modification, these associations and

oppositions form a historically persistent pattern, so that it is desirable to be aware of some of the most fundamental of them.

Beginning with oppositions, we may recall the epithets used of the heroes of the *Chanson de Roland*, where Roland is *proz, pesme, fiers* and Oliver is *proz, gentil, sages,* and *curteis*. Earlier critics, led by Joseph Bédier,[7] tended to represent the difference between Roland and Oliver as one of complementarity: Roland has the virtue of forcefulness, *fortitudo*, whereas Oliver is blessed by the attribute of greater reflectiveness and calm, *sapientia*. These are traditionally two aspects of the heroic character, and undoubtedly have some appropriateness to the characterization in the poem. But more modern critical opinion tends to regard this division as too simplistic,[8] and our own experience of the flexibility in sense of words like *curteis, proz*, and *vaillanz* noted above, may incline us to agree. When Oliver is called 'li proz e li curteis' (3755), we may therefore be uncertain of the nature of the semantic relationship between the two adjectives: association, complementary opposition, or synonymy? The immediate context offers no clarification, and we can only form an opinion from our reading of the motivations and behaviour of the characters in the entire poem. No such uncertainty afflicts the Middle English *Kyng Alisaunder*, which was composed at the end of the thirteenth century and copied into the earliest extant manuscript perhaps a generation later. Here the wily Neptanabus is said to be 'curteys in halle, in werre wiȝth' (1527). The complementary nature of military and peaceful accomplishment is made clearly apparent in this context. This opposition of virtues ideally reconciled in one person was a powerful tradition descending from Late Latin epic,[9] and indeed still forms part of the representation of the Knight in Chaucer's *General Prologue* to the *Canterbury Tales*, of whom it is stated that: 'Thogh that he weere worthy, he was wyse' (68). Any reader unaware of the traditional oppositions between prowess and courtesy, *fortitudo* and *sapientia, auxilium* and *consilium*, could very well overlook the significance here of the word *thogh*, followed by a subjunctive, in the constitution of the character of this controversial knight.

This distinction between chivalric, military skills and domestic refinement, together with the desirability of possessing both at the same time, forms the theme of Hue de Rotelande's long poem, *Ipomedon*, which he composed in Anglo-Norman between 1174 and 1190. The durability of the theme is demonstrated by the fact that the essential appropriateness of its ideals was still recognized in the fourteenth and fifteenth centuries when it was three times translated into English. That it then held interest for a broader and more bourgeois audience is indicated by the abbreviated copy made for the private collection of John Colyns, a London merchant.[10] Although this version is a fraction of the length of Hue de Rotelande's work, it carefully preserves many aspects of courtly conduct which would befit a young gentleman.

In the original poem Ipomedon, the hero, is a young man, a *valez* and a prince, who becomes restless at his father's court and, much as medieval students sought out famous teachers at schools throughout Christendom, he assumes that the perfection of his courtliness will come from experience of a foreign court:

> Mestre, vus savez bien ke dit
> Li sages homme en son repit:
> De affaitement n'avra ja pris,
> Ki n'est fors de une cort appris.
>
> (249–52)

Master, you know very well what the wise proverbially say: he will never get the prize for his skills who has been educated in only one court.[11]

Beside this laudable concern for his own education, Ipomedon is attracted by stories he has heard of a beautiful heiress, La Fiere. Accompanied by his *mestre*, Tholomeu, he makes his way to La Fiere's court, where he is swiftly retained in her service, and soon becomes esteemed by the other courtiers for his accomplishments. His skills at hawking and hunting are outstanding, he is clever in speech, intelligent, filled with every conceivable virtue, and knowledgeable about the customs of the hall. He is appointed immediately to the post of cup-bearer; but, alas, despite all this undoubted excellence, it appears that he is lacking in spirit. He does not go to fence, wrestle, or play the sports of the other young men around the court, and he begins to be mocked that he is not *pruz*. La Fiere, finding herself strongly attracted to this newcomer, admits to herself that he is *plein de curteisie* (683–4) but she too laments his lack of prowess. In due course Ipomedon is forced to leave the court and pursue adventure elsewhere, which will give him an opportunity to prove his true worth. He first returns home and receives arms from his father. His *mestre* Tholomeu is not himself a knight, but he refuses dubbing in order to devote himself to Ipomedon's service, and together with a retinue or *mesnie* they depart to begin Ipomedon's career as knight errant, wandering incognito to win esteem and wealth in tournaments.[12] One day, while passing through the forests of the land of Cecile, he encounters the king of that country, who sends an intermediary, Capaneus, to enquire in the now familiar fashion about his name and lineage, where he is from and where he is going to. Ipomedon, we are told, knew about courtliness (2854), so that the formal correctness of his replies, together with his opulent appearance, immediately decide the king to retain him in his own service. Symbolically sharing a cup of wine with Capaneus, Ipomedon enters into companionship with him as a fellow member of the court of Cecile. Once in the court, however, he deliberately re-adopts his previous eccentric behaviour, exhibiting skills in hunting and civilities to the queen, but avoiding the proper concerns of knights:

> En la curt out mut chevalers,
> De ben vaillanz e pruz e fiers,
> E custume est par tut le munt,
> U chevalers ensemble sunt,
> Ke il parolent d'enveiseüres
> E cuntent de lur aventures,
> De dames e de drueries
> E de beles chevaleries.
> Tuz jurz, quant il issi parlerent
> E les pruësces recorderent,
> Ipomedon tut de el parla
> E la parole aillurs turna;
> Quant il cuntent chevaleries
> Il recounte de veneries,
> Cil parolent de forz esturz
> E il des brachetz e de ostourz,
> Cil cuntent de turneemenz
> E il de chens, igneaus e lenz;
> Cil cuntent de bons chevalers,
> Il de veautres e de levrers.

(3099–118)

There were many very worthy and bold knights in the court, and where knights are gathered together – it is the same all over the world – they talk about amusements and tell of their adventures with ladies, and love affairs, and fine feats of arms. Always, when they spoke of such things, and related these feats, Ipomedon changed the subject, turning the conversation to something else. When they talked of knightly deeds, he told of hunting. They spoke of tight corners in battle, he of hounds and hawks. They told of tournaments, he of dogs swift or slow. They told of strong knights, he of boarhounds and greyhounds.

Once more Ipomedon becomes the object of cheerful derision. He is admittedly handsome and *curteis*, but the first duty of a knight is *chevalerie*, so that he is mockingly referred to as 'li bel malveis', perhaps translatable as 'the handsome coward'. There is no need to labour any further the distinction maintained in this romance between the possession of the qualities of *curteisie* and the esteem to be won from deeds of *chevalerie*. Arising from this, it is worth noting a further important point about Hue de Rotelande's use of the words *pruz* and *pruesce*. Clearly, they are often associated with the force of the armed vassal, with the skills of the military man; and they are then in contrast with the peaceful accomplishments of the *curteis*. But it is equally clear that the word *pruesce* has a broader significance. In this sense, *pruesce* 'worthiness' is considered to include both military and peaceful accomplishments. This is evident in remarks which accept qualities like beauty, open-heartedness, and generosity (880) or hawking and hunting skills as *pruesce*, but also urge the desirability of a more military kind:

> Mes river' e bois tant ama
> De autre pruësce unc ne pensa.
>
> (529–30)

But he loved hawking and hunting so much that he gave no thought to other kinds of prowess.

Thus, there is no redundancy in the statement that Hermogenes was 'pruz en chevalerie' (173). The story of Ipomedon, then, makes clear that *curteisie* and *chevalerie* may be distinct qualities, in opposition, but they are complementary in that man who can truly be called *pruz*. In a world where the courtly man who does not employ military skills can be regarded as ineffectual, and worthy of neither love nor respect,[13] there is no doubt which is regarded as the more fundamental virtue: an outlook which is apparent in the common Middle English use of the word meaning 'worthy' to refer to the latter skills alone.

Setting aside this opposition between *chevalerie* and *curteisie*, let us now consider a second ubiquitous opposition within conceptions of courtliness: that antithesis reflected in the use of the words *curteisie* and *vilanie*. The latter word, like the former, is an abstract noun which connotes a set of real or imagined qualities characteristic of a social group: in this case, not courtiers but countrymen or peasants. Etymologically, the word *vilanie* is formed from the noun and adjective *vilains*, which is itself derived from the late Latin *villanus*, and ultimately from the word *villa*, meaning a 'farm' or 'country estate'. The word *villanus* in medieval Latin meant a 'peasant' or 'rustic', the working inhabitant of a farm. In view of the opposition mentioned earlier, it is not surprising to find that when *curteisie* becomes associated with the characteristics of *urbanitas*, *vilanie* is regularly associated with *rusticitas*. Although this opposition of *curteisie* and *vilanie* was originally founded upon a Latin opposition between sophisticated court administrative circles and simple peasantry, and reinforcement of this distinction was constantly available from Latin sources, the opposition was more commonly understood in vernacular languages as one between the ideals of courtly society on the one hand and the behaviour and qualities which it despised on the other. Both were, of course, re-interpretable according to the courtly virtue being urged in any particular context, but the opposition persists. Thus, in Gaimar, where we have seen *curteisie* associated with military prowess, and more or less synonymous with Hue de Rotelande's *chevalerie*, *vilanie* is perceived as feebleness or cowardice, as in this exploit of Hereward the Wake:

> . . . li chevalier
> Furent suspris [a lur] mangier.
> Cil entrent haches en lur mains,
> De bien ferir ne sunt vilains,
> Normans ocistrent vint e [sis]
> E duze Engleis i ot ocis.

> (5519–24)

The knights were surprised at their meal. They [the English] enter, axes in their hands, and they aren't afraid to strike hard. They slew twenty-six Normans, and twelve English were slain.

In the last quarter of the twelfth century, in the *Romance of Horn*, *vilanie* is clearly in opposition to *curteisie* not in the terms just demonstrated, but in application to refinement and polite behaviour. In the chess game played by the hero of the romance, decorum reigns:

> Or ont joé entr'els par si fete baillie
> Qu'il n'i out un mot dit qui notast vilanie,
> Mes quant ke dit i out, turna a curteisie.

> (2760–2)

Then they played together in such a way that not one word which suggested *vilanie* was spoken, but whatever was said revealed *curteisie*.

In *Ipomedon*, a similar opposition is found between the adjectives *curteis* and *vilains* in the form of a series of inclusive tags, which assert that every imaginable state of womanhood wept at the threat of the forced marriage facing La Fiere: ladies and maidens, widows and young girls, 'vilaines e curteises' (9332). Here, the adjectives are used substantivally, and the senses opposed seem to echo the earliest opposition between those of the peasants and the court.

Such collocations illustrate at the lexical level a conceptual opposition, which, although varied in content, is so immediately recognizable that it can be employed as a rhetorical device of negative understatement. Thus, as she describes a notably decorous social gathering, Marie de France remarks that 'Cil parlementz n'ert pas vilains' (*Lanval*, 252), a statement which serves to emphasize the graciousness of manners displayed. So firmly established is the opposition between courtliness and villainy in medieval thought that her denial of the one is an effective rhetorical affirmation of the other. Some of the further implications of this will be traced in later chapters, but we must turn now to the consideration of some associations rather than contrasts.

Emphasizing the close correspondence between the two words, the first recorded use in English of the word *vilanie* occurs in that text which also contains the earliest example of the use of the word *curteisie*. The *Ancrene Wisse*, which has been dated at about 1225 in the most recent detailed study of its origins,[14] contains the following statement:

> Of ancre curteisie, of ancre largesse, is cumen ofte sunne and scheome on ende.

> From curteisie among anchorites, from generosity among anchorites, sin and shame often come in the end.

The tone of disapproval evident in this quotation cannot be discussed here, and will be deferred until Chapter 10. What must concern us now is the collocation of *curteisie* with the word *largesse*. This latter word, translated 'generosity' above, means readiness to dispense material gifts, usually in a very conspicuous and ostentatious way. On entering La Fiere's hall, as a test of his abilities, Ipomedon was given the task of serving wine to the lady. To everyone's amusement he enters the butlery still wearing his splendid outdoor cape. But derision is swiftly quelled and turned to admiration when he seizes the initiative by presenting the valuable cape to the butler. The scene stands as a demonstration of Ipomedon's nature and capacity to make an impression, and a court anxious to find fault with a new recruit is compelled to praise his *largesce*. The prestige of largesse as a mode of behaviour continued unchanged throughout the middle ages, so that this incident is faithfully reproduced in the fifteenth-century English translations of the poem.

In discussing the virtues of the courtly hero and heroine in Ipomedon, Hue de Rotelande collocates *curteisie* not only with qualities of character such as *largesce* 'ostentatious generosity', *sen* 'intelligence' (155), and *franchise* 'open-heartedness' (196), but also with phrases which indicate learned accomplishments. *De merveillous afaitement* 'of wonderful accomplishment or training' (188), *bien apris* 'well instructed' (504), *anseignee* 'educated, polished' (216) are all phrases which indicate successful instruction in the skills suitable for the courtier and useful to his lord. These would be taught to the young valet by his mentor and guide, his *mestre*, whose instruction extends from hawking to serving at table, and over the whole province of manners and accomplishments. Literacy did not possess the prestige in education that we unhesitatingly grant it today. Ipomedon, we are told, is literate (*lettrez*) but not a scholar. Literacy is an advantage, Hue believes, since it helps to sharpen the wits.[15] To be reckoned *de bon servise* 'helpful and respectful' (195) is, however, of prime importance to the career prospects of any young recruit to the household. Hue comments:

> De tutes les teches ki sunt,
> N'ad nule meudre en tut le munt,
> Ke un pusse fere en nule guise,
> Ke de rendre home sun servise.

(1753–6)

Of all good qualities that there are, there is none at all better in all the world that a man could do than that he should offer service to another.

Such readiness to place his skills at another's disposal deserves recognition, and is indeed the way to advancement in the household. Even in Chaucer's poetry, two hundred years later, the 'servysable' Squire exhibits this characteristic of his station in life, and in the *Canterbury Tales* friars too have learned this lesson (*GP*, 250). Other figures associated with the Canterbury pilgrimage may also echo distantly the twelfth-century vocabulary of courtly education. The Prioress notoriously applied herself to learning the manners of the court, and is ironically called 'wel ytaught' – a phrase echoing descriptions of earlier possessors of a courtly education. Griselda, in the *Clerk's Tale*, was brought up in a cottage but seemed to have been, 'norissed in an emperour's halle' (399). The word *norissed* 'brought up' in this context emphasizes the continuity of medieval social conceptions as it recalls Hunlaf's promise in the twelfth-century *Romance of Horn* to the young hero whom he offers to shelter and educate:

> Vus n'i perdrez par mei; n'i serrez damagez
> Plus que fussez mis fiz de ma char engendrez;
> Ainz vus frai bien norrir e a vos volentez
> . . .
> Quant meuz serrez creüz, si serrez adubez.

(331–5)

You will not lose through me; nor will you be harmed any more than if you were my own son; rather I will have you well brought up and, according to your wishes when you have grown more, you will be knighted.

NOTES

1. Lewis, *Allegory of Love*, p. 2.
2. Press, 'Precocious Courtesy', pp. 267–76. Edgar is smitten by the beauty of Elfthrida in similar circumstances to Hengest and Ronwen, as they kiss while wass-ailing. He proceeds to send her gifts and the stags he takes on the hunting field (3822).
3. Robert Mannyng's account of 1338 echoes the values of the original quite precisely:

> Brenne was yn speche curteys,
> And konnynge knyght by many weys;
> He couþe of chas and of ryuere,
> Inow of game of here manere;
> Gentil of body, wiþ fair visage
> He semed a man of hey parage.

(*Chronicle of England*, 3133–38)

4. The appreciation of witty and eloquent speech as a kind of spectator sport is echoed in *Sir Gawain and the Green Knight* (916–19).

5. Bezzola, *Origines et Formation*, I, pp. 53–4, 74–5. Venantius Fortunatianus (530–609) was born in Northern Italy and moved to the court of the Merovingian Frankish king Sigibert before settling in Poitiers, where he became bishop. Although he wrote the two famous hymns *Vexilla regis* and *Pange lingua*, he was equally celebrated for his occasional poetry, and the works he addressed to the Princess Radegunde and her sisters.

6. Ramage, *Urbanitas*. Ovid seems to substitute the word *cultus* for *urbanitas*, maintaining the contrast with *rusticitas* (p. 87).

7. Bédier, *Legendes épiques*, III, pp. 433–4.

8. Brault, *Song of Roland*, I, pp. 10–14.

9. Curtius, *European Literature*, pp. 170–6.

10. *Lyfe of Ipomydon*, edited by Ikegami; Meale, 'Compiler' pp. 82–103.

11. This is proverbial, and echoed by the assertion that many schools make skilled clerks. See Whiting and Whiting, *Proverbs*, C479 and S90.

12. Duby, *Chivalrous Society*, pp. 114–15. Duby echoes the account given in *L'Histoire de Guillaume le Maréchal*, in which William Earl of Pembroke is shown supporting himself, and indeed prospering through participation in tournaments in France.

13. Frappier, 'Conceptions courtoises', pp. 135–56. On the perspectives on courtliness in Ipomedon, see also Crane, *Insular Romance*, pp. 158–74.

14. Dobson, *Origins of Ancrene Wisse*.

15. Hue de Rotelande's attitude to literate knights recalls Walter Map's well-known statement that Henry II 'had skill in letters as far as was fitting or practically useful'. But M.T. Clanchy points to *milites litterati* from shortly after the Conquest onwards. See Clanchy, *Memory to Written Record*, p. 182.

Chapter 3

The Aesthetic Ideal: Personal Beauty

To the various skills, accomplishments and natural advantages which constitute courtliness and which were mentioned in the last chapter, a final and very important association must be added: that with physical beauty. The beauty of women had, of course, long formed the subject of poetic inspiration, and lacking inspiration – or perhaps on occasion beauty – of rhetorical exercises too. Geoffrey of Vinsauf, in his twelfth-century handbook of Latin poetic composition, regards it as an 'old and even trite theme' (*Poetria Nova*, 622–3), but all the authors of arts of poetry nevertheless felt compelled to include exemplary descriptions of feminine beauty. The flavour of them can be gained from the following description of Helen of Troy given by Matthew of Vendôme:

> Her beauty knows no equal; it has earned commendation of hatred, the praise of envious judges. Her hair, resembling gold, runs freely, ungoverned by a knot. Freed to distribute its radiance to the shoulders, it unfurls its beauty; outspread, it is the more pleasing. The page of her forehead contains, as it were, friendly words and, unmindful of wicked-ness, without a flaw, it attracts glances. A milky way separates her black eyebrows; the divided arcs forbid the hairs to run wild. Her eyes outshine the stars and with a favouring frankness promise to be the ministers of Venus. Red mingled with kindred white contends in her face and demands tribute of the rosy flower. Not as a stranger does colour abide in her face; lest her face lack colour, the red and snowy white strive therein. The lines of her nose do not dare to lie too low or rise too high. The charm of her rosy mouth desires kisses . . .
>
> (*Ars Versificatoria*, I, 56; trans. Gallo)

As Geoffrey of Vinsauf notes, physical description is a process of the accumulation of detail, descending from the head to the toe. In addition, traditional rhetorical practice divided description into *effictio*, dealing with physical attributes on the one hand, and *notatio*, which assembled moral qualities, on the other. Descriptions of both men and women can be found in rhetorical sources, but in fact, the exemplary descriptions provided by the arts of poetry contain very little on masculine physical appearance, concentrating instead on moral qualities and more general attributes. Matthew of Vendôme describes the Pope, Caesar and Ulysses with no mention of their physical appearance. Although feminine beauty and virtue was the subject of many such exemplary descriptions,[1] the appreciation of male physical elegance is very restricted in medieval Latin tradition. Historical portraits of important men may give a few significant details of their physical appearance, but naturally concentrate, in the Ciceronian manner, on those moral attributes and achievements which have been the foundation of their greatness. We learn, for example, of the Yorkshire baron Walter Espec that he was large, but well-proportioned, 'bearded, with black hair, a frank and open look, large, penetrating eyes, and a very handsome face', but his admirer, Aelred of Rievaulx, is more concerned with his eloquence, which he proceeds to demonstrate by lengthy quotation.[2]

In early Anglo-Norman romance the role of women in the story is relatively small, since authors tend to concentrate instead on the adventures and maturation of the hero. Nevertheless, women may be the instigators of the hero's adventures, the recompense for his exertions or suffering, and above all the witnesses to his attractiveness. In this last function a different kind of description is required from those official portraits which celebrate the status of popes, kings or heroes. Unlike the Latin rhetorical models, the presentation of the young hero is felt to require the description of his physical appearance. This presented some problems, since, in describing the physical beauty of men, authors were, to a considerable degree, attempting a new literary procedure. New canons of masculine beauty had to be developed. They borrowed from the suggestions of rhetorical tradition, but were not necessarily constrained by them.[3] Thomas, in the *Romance of Horn*, hyperbolically asserts his hero's attractiveness by repeated reference to its supernatural quality, appropriating religious language and concepts to his purpose. The whole house shines with his beauty, and when he enters her chamber, Rigmel believes that she must inadvertently have summoned an angel to her room (1052–9). On the whole, Thomas contents himself with these hyperbolic claims, and does not offer extended explanation of what he believes to constitute beauty, but he does place an extended description of Horn on to the lips of Rigmel:

Cheveus ad lungs e blois, que nul n'en est sun per;
Oilz veirs, gros, duz, rianz pur dames esgarder;
Nies e buche bien faite pur duz beisiers prester;
La chiere ad riaunte e le visage cler;
Mains blanches e braz lungs pur dames enbracer;
Cors bien fait e deugé, ke n'i ad qu'amender;
Dreites jambes, beaus piez, set sei [tres] bien chaucer.

(1255–61)

He has hair long and fair without equal; large, bright, twinkling eyes, sweet for ladies to look into; a nose and mouth well formed for bestowing sweet kisses. He has a good-humoured appearance and frank and open look; white hands and long arms to embrace ladies; a body so well formed and elegant that it cannot be bettered; straight legs, fine feet, and he knows just how they are best shod.

Thomas's conception of masculine attractiveness to women seems to modern taste rather bizarre. The organization of this description, proceeding more or less from head to toe, betrays its dependence upon rhetorical exercises, and some of the details suggest that it has been adapted from the more familiar descriptions of beautiful women, such as that of the beauty of Helen of Troy. In particular, the long blonde hair, white hands, and the mouth, here transformed to bestow rather than receive kisses, all belong to feminine descriptions, resulting in an impression of effeminacy, which, when construed as representing actuality, was the subject of criticism by clerical commentators and of satire in later authors.[4] As he reaches his hero's feet, Thomas significantly mentions the detail of his hero's awareness of fashion, of the advantages of well-chosen footwear in attracting approval. Hue de Rotelande echoes this sophistication, but has a surer touch in the description of his hero, beginning with the general impression of his appearance derived from his clothing:

Ypomedon en la sale entre
E si mestres veneit soentre.
De un purpre cendal iert vestu,
Mes pur le grant chaud ke adonc fu
Li bliaus pas furé ne esteit,
A merveille li aveneit;
Li mantel iert furé d'hermine
Ke mult iert blanche e bone e fine,
E fu un poi [?]ditablé,
Od vermail cendal adenté.
La blanche hermine mult avent

Kant a purpre vermail se tent;
Mult iert le bliaut bien seant
E mult bien veneit a l'enfant,
Mult li aveneient ses dras.
Li valet vint les petit pas,
Touz l'esgardent a grant merveille;
Il out la face aukes vermaille
Pur la honte ke il aveit,
Durement bien lui aveneit.
De sa beauté, quant il entra,
Tute la sale enlumina;
Si cum le solail done au jor
Clarté aprés grant tenebror,
Si revent leyns la clarté
Et la lume de sa bealté.
Il out bloie la chevelure
E si duce la regardure,
Nïent trop simple ne trop fiere,
Assez ert de bone maniere;
Plener e large aveit le frunt,
Al visage assez bien respunt,
Cum au cors fu plus avenant;
Les oilz ot clers, bels e rians
E le nes si amesuré,
Par grant estudie fu formé,
E la bouche si bien li sist,
Tuz jors vus fust vis k'ele offrist
A beiser dame ou dameisele,
Tant par fu moulé e bele,
Le col out long, blanche petrine,
Assez plus ke ne fu hermine,
Espaules ot il bien seauntes,
Par mesure bien avenauntes.
Le cors out de bel'estature,
E aukes longe la forcheüre,
E beles mains e les braz beaus,
Tut entrelacé de freseaus,
Pis ot espés avenauntment
E par ses flankes auqes gent,
Les jambes dreites, e les piez
Bien fet sunt e bien tailliez;
Jeo ne quid pas qe unkes nature
Feïst plus bele creature.
K'en dirrai? Ceo est la sume:
En tot le mund n'out si bel homme.

(375–430)

Ipomedon enters the room and his *mestre* with him. He was dressed in purple silk, but because it was then so hot, the tunic was not adorned with fur. It became him extraordinarily well. The mantle was trimmed with ermine, very white, fine and good, and was a little [? (MS corrupt)] with indented purple silk. White ermine goes very well with royal purple. The surcoat was well-fitting, and suited the young man very well, as also did his [other] clothes. The lad moved slowly forward and everyone stared at him in wonder. His face was scarlet with embarrassment, but it suited him marvellously well. As he entered, the whole room lit up with his beauty; just as the sun gives brightness to the dawn after the gloom of night, so came in there the light and brightness of his beauty. He had light hair and so mild a look: not too reserved and not too assertive. He had an excellent manner. His forehead was broad and full, commensurate with his face and his body. His eyes were bright, attractive, and twinkling, and his nose was proportioned as though by careful design; his mouth became him so well, and would seem to you that it was always ready to kiss a lady or maiden, it was so soft and fine. His neck was long, his chest whiter than ermine. His shoulders were well formed in proportion and elegantly; his body of fine stature and the lower part of his chest was long. Fine hands and arms, all wound round with ribbons. He had an elegantly deep chest, and from his neat hips his straight legs and his feet are well formed and sculpted. I do not believe that ever Nature made a more beautiful creation. What more can I say? He was the ultimate. There was no more handsome man in all the world.

This lengthy *effictio* then moves on into a briefer description of Ipomedon's qualities of character (*notatio*). There are many similarities of detail here with Thomas's description of Horn, but the whole has been greatly elaborated. Careful reading of this description would pay useful dividends in understanding both early canons of masculine beauty and rhetorical techniques of elaboration, but two particular aspects are worthy of special note. First, the emergence of a conception of beauty based upon proportion, moderation, and appropriateness; the idea of a physique well and proportionately formed is usually present in such descriptions.[5] Secondly, there is a heavy emphasis on external finery. The passing reference to Horn's taste in shoes is now overshadowed by a fully developed and urbane awareness of the allure of fine and well-chosen clothing.

Such descriptions well illustrate the changes which had taken place in the three generations since the making of the Bayeux tapestry. The relationship between men and women has changed. Men have emerged as courtiers as well as knights, found themselves

in the social milieu of women as well as warriors. The attraction
between men and women which can be felt in these new social
circumstances has become the subject of poetry, and poets have
been forced to seek means of describing and accounting for the
grounds of such attraction at the physical as well as the moral level.
The ideal qualities of the courtier, then, include not only those of
his moral character, but his acquired accomplishments, and his
physical attractiveness. Courtliness, in short, has both a moral and
an aesthetic dimension, concerned with inner beauty and external
grace, and these, sometimes contrasting, dimensions will be encountered often in the course of this book.

Within the same generation in which Hue de Rotelande wrote
his description of his hero, Ipomedon, an author close to the royal
court produced the following description of the dramatic entrance
made into the court not by a man, but by a beautiful woman. In
terms of the impact on bystanders made by her appearance, the
technique is comparable to Wace's description of the entry of
Ronwen.

> Ja departissent a itant,
> Quant par la vile vient errant
> Tut a cheval une pucele,
> En tut le secle n'ot plus bele.
> Un blanc palefrei chevachot,
> Que bel e süef la portot:
> Mut ot bien fet e col e teste,
> Suz ciel nen ot plus bele beste.
> Riche atur ot al palefrei:
> Suz ciel nen ad cunte ne rei
> Ki tut [le] peüst eslegier
> Sanz tere vendre u engagier.
> Ele iert vestue en itel guise:
> De chainsil blanc e de chemise,
> Que tuz les costez li pareient,
> Que de deus parz laciez esteient.
> Le cors ot gent, basse la hanche,
> Le col plus blanc que neif sur branche,
> Les oilz ot vairs e blanc le vis,
> Bele buche, neis bien asis,
> Les surcilz bruns e bel le frunt
> E le chef cresp e aukes blunt;
> Fil d'or ne gette tel luur
> Cum si chevel cuntre le jur.
> Sis manteus fu de purpre bis;

Les pans en ot entur li mis.
Un espervier sur sun poin tient,
E un levrer aprés li vient.

(Lanval, 547–74)

They would have given judgement then, when through the town there
came riding a maiden without equal in all the world. She rode a white
palfrey, which bore her soft and gently. Its head and neck were
perfectly formed: there wasn't a finer animal under heaven. The horse
was well caparisoned: no earl or king on earth could have afforded it
without selling or mortgaging his lands. She was dressed in this manner:
with white linen and a smock which revealed all her flanks, which
were laced over on both sides. Her body was elegant, with low-set
hips; her neck whiter than snow on the branch. She had bright eyes
and a fair complexion, pretty mouth, and a well-fashioned nose, dark
eyebrows and a fair forehead, a curly and blondish head. Gold thread
never cast forth such a gleam as her hair in the sunlight. Her mantle
was of deep purple; she had arranged its folds around her. On her wrist,
she bore a sparrow-hawk, and a greyhound followed after her.

This description, written at some time during the last three
decades of the twelfth century, is in effect the feminine equivalent
of that produced by Hue de Rotelande. It shares with it an
appreciation of the condition of living a life in public, of the
importance of appearance, and of making an entrance. Like the
description of Ipomedon, it is idealizing, but this time it is not
simply the representation of some human creature presumed to
have once existed in some foreign land remote in time and space.
In this portrait there is no pretended actuality; rather, it is admittedly an imaginary construct, the description of a supernatural
inhabitant of the other world of enchantment. Lanval's mistress,
then, is in double measure a creature of fantasy: an ideal lady from
a world of imagination, whose beauty surpasses all reality, and who
is ever-ready at his bidding, inexhaustibly wealthy and no less
generous. The fact that the benefits which she offers are crucially
dependent upon his discreet silence about her existence need not
concern us at present. At this stage in our discussion, it is more
significant that this pure ideal of contemporary feminine beauty and
attractiveness is the creation of a woman, Marie de France. Nothing
about the description would advertise its feminine origin. Placed
alongside Hue de Rotelande's similar description of his heroine, La
Fiere (Ipomedon, 2203–72, not quoted here), one may be aware of
certain differences of emphasis: Marie perhaps pays more attention
to richness of appearance at the expense of physical detail, whereas

Hue gives greater emphasis to erotic impact, descending indeed to prurient speculation of a quite intimate nature at the close of his physical description.[6] Some scholars have seen a conflict of perception within Hue's description between the idealizing and the vulgar, and sought to explain this conflict by assuming an irony which pokes fun at the established rhetorical descriptive procedure.[7] Yet the frank appreciation of sexual possibilities, although unusual outside southern France, is not necessarily at odds with the more delicate expression of sensuality common in these descriptions. Hue differs from Marie, certainly in gender, more likely in personality; but similarities outweigh differences. Hue, like Marie, describes his lady's fine clothes, and much of the detail, phrasing, and similes are the same: the hair like gold thread, the elegant body with low-set hips, the flesh white as snow. Both authors touch delicately on the same erotic theme of the revealing dress:

> N'esteit pas furré li bliauz,
> Nel voleit pas pur le grant chauz;
> De chef en chef lacé esteit,
> Sa nue char parmi pareit
> Tut des la centure en amunt.
>
> (*Ipomedon*, 2219–23)

The tunic wasn't furred; she didn't want that on account of the heat. It was laced from top to bottom, and from the waist up her naked flesh showed through.

This particular detail was to become very widespread in such descriptions, recurring not only in the fourteenth-century English adaptation of *Lanval*, but also in alluring feminine description in so morally earnest a work as *Sir Gawain and the Green Knight*. It represents some sophistication in the perception of a woman as the object of desire: interestingly revealed, yet imperfectly known, promising but withheld.

Although we might seek to tease out the threads of distinctively feminine consciousness from Marie's poetry, what is more remarkable about it is the extent to which she has appropriated to her own artistic and communicative purposes a viewpoint which might reasonably have been considered to be more characteristically a masculine one. Thus, to know that this description was the work of a woman marks it as a testament to the self-awareness of her society to a quite different degree from that of similar descriptions by men. Marie is indeed justly celebrated for her psychological insight, but whatever is implied about her individual achievement by this imaginative revision of what we must assume to have been her own proper perspective, the inevitable implication of descriptions such as these is that of an integrated society thoroughly aware of the importance of the attraction between individuals, and ready to raise it to a theme of poetry, in which it had already developed characteristic devices of expression. These devices were well enough established to surmount any differences between masculine and feminine viewpoints, and to be deftly used by a woman aiming her writing at a mixed audience.

The attractiveness of the opposite sex as represented in these physical descriptions of both women and men is unquestionably an erotic one, but the plain statement of this fact is artfully concealed in the material richness of the setting. Sexual desire becomes refined by its association with aesthetic criteria, which at their simplest find canons of physical beauty based on erotic function: lips well-formed, full, and therefore adapted for kissing (*Ipomedon*, 2247); eyes which cause the onlooker to be seized by love (*Ipomedon*, 2241), messages which can be read in an aspect. Above all, the description of physical beauty often functions in the narrative to explain the origins of that love affair which is so important to the motivation of the plot in the romance genre. Nevertheless, in such descriptions the evocation of beauty often plays a more complex role too. This is evident in such remarks as these by Hue de Rotelande:

> Les espalles out si bien faites,
> Cum se fussent de mains purtrettes,
> Les hanches basses, le cors gent:
> N'i out a reprendre neent.
>
> (*Ipomedon*, 2255–8)

She had shoulders so well-formed as though they had been made by hand; low-set hips, an elegant body: there was nothing to criticize.

> Les oilz ot clers, bel e rians,
> E le nes si amesuré
> Par grand estudie fu formé.
>
> (*Ipomedon*, 408–10)

He had bright, beautiful, laughing eyes, and the nose proportioned as though by careful deliberation.

Les jambes dreites, e les piez,
Bien fet sunt e bien tailliez:;
Jeo ne quid pas q'unkes nature
Feïst plus bele creature.

(Ipomedon, 425–8)

His straight legs and his feet are well formed and sculpted: I do not believe that Nature ever made a more beautiful creation.

Passages in which – following the opinion of Alan of Lille – Nature is represented as the creator of beautiful human beings are not uncommon. Nature is an artist; men and women her artefacts. Like other works of art or indeed architecture, they should appear to be the product of prolonged meditation, and their beauty should conform to those ideals of proportion and congruity expected in any work of art. Portraits, including those of a more formal kind, such as that of Walter Espec noted above, frequently insist on the proportion conforming in a very general way to a tradition of artistic appreciation which descends from the Greeks through Augustine and Boethius.

The implication of this is that the beauty of the hero or heroine of romance was already seen to have an importance beyond its purely functional role in the motivation of narrative. Physical beauty was susceptible to analysis into abstractions, and could be valued at a higher level of perception. Vernacular literature does not analyse this in abstract terms, but scenes in which uninvolved bystanders gaze in pleasure and approval on the beauty of the heroine, as though upon the beauty of a work of art, are common in early romance, and are found in both *Lanval* and *Ipomedon*. Beauty is therefore appreciated not simply by the lover, but although it is never completely detached from erotic associations, it is appreciated by courtly society at large. Beauty has become a social benefit, a quality which enriches the life of all who are privileged to witness it. Canons of beauty developed in literary sources have been incorporated into the aspirations of fashionable society, and are reciprocally held up as ideals in the literature produced for that society's entertainment.

That physical beauty has been incorporated as an essentially social ideal is amply confirmed by the pictures offered in the literature of the *vilains*, that character who, by definition, is opposed to the *curteis* in all his aspects. Descriptions of *vilain* are almost always physical portraits of conventional ugliness, and as such are devoid of all but a few defining moral characteristics. The *vilain*'s skin, rather than being as white as the hawthorn blossom or as snow, is dark and brown; his body lacks the elegance of the courtly, and is thick-set and solid, and his limbs and features are disproportionate. In the estimate of the canons of courtly beauty, he is a botched work of art. The late fourteenth-century Middle English *Ywain and Gawain* describes such a creature:

> I saw sone whare a man sat
> On a lawnd, þe fowlest wight
> Þat euer ȝit man saw in syght.
> He was a lathly creature,
> For fowl he was out of mesure;
> A wonder mace in hand he hade,
> And sone mi way to him I made.
> His hevyd, me thoght, was als grete
> Als of a rowncy or a nete;
> Unto his belt hang his hare,
> And efter þat byheld I mare.
> To his forhede byheld I þan,
> Was bradder þan twa large span;
> He had eres als ane olyfant
> And was wele more þan geant.
> His face was ful brade and flat;
> His nese was cutted als a cat;
> His browes war like litel buskes;
> And his tethe like bare-tuskes.
> A ful grete bulge opon his bak
> (Þare was noght made withowten lac);
> His chin was fast until his brest;
> On his mace he gan him rest.
> Also it was a wonder-wede,
> Þat þe cherle yn ȝede;
> Nowther of wol ne of line
> Was þe wede þat he went yn.

(244–70)

This picture of a giant and deformed churl is an uncharacteristically lengthy adaptation by a Middle English author of a description in a French source, Chrétien de Troyes' *Yvain*:

> Un vilain, qui ressanbloit mor,
> Grant et hideus a desmesure,
> (Einsi tres leide creature,
> Qu'an ne porroit dire de boche),
> Vi je seoir sor une çoche,
> Une grant maçue an sa main.

Je m'aprochai vers le vilain,
Si vi qu'il ot grosse la teste
Plus que roncins ne autre beste,
Chevos meschiez et front pelé,
S'ot plus de deus espanz de le,
Oroilles mossues et granz,
Autés come a uns olifaunz,
Les sorcis granz et le vis plat,
Iauz de çuëte et nes de chat,
Boche fandue come los,
Danz de sangler, aguz et ros,
Barbe noire, grenons tortiz,
Et le manton aers au piz,
Long eschine, torte et boçue.
Apoiiez fu sor sa maçue,
Vestuz de robe si estrange,
Qu'il n'i avoit ne lin ne lange,
Ainz ot a son col atachiez
Deus cuirs de novel escorchiez
De deus toriaus ou de deus bués.
An piez sailli li vilains lués
Quant me vit vers lui aprochier.

(288–315)

A churl who looked like a Moor, excessively huge and ugly (more hideous than could be expressed) I saw sitting on a stump, a great club in his hand. I went towards the peasant and saw that he had a head bigger than a packhorse or any other beast, with hair tufted and brow hairless, and his forehead was more than two spans in breadth. [He had] huge and hairy ears just like an elephant, large eyebrows and flat face, with eyes like a screech-owl and nose like a cat, a wolfish wide-cleft mouth with teeth like a wild boar, sharp and yellow, a black beard, twisted moustache, and the chin pressed to his chest, his back long, bent and humped. He was leaning on his club, dressed in a gown so strange, which was neither linen nor wool, rather he had fixed round his neck the skins of two newly flayed bulls or oxen. When he saw me approach him, the churl at once sprang to his feet.[8]

The Middle English version preserves much of the detail of its French source. Some omissions, such as the failure to mention his eyes or the nature of his uncouth dress, seem unmotivated; others, such as the hair descending to the waist which replaces the tufty hair of the original, may be due to changes in fashion, but what is remarkable is the stability of the underlying aesthetic. The passages are separated not only by language and the sea, but by more than two hundred years, and yet most of the details which constitute ugliness are held in common: the disproportionately large head, the broad, flat face, huge ears and teeth, the crippled back, the chin pressed to the chest from the shortness of his neck. Chrétien alludes to the darkness of complexion, which makes the churl look like a Moor, and although this detail is omitted in the English, it is a characteristic resumed in Chaucer's Miller in the *General Prologue* to the *Canterbury Tales*, whose colour is imaginatively reconstructed by the artist of the Ellesmere portrait.[9] Even some minor details survived well in the transmission of the traditional portrait of the *vilain*. It may be that the word *çuete* 'screech-owl', which he may not have known, suggested to the English adaptor the phrase 'cutted als a cat'; but whatever the significance he found in it, comparison of the nose to that of a cat was a traditional mark of ugliness found also in *Of Arthour and of Merlin* (8716). Noses must be proportionately long, and the existence of the Middle English words *camus*, *cammish* and *cammede* (see *MED*) are testament to this prejudice. All are restricted to descriptions of noses which are flat, snub, and associated with uncouth owners. The fifteenth-century Anglo–Latin dictionary, the *Promptorium Parvulorum*, demonstrates a link to the Latin word *simus*, which is used technically by Pliny of a class of animals including apes, which have flattened noses. To the courtly observer, the churl in *Yvain* looks like an animal or some indescribable creature against whom he may have to defend himself; indeed, he seems to lack reason and thus may not be able to speak. Nevertheless, to the observer's question he describes his function as a herdsman, and in the French text he protests his humanity. He apparently possesses the fundamental qualities of humanity, reason and speech, but the condition of humanity to which he belongs is left in both versions to the judgement of the observer. In practice, more sophisticated authors were often concerned with the moral implications of imposing an irreconcilable division upon humankind, and this is echoed by the herdsman's claim to shared humanity with the knight. Alternatively, as in *Ipomedon* or the romance of *Fergus*, a courtly *burgeis* or a hero of mixed noble and *vilain* ancestry is envisaged as an intermediate condition. But these are conscious anomalies, and here we are concerned with establishing the fundamentals of the courtly mindset and not with such critiques of it. Courtly conceptions of refinement asserted the breadth of the divide separating human from animal; descriptions of the *vilain* consequently partake more fully of the bestial, and the judgement of courtliness, as distinct from simple humanity, depends on the aesthetic sense of the observer. The recognition of humanity may or may not invoke a parallel moral judgement or an impulse of charity.

Courtly opinion in the last decades of the twelfth century asserted the worth of beauty, but the appreciation of it was not restricted to personal appearance. Equally as prominent as the natural beauty of the individuals who populate romance is the richness and sensuous appeal of the settings in which they move, as well as the elegance with which they move through them. The aesthetic ideal encompasses not only the physical beauty of the protagonists in the story, but also the grace of their demeanour, and the appreciation of those concrete artefacts by which they are surrounded. In most direct connection with the formal descriptive passages, this means of course their clothing, which is often described in loving detail, clearly representing the fashionable wear of the day. Women may wear a white linen undergarment and a chemise or smock, and have their hair adorned with gold. Both sexes wear *samit* or *cendal*, 'silk', a *bliaut* or tunic, or a mantle trimmed with ermine, sable or martin fur, and variously *vermeil* 'scarlet' or *purpre* 'purple' in colour. A special point is often made of the fact that the *bliaut* fits neatly and that the ensemble suits the wearer. Silk features prominently in the description of clothing, and may be further identified as of Phrygian (*Lanval*, 511), Alexandrine (*Lanval*, 102), or Russian (*Horn*, 1580) origin. This air of connoisseurship in textiles is repeated in similar references to Cordovan leather, swords of Poitevin steel, and horses from Frisia. Gold cups of *oevre Salemun* are apparently gold incised with a chisel[10] and may be made of African gold, while other jewellery is attributed to the legendary goldsmith, Marcel (*Horn*, 561). The heroine's chamber is floored in a mosaic of marble and lias (*Horn*, 853–4) and has a carved ceiling with vaults constructed by a good engineer (*Horn*, 2709–10). Personal beauty is complemented by the sensuous beauty of the world it inhabits.

Such things are not simply beautiful: they are also emphatically expensive. Rings may have stones beyond the worth of a castle, and in *Lanval* even a tent is said to have trappings beyond the means of earthly princes. Although much is made of proportion as a sign of beauty, intricacy of design, revealing the skill of the craftsman, and the time spent on the work, is equally important. Indeed, the semantic development of the word *cointe*, which implies both refinement in manners and intricacy and 'finish' in material objects, emphasizes the conjunction of skill, complexity, and wealth which underlies approval of the beautiful artefact. Courtly people and their imagined world formed one continuous ideal of sensuous beauty and refinement. Marie de France does not overlook the opportunity of asserting the contribution of craftsmanship to a scene whose main import is in fact the decorousness of manners of the human participants, when she describes the queen looking down from a carved window, *une fenestre entaillie* (*Lanval*, 237) on to knights in the orchard before descending to join them for a meeting which *n'ert pas vilains*.

NOTES

1. De Bruyne, *Esthétique médiévale*, II, pp. 173–202; Brewer, 'Ideal of Feminine Beauty', pp. 257–69.

2. Howlett, *Chronicles*, p. 183. Marie Collins claims that in ME literature too, the emphasis in the presentation of male attractiveness to women seems once again to be on aspects of personality rather than simply physical appearance. Collins, 'Feminine Response', pp. 12–28.

3. Colby, *Portrait*, p. 14. As Colby points out, early French romance does not necessarily follow very precisely the top-down order enjoined by the Latin arts of poetry. In fact the rigidity of procedure recommended by the poetical handbooks is rarely followed in practice except for comic effect, as, for example, in Hoccleve's address 'To His Ugly Lady'. For further examples, see Stemmler, 'My Fair Lady'.

4. Compare, for example, Chaucer's representation of Absolon in similar terms in the *Miller's Tale*.

5. The description incorporates the three main factors in the contemporary conception of beauty: colour, light, and proportion. The theory of beauty based on proportion goes back to Plato and Pythagoras, but was transmitted to the middle ages in Boethius's commentary on Aristotle's *Topica* (PL 64, 933–5), where he remarks *pulchritudo est quaedam membrorum commensuratio* 'beauty is a certain symmetry of the parts'. This conception of proportion and symmetry was extended to the human body and to architecture by Vitruvius, and was also exploited by physiognomists, who saw external proportion as the reflection of inner harmony. The most elaborate accounts, intended as guides to painters and sculptors, represented each part of the body as a proportion of another part: for example, the face should ideally constitute one-tenth of the total height. The face itself was divided into three equal zones, from the hairline to the eyebrows, from the eyebrows to beneath the nose, and from there to the chin. Villard de Honnecourt's thirteenth-century album contains drawings showing the vertical extent of the human face as three nose-lengths. De Bruyne, *Esthétique médiévale*, I, 291–305; III, 255–61.

6. 'Quant si beaus out les membres tuz, / K'en dites vus de cel desuz / Ke nus apelum le cunet? Je quit qe asez fut petitet' (2268–70). It is worth noting that Hue's reference to his heroine's private parts is highly untypical of courtly poetry. Indeed, Colby, in her survey (*Portrait*, p. 62), found only this one reference.

7. Field, 'Ipomedon', pp. 135–41. See also Crane, *Insular Romance*, p. 165.

8. On the social significance of this portrait, as well as for a list of the characteristic features of the description of the *vilains* in general, see Specht, 'Beautiful'. This article includes a particularly extensive bibliography.

9. For an account of the representation in art of those outside the courtly canons of beauty, see Mellinkoff, *Outcasts*. On the representation of the peasant, see Vol. I, pp. 137–40.

10. *Romance of Horn* edited by Pope and Reid, p. 132.

Chapter 4

Courtly Values

Nobility, which later medieval sources sometimes defined as the legacy of ancient riches,[1] was inherited, but courtliness of demeanour, which provided the complement to physical beauty was, as we have seen, also the product of education, of nurture. Yet it could be maintained and cultivated only by the enjoyment of leisure. Preoccupation with wars, administration, commerce, or even religious observances might detract from the unhindered cultivation of the individual's refinement. Guillaume de Lorris recognized this in allegorical statement when he made Oiseuse, 'Leisure', the guardian of the gate to his garden of courtliness in the *Roman de la Rose*. The leisured life which Chaucer imagined to be suitable to the aristocracy of Troy, where Criseyde sits with her ladies listening to one of them reading the story of Thebes, is a life prefigured in the romance of *Galeran de Bretagne*, where genteel idleness is the lesson of the noble heart:

> Mon cuer, madame, si m'aprent
> Que je ne face aultre mestier
> Le jour fors lire mon saultier
> Et faire euvre d'or ou de soie,
> Oÿr de Thebes ou de Troye,
> Et en ma herpe lays noter,
> Et aux eschez autruy mater,
> Ou mon oisel sur mon poïng pestre:
> Souvent ouÿ dire a mon maistre
> Que tel us vient de gentillesse.

(3878–87)

My heart, madam, teaches me this, that I should do no other work each day than read my psalter and make embroideries with gold or silken thread, or listen to stories of Thebes or of Troy, and play *lais* on my harp, and beat another at chess, or feed my pet bird on my wrist: I have often heard my *mestre* say that this manner of behaviour arises from nobility.

The everyday life of a noble lady is here visualized in exclusively aesthetic terms. Her accomplishments are essentially unproductive, contributing only to an enhancement of the quality of life for herself and those immediately around her. Her skills centre on entertainment and the production of luxurious and beautiful articles. In the context of personal refinement and accomplishment, the cultivation of her soul is perhaps represented by her private reading of the psalter, although of all Scriptural works this was that with the most secular and sensuous appeal, commonly produced in appropriately *de luxe* form for private contemplation. In the fourteenth century, the contributor of the Prologue to the later version of the Lollard Bible found it beyond all other books of the Old Testament the most difficult for lay readers to understand in simple terms.[2]

For young men, knowledge of the techniques of hunting and the skills of woodcraft are the insignia of a cultivated gentleman. At the age of fifteen or sixteen, the young Amadas was skilled not only in fencing and board games, but also those of the field:

> De afeitement, de curteisie,
> D'eschés, des tables, de eschermie,
> De tuz deduiz, de chens, de oiseaus,
> Ert si apris li damiseus
> Que nul de lui plus savait.

(Amadas et Ydoine, Vatican Frag., 73–7)

Of accomplishments, of courtliness, of chess, of backgammon, of fencing, of dogs, of hawks, the youth was so well informed that none knew more than he did.

But of all the heroes of romance, Tristan is reckoned to be superlative in hunting and woodcraft. According to Béroul, while hiding from King Mark in the woods, he trained his hound to hunt silently (1527–1626); and the author of the *Donnei des Amanz* has him learn to imitate the calls of the birds (465–78). Authors clearly expected their readers to be interested in such accomplishments, and often incorporated the stories of hunts into their narrative, sometimes with effects crucial to the development of the plot. The young Ipomedon, although he is judged deficient in ultimate prowess because of his neglect of *chivalerie*, is nevertheless *corteis e affaité de bois* (649). Hue presents a long hunting scene in which his hero displays his particular prowess in the field. The lady La Fiere sits in a pavilion set up in a clearing to see the sport. A deer falls at bay beside her tent:

La fiere regarde la beste,
Que de sa lachesce s'areste,
E reveit le brachet gisaunt
E oit celui venir cornant;
As autres dit: 'Avez veü,
Cest cerf n'ad nul repos eü,
E li brachet ne boisa mye,
E cil reciet de venerie
Ki cest brachet si affeita,
N'est mie loinz, tost avendra.'
Ypomedon avant i vint,
La fiere vit, mes plait ne tint;
Donc sun serf outre passa,
Mult affeiteiement corna
De prise n'i ot autre aïe,
Ffors sun brachet qe od lui crie.
Ypomedon est descendu,
Bien est cum veneür vestu,
Cote ot qe de [?]sursegle esteit,
Deke a genoil l'ateigneit;
Son serf ad mult tost acuré,
Puz li ad la teste atourné
Sor les perches, com fere deit,
Come cil, qi assez saveit.
'Or poez, seignurs,' fet la Fiere,
'Veer valet de grant maniere,
Corteis e affaité de bois;
Or me suez, qe jeo me voiz
Veer come cil vodra fere
E cum il siet son serf defere.'
E veit le valet regarder.
Il ne vot pas tant demorer,
Mes son cerf ad mult tost deffet,
Son brachet pest, iloec le lest;
Il s'en vait quatre moz cornaunt
Pur son mestre, qil vait suaunt.

(623–58)

La Fiere looked at the animal, which had stopped from exhaustion, and again at the hound lying there, and she heard the huntsman coming, blowing his horn. She said to the others: 'Look, this stag has had no rest, and the hound did not lose the scent at all, and whoever trained this hound like that knows all about hunting. He isn't far away; he will come up soon.' Ipomedon appeared. He saw La Fiere, but did not speak, and passed by to his stag, very skilfully sounding the kill without any other help than that of his hound, which announced it with him.

Ipomedon dismounted. He was correctly dressed for hunting. He wears a [?] coat with a belt [alternative reading, *grisein* '[?]of grey'], reaching to the knee. He very soon approached his stag, then he arranged the head on the branches as he ought to do, as one who knew well what he was about. 'Now lords, you can see,' said La Fiere, 'an accomplished valet, courtly and skilled in woodcraft. Now follow me, I am going to see what he's going to do and how well he knows how to break his deer.' And she went to watch the lad, but he did not wish to delay, and very quickly dealt with his stag, rewarded his hound, and departed. He went, blowing four long notes on his horn for his *mestre* whom he saw following.

At the end of the day Ipomedon presents the heads of the deer he has taken to La Fiere, who receives them and takes this opportunity to get a better look at the man presenting them, for even more than his largesse and service in the hall, his skills as a huntsman have recommended him to her. Already her reason is striving with her heart, which is protesting its love for Ipomedon. Thus Hue makes skill on the hunting field the immediate cause of that recognition of virtues which leads on to love. Nor is he alone among Anglo-Norman *romanciers* in finding this motivation for his plot: in *Boeve de Hamtoun*, Josiane likewise falls for Boeve after he demonstrates his skill in a boar hunt. The importance lent to hunting as a skill *par excellence* of the courtly gentleman evolves throughout the middle ages, and is to be found as much in the technical descriptions of *Sir Gawain and the Green Knight* or the *Parlement of the Thre Ages* as in the technical vocabulary and the allusion to knowledge of horn calls in Chaucer's *Book of the Duchess*, the poem in which he comes closest to presenting himself as a participant in the world of courtly refinement.[3]

Despite later appropriation of them to more general social benefit (see Chapter 11), the lady's skill at sewing silk, or the knight's prowess in the pursuit of wild game, were not normally envisaged within the courtly ethos as useful accomplishments. Utility, whether directed towards the common good or the salvation of the individual soul, is not the measure of worth in the estimation of the authors of early romance. Rather, they exhibited, and by exhibiting advocated, the refinement of accomplishments for purely aesthetic ends. The goal is refinement, elegance, beauty; the arena within which it is to be won is the secular world, and specifically within that restricted company who are adjudged to be *curteis*.

Membership of a social group, originally dependent upon a single household or court, requires of course more than either the natural gifts of physical beauty or the individual skills of musical composition, fencing, hunting, or sewing. The larger court is a complex social and administrative unit, and the courtier must be competent in a range of social skills at various levels of formality, and with differing ultimate aims. In the one case, personal skills such as eloquence and affability, both of which are recommended by later and more analytic works on courtliness, may be exploited in the cause of personal advancement. In the other, an awareness of formalities and procedures of the court contributes to its order and stability at the social level, and refinement of behaviour promotes the pleasantness of everyday life. Since personal qualities and accomplishments such as eloquence will be discussed in more detail in later chapters, the protocols of court behaviour are what concern us now. Essentially it is a question of manners appropriate to the various situations of public life in the hall; at feasts, for example, where the role of the young valet is to serve wine to the lord and his lady. Horn excels in this accomplishment and, after his success in the hunting field, Ipomedon too returns to the butlery, bringing a cup to set before La Fiere. His advancement is marked by the fact that he is then excused the task after his triumph at hunting and set in a place of honour before the lady.

Seating is, of course, of great importance, because its position relative to the place occupied by the lord and lady is symbolic of status or of special honour. This is as true in the late fourteenth-century *Cleanness* as in the twelfth century.[4] Preparatory to a parliament in the *Romance of Horn* (442–4), we are given a glimpse of the seneschal, Herland, arranging carefully that lodgings too are appropriate to status. Consciousness schooled to the awareness of position in a hierarchy led to a very tender sensitivity to hints of preference or traces of a slight (see Chapter 8). If honour were besmirched, violent disruption might ensue. Hence care had to be lavished on observing those ceremonious formalities which court society had evolved for its own protection. Departure from the lord's household presupposed the need to ask formal leave to go. The asking and granting of *cungié* is a legacy of early feudal practice attested in the *Chanson de Roland* and appropriate to a society in which custom imposed a formula of parting to forestall abrupt or ill-considered withdrawal from a household if a vassal felt aggrieved. Once the institution of *cungié* was established the ambiguity in behaviour was clarified, and sudden and unannounced desertion could be interpreted as equivalent to *défiance*. The ceremony of leave-taking is so generalized by the end of the twelfth century that Lanval, when leaving his mistress, asks *cungié* (193). In the reverse circumstance, when meeting, courtly etiquette required that a greeting should be given, and that such greetings should be pleasantly returned. In prescriptive passages, such as that to be found in the *Roman de la Rose* (2099–108), this is clearly stated as a precept. In Marie de France's *Lanval* it is already assumed in practice, when the narrator comments that the hero is *mut . . . enseigniez*, and the evidence offered is that he rises to his feet to greet two ladies, who courteously greet him in return (67–8).

When leaving a court, having duly taken leave to go, his colleagues would normally turn out to set a man on his way. This practice of seeing a traveller off on his journey is so well established that it seems to have attracted a special contextual sense of the verb *cunveer* 'to escort' and its associated noun *convoi*. It is a courtly custom still observed in *Troilus and Criseyde* when the important figures of Troy accompany Criseyde on her departure for the exchange with Antenor, and the word retains its technical sense in the *Knight's Tale* (2737) where 'Duc Theseus . . . conveyed the kynges worthily / Out of his toun'; in *William of Palerne* (5111) where 'þe king of spayne . . . went wiþ him . . . to conveye him curteisli, as kindnesse it wold'; and in *Sir Gawain and the Green Knight* (596) where we have both leave-taking and escort: 'Syþen he . . . Lachez lufly his leue at lordez and ladyez; And þay hym kyst and conueyed, bikende hym to kryst'. Indeed, these technical connotations still cling to the word in the burlesque of courtly manners in Shakespeare's *Henry IV*, Part One, Act II, scene iv, where Falstaff, playing the role of the king, instructs his fellow revellers to 'convey my tristful queen', using what he fancies to be language characteristic of the court.

The formal aspects of courtly behaviour, which can be subsumed under the heading of etiquette, were preserved in the later middle ages in England in the form of manuals of behaviour known as courtesy books, and these are discussed in Chapter 8. Earlier romance pays little detailed attention to the minutiae of courtly manners, but it is worth noting how many narrative works feel it worthy of mention as a mark of refinement that cloths are spread on tables, or that diners pause to wash before a feast. In *Lanval*, before the hero's encounter with the *fée*, two maidens advance upon him, one bearing a towel, and the other a pair of basins. The relevance of this incident to the story is not made clear, and scholars have been tempted to see in it some distant echo of Celtic myth and water nymphs.[5] But whatever purification rituals might have been distantly involved in this scene, it is by no means dissonant with the emphasis on cleanliness preceding feasts in other romances, prescribed in the *Roman de la Rose*, and explicit later in *Lanval* before he eats:

> L'ewe li donent a ses meins
> E la tuaille a essuer.
>
> (178–9)

They give him the water for his hands and the towel to wipe them with.

The conception of courtly society and its formality and refinement which we have discussed so far has been one closely dependent upon the hierarchies of feudal allegiance: those qualities which promote the secure and equable running of a major household in which the lord's vassals are gathered to form a court. Wace's description of such a court *en fête* has become famous and it is worth quoting some excerpts as a postscript to this conception of the court. First, the preparations for the gathering:

> Quant la curt le rei fu justee,
> Mult veïssez bele assemblee,
> Mult veïssez cité fremir,
> Servanz aler, servanz venir,
> Ostels saisir, ostels purprendre,
> Maisuns vuider, curtines tendre,
> Les mareschals ostels livrer,
> Soliers e chambres delivrer,
> A cels ki n'aveient ostels
> Faire loges e tendre trés.
> Mult veïssez as esquiers
> Palefreiz mener e destriers,
> Faire estables, paissuns fichier,
> Chevals mener, chevals lier,
> Chevals furbir e abevrer,
> Aveine, foerre, herbe porter.
> Mult veïssiez en plusurs sens
> Errer vaslez e chamberlens,
> Mantels pendre, mantels plaier,
> Mantels escurre e atachier,
> Peliçuns porter vairs e gris,
> Feire semblast, ço vus fust vis.
>
> (10337–58)

When the royal court was gathered together you would have seen a
fine crowd, the city agog with servants going hither and thither to take
and secure lodgings, emptying houses and setting up pavilions. Marshals
allotting lodgings, chambers and rooms to those who had nowhere to
go, preparing cabins and tents. You would see hosts of squires attending
to stables, fixing pasturage, leading horses and tethering them, grooming
and watering them, bringing hay, straw, and grass. Everywhere you
would see valets and chamber servants going to hang up mantles, fold
them, clean and care for them, carrying tunics trimmed with grey fur.
It would seem to you like a fair.

A solemn religious ceremony now takes place, accompanied by
elaborate ritual and music:

> Mult veïssiez par les mustiers
> Aler e venir chevaliers;
> Tant pur oïr les clers chanter,
> Tant pur les dames esgarder,
> D'un mustier a l'altre cureient,
> Mult aloent e mult veneient;
> Ne saveient certainement
> Al quel fussent plus lungement;
> Ne se poeient saüler
> Ne de veeir ne d'esculter;
> Se tuz li jurs issi durast,
> Jo qui, ja ne lur ennuiast.

(10425–36)

You would see many knights coming and going through the churches,
partly to hear the clerks singing, partly to look at the ladies, they ran
from one church to another, with much coming and going. They
didn't know where to stay longest, nor could they have enough of
looking and listening. If it had lasted all day in this manner, I think it
wouldn't have bored them.

After the mass is completed, the guests proceed to a banquet:

> Quant li reis fu al deis assis,
> A la custume del païs
> Assis sunt li barun entur
> Chescuns en l'ordre de s'enur.
> Li seneschals, Kei aveit nun,
> Vestuz d'ermine peliçun,
> Servi a sun mangier le rei,
> Mil gentilz homes ovec sei

Ki tuz furent vestu d'ermine;
Cil serveient de la cuisine,
Suvent aloent e espés,
Escueles portant e més.
Bedoer, de l'altre partie,
Servi de la buteillerie,
Ensemble od lui mil damaisels
Vestuz d'ermine, genz e bels;
Od cupes e od nés d'or fin
E od hanaps portoent vin.

(10459–76)

When the king was seated on the daïs, according to the custom of the country the barons are seated around him each in order of his status. The seneschal, who was called Kay, dressed in an ermine tunic, served the king at his meal, and a thousand men with him, who were all dressed in ermine; these served from the kitchen, going continually bearing knives and table settings, and dishes. Bedivere on the other hand, served from the butlery together with a thousand maidens dressed in ermine, elegant and beautiful, with cups and vessels of pure gold, and they bore wine in goblets.

After the meal come the sports: horse-racing, fencing, putting the stone, throwing the javelin, and wrestling. The ladies climb on to the castle walls to watch their men compete, and the king richly rewards the winners. Entertainment is provided also by a formidable list of jugglers, singers, and instrumentalists, tumblers and illusionists. Minstrels tell tales, and some of the guests play chess, while others waste their money at dice, lose, and become irritable. This, of course, is the court of King Arthur, but the graphic pieces of detailed observation and the mundane realism, even cynicism, interspersed amid the conventional hyperbole, have persuaded scholars that Wace was here drawing on his experience of festivities at the coronation of Henry II. In a somewhat attenuated form, a similar scene is described in Middle English in the celebrations of the coronation of Havelok (2321–46).

This then is the court conceived of as a household and its guests meeting in celebration. But, as Walter Map well knew when he puzzled over the significance of the word in the 1180s,[6] the court is more than the sum of its personnel at any given moment. The conception of courtliness and of membership of a courtly elite was a much more extensive one than could be defined by participation in any particular household or feudal allegiance: it was defined rather by a community of culture, of aspirations, and beliefs, and this view was already well established by the end of the twelfth

century. Although not expressed as rules for self-improvement, as
came to be the case in later times, the awareness by that society of
its own distinct existence, and a consensus upon its ambitions is
strongly implied by the consistency of the aesthetic vision presented
in the romances. Even more impressive than this is the repeatedly
expressed opposition between the *curteis* and the *vileins*, made no
longer in terms of social position alone, but rather in terms of
outlook and aspirations. But probably the most eloquent testimony
of courtly society's self-recognition, and indeed self-absorption, is to
be found in the repeated instances in which the authors of these
early romances concern themselves with the historical origins of
those customs and observances which they feel to distinguish the
social circles in which their intended audience moves. It is apparent
that they can anticipate an audience whose interest in its own
customs extends to furnishing them with a history. The prestige of
contemporary social practice both encourages the invention of an
illustrious historical background and benefits further from its consequent existence. The veneration accorded to ancient custom is of
course always implicit in the antique settings of many romances,
and Horn, Ipomedon, and Tristan, all heroes of the past, excel in
the training of hounds in a way which contemporary aspirations
would have approved. But the myth of ancient origins may be
more explicitly stated, as when Wace discusses the beginnings of
'wassail' in England, or contrasts the custom of men and women
eating separately at Arthur's court with practice in his own time.
Hue de Rotelande also pauses to explain to his audience the
contrast between local custom in ancient Cecile and that of his own
day. The king of Cecile is disturbed by hearing the sound of
Ipomedon's progress with his retinue through a forest. Can this
mean an attack by an enemy?

> Kar a cel tens custume esteit
> Ke nul chevaler ne menout
> Herneis, ki pris cunquere vout;
> Sul sout venir, sul sout aler
> E sul sout ses armes porter;
> Si firent en chescune terre
> Chescuns ses aventures quere.
> En livre ai truvé e veü,
> Ke Ipomedon li primers fu,
> Ki unc od lui herneis mena
> E ki si fetement erra.

(2776–86)

For in those days the custom was that no knight who wished to win honour took with him a baggage train; he used to come and go and bear his arms alone. Thus they did in every land, each man seeking his fortune. I have found it in a book and seen that Ipomedon was the first ever who took equipment with him and who travelled so elegantly.

It may be that the celebrated remark in the *Ancrene Wisse* (pp. 21–2), which describes an earlier custom by which knights once fought on behalf of their ladies, adapting this to an allegory of Christ and the soul, should also be seen as owing something to this complex interplay of past and present custom, idealized history and social precept. Slight as these aetiological passages are when placed in the context of the major myth of European nobility which proclaimed its origin in the fall of Troy and a series of heroic foundations modelled upon that established for Rome on the authority of Virgil, yet they are further confirmation of the sense of corporate existence felt by those who sought to practise and promote courtly values. Corporate existence demands history, for the ideals of its incorporation are validated by the claim of prolonged and prestigious existence: such myths fulfilled this need.

NOTES

1. Gower, *Confessio Amantis*, IV, 2204ff; Chaucer, *Gentillesse* and *WBT* 2 1090–1.
2. Forshall and Madden, p. 38. The implication in the Prologue is that, since the interpretation of the text is difficult, commentators tend to turn to fantastic significances: 'Noo book in the eld testament is hardere to vndirstonding to vs Latyns, for oure lettre discordith myche fro the Ebreu, and many doctouris taken litel heede to the lettre, but al to the goostly vndirstonding'.
3. Compare also *The Avowing of King Arthur* (257–64) and especially, *The Awntyrs off Arthure* (33–52), where the rare technical term *queste* 'searching' is paralleled in *Sir Gawain and the Green Knight* but treated as needing explanation in the *Master of Game* (p. 6).
4. Nicholls, *Matter of Courtesy*, p. 88. At a more practical level, Geraldine Barnes (*Counsel and Strategy*, p. 21) notes that preparations for the parlement of May 1265 involved the provision of a hundred tuns of wine. That at Lincoln in 1301 consumed more than ten thousand gallons of ale.
5. Cross, 'Celtic Element'.
6. Scattergood and Sherborne, *English Court Culture*, p. ix.

Chapter 5

The Qualities of Courtliness

The acknowledgement of generalized courtly custom, as also Ipomedon's assumption mentioned in Chapter 2 that courtliness could be perfected by the experience of various courts, is an indirect statement of the existence of an abstract ideal of *curteisie*. A further abstraction from the circumstances in which the word had simply designated the customs of a particular household occurs when characteristic psychological qualities frequently attributed to a member of such a community are accepted as part of this ideal of *curteisie*. Such qualities are numerous, and the words used to denote them are still more legion. However, we shall restrict our discussion at present to a handful of the more important of them, in particular *pite*, *mesure*, and *largesce*. All three are considered courtly virtues, and are consequently valued for the contribution which they make to the refinement, amenity, and sense of community of courtly society. Inevitably, since literacy at the time involved close awareness of Christian moral values, these three conceptions of secular virtue were intimately connected with virtues as conceived by the Church. *Pite*, closely related to compassion and charity, was valued as much by religious authors as by secular.[1] *Mesure*, dependent as it was upon a rationalistic conception of what constitutes good behaviour defined by the avoidance of excess, was as much a virtue of clerks as courtiers. It was urged by authors with ethical concerns in works *destined* for a courtly audience rather than arising from the values intrinsic to that audience itself. *Largesce*, which involves the liberal distribution of wealth, bears a somewhat uncomfortable relationship to Christian notions of the charitable nature of alms-giving, since it is not necessarily inspired by the same motives as charity.

The word *pite* occurs frequently in late twelfth-century sources. It is much associated with tenderness of heart, weeping, and lamentation. Characteristically, it is the heart-felt regret at the over-throw of someone considered worthy of esteem: perhaps a worthy adversary killed in battle (e.g., *Roman de Toute Chevalerie*, 3642; 1993). As if echoing etymology, where Latin *pietas* may refer to the solidarity of the family, many early uses are to the inadvertent slaying of a father (*RTC*, 505) or a brother (*RTC*, 3213). Wace tells a brief and ultimately happier tale of family piety. King Argel is deposed for maladministration, and his brother Elidur is crowned king, a man 'de mult grant amistied, / Pleins de dulçur e de pitied' (*Brut*, 3499–500). Argel's attempts to raise help to recover the throne are fruitless and he is forced to fall back on his brother the king's charity. Elidur is sorry for him (*pitos*) and secretly grants him succour. Wace remarks: 'Lord, who ever saw such *pieté*, such love, such brotherly feeling' (3523–4). Not only does Elidur support his brother, now reformed, but in due course restores him to the throne: an act which gains him a general reputation as a *pitus* (3564) man. Ending the tale, Wace concludes on Elidur that:

> Il fu essample de justise
> E de pitied e de franchise.
>
> (3605–6)

He was an example of justice, compassion, and generosity.

It would be naïve to read this as anything other than a statement of the rationale for telling this story. Like other writers of legendary history and fantastic geography, Wace introduces numerous figures whose major role is to exemplify approved or deplorable behaviour. Elidur is intended to illustrate fraternal piety, but we should be aware of two other aspects of the use of the word *pite* in these excerpts. First, that it is closely associated with *amistié* 'friendship'– and indeed the two words frequently occur in rhyme in Anglo-Norman sources. Secondly, that *pité* – and the associated adjective *pitos* – may be used to describe a habit or quality of character distinct from the simple emotional reaction to particular disturbing events. Indeed, *pité* may designate not simply the emotion but also the reason for feeling; that quality of personality which makes the experience of feeling possible:

> Aldroën, ki fu mult pitus,
> Devint tut tristes e plurus
> De la tristur que il oï.
>
> (*Brut*, 6397–9)

Aldroën, who was very *pitus*, became all wretched and tearful for the sad event that he had heard.

That a sorry tale has such an effect is the consequence of Aldroën's *pitus* nature. *Pité*, then, may denote the feeling itself, but is also considered to designate that quality which predisposes a man to suffer strong feelings. The power of this emotion may be dispersed in tears, or it may explode into action: some form of political help, perhaps,[2] as is the consequence of the example just quoted, or perhaps even to greater efforts in battle:

> E veit la Fiere e veit Ismeine,
> Ki sunt en eines e en peine,
> E ces dames e genz plusurs,
> E ot ces criz e ot ces plurs;
> Al quer en ad mut grant pité,
> Le bon brant furbi ad haucé,
> L'escu leve, pur sei cuvrir,
> Leonin fert par grant aïr.

(Ipomedon, 9621–8)

And he sees La Fiere and Ismeine, who are in misery and anxiety, and her ladies, and many others, and he hears her cries and weeping. In his heart he feels very great emotion. He raised his good, burnished blade, lifted his shield to protect himself, and strikes Leonin with great force.[3]

Pité, then, implies powerful emotion, or the capacity to feel such emotion, often sympathetically; it is frequently associated with dolour, chagrin, and wretchedness. But this association is not a necessary one, and *pité* is not incompatible with joy. Such *pitos* joy is often associated with emotional reversal or the release of pent-up emotion which comes at the end of suffering. In the Anglo-Norman *Ami e Amilun* (489–90), two separated brothers are re-united after many years with expressions of joy and pity, and in *Ipomedon* when, after lengthy separation, it is discovered that the re-united Ipomedon and Capaneus are in fact half-brothers, they weep 'de joie e de pite' (10291) at this revelation. Hue goes on:

> Il n'ad si felun quer el mund,
> Ki veïst la joie, k'il funt,
> Ki d'eus mut ne se rehetast
> E de la pité ne plurast.

(10303–6)

There is no so unfeeling heart in the world who, seeing the joy that they felt, would not have rejoiced greatly with them, and wept for the pathos.

Their re-union and its accompanying emotions is a challenge to any observers to demonstrate their sympathy by matching these emotions. The instability of earthly things, alternating misery and happiness, is not infrequently the occasion of joy and pity.

The adjective *pitos*, then, may have objective reference to those circumstances which provoke an emotional reaction, or it may have subjective reference to the individual who feels this reaction. In the latter case, the feeling may be viewed either as a temporary emotional response to a stimulus, or as an enduring predisposition of personality.[4] This last is a courtly virtue which makes one ready to feel sympathy with any who are perceived as worthy through family or feudal relationships, or merely through their apparent *proesce*. In the opinion of Wace, *pité* is especially commendable in a lord:

> Mult valt a seinur pieté
> Mielz que ne fait altre bunté.
>
> (*Brut*, 4781–2)

Pity is of great worth in a lord, better than any other good quality.[5]

It is one of the virtues which he ascribes to the fifteen-year-old King Arthur:

> Cuntre orguillus fu orguillus
> E cuntre humles dulz e pitus;
> Forz e hardiz e conqueranz,
> Large dunere e despendanz;
> E se busuinnus le requist,
> S'aidier li pout, ne l'escundist.
> Mult ama preis, mult ama gloire,
> Mult volt ses faiz mettre en memoire,
> Servir se fist curteisement
> Si ce cuntint mult noblement.
> Tant cum il vesqui e regna
> Tuz altres princes surmunta
> De curteisie e de noblesce
> E de vertu e de largesce.
>
> (9019–32)

He was haughty to the haughty and gentle and compassionate to the humble; bold and strong and successful, a generous giver and liberal. And if a needy person approached him, he did refuse him if he could help. He greatly loved reputation and glory, and much desired that his deeds should be put on record. He set himself courteously to serve, and bore himself nobly. As long as he lived and reigned, he surpassed all other princes in courtliness, nobility, virtue, and generosity.

The connection between *pité* and *amistié*, which is formally represented by their frequent collocation in rhyme, is also evident in similarity of sense. The relation between the capacities for sympathy and for friendship is obvious, but less apparent is the fact that *amistié*, like *pité*, can be considered a quality of character: friendliness rather than friendship. This sense is found in a variety of situations, from the suitor's approach to his lady (*RTC*, 8594) to the political relationship between two states (*RTC*, 2532). Like *pité*, it can be that characteristic of an ideal lord from which his mercy springs:

> Tendent lur meins au roy e dient: 'Ore entendez.
> Aiez merci de nous pur vos granz amistez,
> Pur amur cely dieu par qui estes formez,
>
> (*RTC*, 7062–4)

They hold out their hands to the king and say: 'Now hear. Have mercy on us through your great friendliness, for the love of that God by whom you were created.

By contrast with the affective virtue of *pité*, the quality of *mesure* is associated with rational judgement and control. As we have seen in the physical descriptions of heroes and heroines, *mesure* possessed an exclusively aesthetic dimension expressed in terms of proper proportion, but it is more frequently found with moral significance. *Mesure* is associated with the approved mean between those excesses which constitute vice: it is that rational moderation from which virtue springs. In romances the word is commonly used to refer to rational self-restraint resulting in moral behaviour. Its function is well illustrated by two of the imaginary and exemplary nations which help to populate the *Roman de Toute Chevalerie*. The Mastiens are the basest people conceivable:

> Ne gent n'ad al siecle de si laide faiture,
> Car il n'aiment reson ne vivent en mesur[e].
>
> (6712–13)

There is no people in the world of such evil constitution, for they do not respect reason nor live according to *mesure*.

On the other hand, the Seseres live a life of virtuous ascetism, free
of all self-indulgence and crime:

> Nul n'i est avoutre, faimenti ne parjure,
> Ne ivere ne homicide, nul n'i vit en luxure,
> En tort ne en errance; lai tenent e mesure.
>
> (C., 135–7)

No one there is an adulterer, traitor nor perjuror, neither drunk nor
homicide, no one lives in lechery, wrongdoing, nor in error; they maintain law and *mesure*.

As the law imposes external restraint upon behaviour, so *mesure* is
that inward restraint, imposed by individual reason, which leads to a
virtuous life. It is intimately associated with justice (*Brut*, 10829–30)
and is contrasted with the lack of self-regulation which is associated with madness (*Brut*, 12669–70). Its value as a social virtue
within the courtly context is obvious, and indeed Chrétien de Troyes
goes so far as to equate *curteisie* with the possession of *mesure*
(*Perceval*, 6684; 8127). Hue de Rotelande uses this same equation in
a more limited application to moderation and discretion in speech:

> Mestre, sovent fet cil qe sage,
> Ki set ben cuvrir sun curage,
> Meint home en tel liu se descovre
> Ke meulz li vaudreit celer sa ovre;
> Meins valt trop dire ke celer,
> Ki s'i savreit amesurer;
> Cil ki mut parole sovent
> Ne se pot astenir neent,
> Ke aukune feiz folur ne die:
> Le bel teisir est curteisie.
>
> (*Ipomedon*, 2621–30)

Master, he often acts wisely who knows how to conceal his desires;
many a man in such circumstances reveals himself, who would have
been better to hide his actions. Whoever knows how to apply self-
control, talking too much is worth less than concealment. The man
who speaks too much often cannot restrain himself from saying folly on
some occasion: courtliness is judicious silence.

Although it is so esteemed, yet in romances with a courtly setting *mesure* often presents a moral problem in the treatment of a
narrative which tells of love. Rational *mesure* is opposed to the

extremity of the emotions associated with sexual love, and authors may pursue this opposition in any way they think appropriate. But for good or ill – and always for the good of the story – authors tend to agree that the power of love overcomes *mesure*:

> Merveille est d'amur; nul ne garde reson,
> Mesure ne honur quant vient a la seson.
> N'ad si sage al mond, se le tient en son laçon,
> Quel talent qu'il eit, nel face estre bricon.

(*RTC*, 7611–14)

There's an extraordinary thing about love: no one retains reason, *mesure*, nor honour when the moment comes. There isn't such a wise man in the world that, if it holds him in its snare, it doesn't make a fool of him whatever his own intention may be.

One response, like that of Thomas of Kent to the deliberations quoted, is to deplore this whole regrettable circumstance and go on to a passage of conventional anti-feminism, lamenting the susceptibility of men to the wiles of women. An alternative is to adopt an amoral posture, marvelling at the irresistible force of love. Most frequent, perhaps, of all is a third course which acknowledges the overwhelming amoral force of love, states examples which can be easily moralized, but leaves the reader to choose whether love is a wonder or an atrocity:

> Mut ad grant valur amur fine,
> Ki set danter rei e reïne
> E prince e duc, cunte e barun,
> Vers lui ne valt sens ne resun:
> Ke valut Adam sa beauté?
> Ke valut David sa bunté?
> Ke valut le sens Salemun?
> Ke valut la force Sançun?
> Adam par femme fut vencu,
> David par femme fut desceu,
> Salemun refut engigné
> E Sançun a femme boisé:
> Quant force ne vaut ne beauté,
> Sens ne cointise ne bunté,
> E qe vaudra dunc cuntre amur?
> Certes, ren nule al chef de tur.

(*Ipomedon*, 9095–110)

Great is the efficacy of intense love, which knows how to subdue king and queen, prince and duke, earl and baron. Neither wisdom nor reason is of any account against it: what was Adam's beauty worth? What was David's virtue worth? What was Solomon's wisdom worth? What was Samson's strength worth? Adam was brought down by a woman, David was deceived by a woman, Solomon was ensnared and Samson was tricked by a woman: when neither strength nor beauty, wisdom, intelligence, nor virtue are of any avail, what will then prevail against love? Indeed, nothing in the end.

But love is not the only characteristic of the courtly experience which may surpass *mesure* and thus raise moral qualms. Amidst a predominantly approbatory account of King Malgo, Wace mentions as one of his good qualities that 'larges fud mult a desmesure' (*Brut*, 13365). Later authors in the vernacular, including Chaucer in the *Parson's Tale*, were very positive that *largesce* should not exceed *mesure*.[6] But authors of Anglo-Norman romance are inclined to be less moralistic in this respect. Indeed, Wace is particularly insistent upon *largesce* as a significant virtue of the lord. The courtliness of Bledudo is exemplified chiefly in his *largesce*; he resembled his father, we are told:

> Mais plus larges fu de duner,
> Nule rien ne saveit veer
> Ne a suen ués rien retenir,
> A tuz vuleit le suen largir;
> Mult out en lui gentil seinur.

(Brut, 3685–9)

But he was more generous in giving; he didn't know how to refuse or retain anything of his own, he was willing to distribute his goods to all. He was a very noble lord.

Here we have a picture of what Chaucer and Gower, following moralistic writers, would later identify as *fool-largesse*, but there is not a trace of criticism in Wace's account. Indeed, in Part 3 of the *Ancrene Wisse*, reckless generosity is used as an analogy to the anchoresses' renunciation of worldly possessions. Nevertheless, in Anglo-Norman romance, a connection between *largesce* and a Christian or humanitarian desire to support the needy is only occasionally apparent. *Largesce* in these sources is often much more reminiscent of bounty in the mead hall described in Anglo-Saxon verse than of alms-giving. Arthur's court in Wace's *Brut* (10589–620) is represented as a veritable orgy of *largesce* in which fiefs and castles are bestowed on his own retainers, and visitors from outside his dominions are given all manner of rich gifts of a portable kind:

> N'i out hume qui rien valsist
> Qui d'altre terre a lui venist
> Cui li reis ne dunast tel dun
> Qui enur fust a tel barun.

(10617–20)

There was not a man who was worth anything who had come from another land to whom the king had not given such a gift as would be an honour to such a lord.

It is significant that these gifts are given on the principle of appropriateness to social standing. Their recipients are not men of no worth; we are not dealing here with charity. In *Lanval*, the hero, although a foreigner in a strange land and certainly needy, does not benefit from royal *largesce*. Indeed, he is shunned and forced to withdraw from court. When, however, he becomes rich as the result of his acquisition of a fairy mistress, he spends this wealth in a notably unstinting way and is accepted again into the court circle. Some of the recipients of his generosity are among those approved by Christian tradition, the ransomed prisoners, for example, but there is no suggestion that his behaviour is motivated by Christian charity. It may be deduced that such liberality proves a man to be free of avarice, but this is not stated, and indeed is not a necessary assumption, as we shall see. Instead, the difference in his position in the court is stressed: for being alone and avoided, he becomes 'nostre cumpainun Lanval, ⁄ Que tant est larges et curteis' (230–1). It seems that *largesce* functions essentially to buy golden opinions and impress by the wealth and consequence of the giver. Hue de Rotelande mentions in passing a proverb which he attributes to men of low birth, and which he himself can well endorse:

> . . . povres hom n'at en curt lai:
> Mal dehez eit tuz jurz poverte,
> Sur povre chet tut jurz la perte;
> Ore est merveile ke riche hume,
> Se il ne valt une bele pume,
> Si ert il avant apelez
> E pur sun aveir enurez.

(*Ipomedon*, 8406–12)

A poor man has no justice in the court: may poverty be accursed for ever; loss always falls on the poor man. Now this is a marvel, that a rich man, even if he isn't worth a good apple, will be called forth and honoured for his wealth.[7]

Wealth is indeed a courtly virtue in itself, and this Guillaume de Lorris recognized when he excluded poverty from his courtly garden in the *Roman de la Rose*, and placed the figure Richesse within the gate guarded by Leisure. This unashamed celebration of liquidity no doubt placed serious strain upon those whose means did not stretch to the expectations held of them. In this connection Walter Map tells a story which is no doubt susceptible of other interpretations than that he places upon it.

One day, while hunting, King Æthelred pauses for refreshment at a shepherd's cottage where he is royally entertained by the owner's young son, Godwine, who by instinct reveals all the traits of good service expected of a squire. Æthelred is so impressed that he adopts the boy, taking him into his household, and later elevating him to the earldom of Gloucester. Godwine fulfils all expectations, becoming both a great warrior and a respected courtier. Map, however, will not acknowledge that he was a good man (*uirum bonum*) on account of the humbleness of his birth; only that he shows prowess (*probitas*). Goodness is crucially dependent upon nobility, and Godwine's superficial virtue had to contend with the defects of his origins. Inevitably, vice emerged in his character: covetousness and avarice (*cupiditas* and *aviditas*), which Map explains as arising from his need to subsidize his *largesce*:

> affectabat enim quocumque modo rem lucri facere,
> quatinus modis habundaret omnibus dare, nec puduit
> rapere quod posset erogare, cum non debeat largitas
> facultatis excedere modum, nec sit dare laus quod
> adquisiuit fraus.
>
> (*De Nugis Curialium*, Dist. V, c. 3)

for his object was to acquire money at any price, that he might by all means have much to give away: nor did he blush to seize that he might be able to distribute, whereas liberality ought not to exceed the measure of one's resources, and it is no laud to give what is gained by dishonesty.[8]

The distortion of the courtly virtue of *largesce* which Walter Map alleges in Earl Godwine arises in his estimation not from economic causes but from the rusticity of his birth, which he equates with a moral flaw: this is the result of raising a peasant to courtly circles. But such a lesson raises a problem which reverberates throughout the middle ages and beyond: if *curteisie* can be abstracted as a set of virtues reflected in behaviour, would it not be the case that anyone exhibiting those virtues must be considered *curteis* regardless of whether or not he is a member of anything which could be called a court? This implicit question is answered in the affirmative by Marie de France, who refers to a courtly burgess in *Eliduc* (132–3) and by Hue de Rotelande. The latter in fact gives an important role to a burgess, a town-dweller who lives by trade outside the court, but who 'mut ert curteis' (*Ipomedon*, 6782), and shows him discharging his duty as messenger with courtly grace. Evidently one who is not a courtier may exhibit courtly virtues; but this in turn raises a further question. If *curteisie* is to be associated with qualities of character, does this not tend to equate it with nobility of soul? If so, can such nobility be considered distinct from nobility of birth? We have already seen Walter Map's opinion on the matter, and indeed in *Ipomedon* Hue de Rotelande makes La Fiere assume with Map that true nobility of soul is inseparable from nobility of birth when she says

> Si curteis hom, mien escïent,
> Ne nasqit unc de base gent,
> Ne fut onc engendré, se crei,
> D'autre homme qe de riche rei.

(1003–6)

In my opinion so courtly a man was never born of lowly stock, nor was he ever engendered, so I believe, by any but a rich king.

But Hue makes it clear that this is the fond belief of a love-struck woman, and much of the poem is subsequently interpretable as an extended demonstration of the intrinsic worth of the hero in a series of adventures undergone incognito. The relative importance and the relationship between birth and worth were to become one of the great themes of medieval courtly literature.

NOTES

1.   At the end of the third century AD, as the Roman Empire became Christianized, Lactantius attacked the Stoicism of Zeno by elevating *pietas* to a defining feature of humanity. The ability to feel compassion is what unites the brotherhood of Christ, and indeed *pietas* is presented as a synonym of *humanitas*

(*Divinarum Institutionum*, III, xxiii). A similar view is held by St Augustine (*De Doctrina Christiana*, I, xxix, 30). Burnley, *Philosophers' Tradition*, pp. 134–7.

2. Mathew, *Court of Richard II*, p. 122.

3. *Pitee* is the stimulus for help in aid of justice also in *Ipomedon* (8038ff) and, more famously, in Chaucer's *Knight's Tale* (912ff).

4. In terms of Aristotelian and medieval scholastic psychology, the established feelings and attitudes form a *habitus* or *dispositio* of the soul; what Chaucer calls a *habit . . . and disposicioun* (*KnT*, 1378).

5. The view is repeated frequently in the poetry of Chaucer (*KnT*, 1774–83; *Melibee*, 1860–65; *ParsT*, 468) and is stated explicitly by Gower:

> For Pite makth a king courteis
> Bothe in his word and in his dede.
> It sit wel every liege drede
> His king and to his heste obeie,
> And riht so be the same weie
> It sit a king to be pitous
> Toward his poeple and gracious
> Upon the reule of governance,
> So that he worche no vengance,
> Which mai be cleped crualte.
> Justice which doth equite
> Is dredfull, for he noman spareth;
> Bot in the lond wher Pite fareth
> The king mai nevere faile of love.
>
> (*CA*, VII, 3120–33)

In the *Parson's Tale*, it is ascribed to Seneca (*De Clementia*, I, 3, 3 and I, 19, 2).

6. In Anglo-Norman, the phrase *a desmesure* is an idiomatic intensifier, and does not necessarily evoke the moralistic associations of *mesure* and *outrage* 'excess'. Nevertheless homiletic objections to excessive *largesse* are common in later works. Chaucer's Parson characterizes it as 'wast' (*ParsT*, 813).

7. Compare *St Modwenna* (2085–96), where *largesse* is the determinant of social acceptability, and the poor are shunned; or the misery of Lanval as a stranger at the king's court, who does not benefit from *largesse*. Although the religious orders adopted poverty as morally invigorating, and Langland and Chaucer in the *Wife of Bath's Tale* (1151–80) adopt this view, yet the latter also puts the other side of the argument in the Man of Law's Prologue and in *Melibee*, where numerous authorities are quoted for the view that 'by richesses ther comen manye goodes' (*Melibee*, 1561).

8. See the similar story of Conan in *St Modwenna* (2137ff).

Chapter 6

Courtliness and the Individual

In the Anglo-Norman *Life of St Modwenna*, the author develops a long comparison between a serf who has attained power and a mastiff which has slipped its chain by night:

> Tant cum est povre, se humilie
> Mais quant il est munté en baillie,
> La u il poet aver maistrie,
>
> Nen avra fei ne amisté
> Vers hum, que seit de mere né;
> De orguil avra le queor enflé
> E fel serrad e surquidé.

(8538–44)

> So long as he is poor he abases himself, but when he is risen in estate, where he may have power, he will have neither faith nor friendship towards any man born of a woman. His heart will be swollen with pride, and he will be both treacherous and overbearing.[1]

Such a man exhibits malice and envy towards those over whom he has no power, and lacks fellowship (*cumpainie*) with those who fall under his dominion. People with a *quoer felun* 'ignoble heart', concludes the author, do not have companions and are by nature malicious. Clearly the writer of these opinions would agree with Walter Map: a *vilain* is a *vilain* not simply because he is poor, or ugly, or lacks *afeitement* 'education', but for some more fundamental reason. *Vilainie* is in essence a question of personality, an inherent defect of the heart, which separates the *vilain* from the courtly. Such persons are not to be tolerated in the court by rulers of sound judgement.[2]

In the *Romaunt of the Rose*, the dreamer walks out on a fresh spring morning, sewing his decorative sleeves on to his tunic, and emotionally revelling in the poignancy of the birdsong. No heart could fail to be moved by such springtime melody, remarks the poet. This view is widely endorsed, for the bright sun and the dew are still as restorative to the spirits of the fifteenth-century hunter in the *Master of Game* (6–7) as they were to Guillaume de Lorris. The song of the birds, and especially of the nightingale, often incites the *gentil* hearer to thoughts of love. This view was shared by a disapproving thirteenth-century owl (*Owl and the Nightingale*, 895–900), as it is borne out in Chaucer's account of Criseyde, who is similarly affected by the human singing of her friend Antigone (*Troilus and Criseyde*, II, 827–903). But for the songs of spring to take any effect one must possess the sensitive nature of the *gentil*. The author of the *Donnei des Amantz*, composed towards the end of the twelfth century, reflects upon the heart of the *vilain*: walking barefoot in the dew is a delight (*joie*) and is a restorative to the noble soul, but the *vilain* is oblivious to this, and is indeed opposed to joy of any kind, because it is foreign to his nature, which is to complain and grumble (*grucer*). Pursuing his picture of the *vilain* as life-denying killjoy, the author turns to the stock character of *li gelus* 'the jealous one', often the figure who intervenes to frustrate the enterprises in love of the young *gentil* man, and he undertakes to explain the etymology of this word:

> Gelus est nomé de gelee,
> Ke l'ewe moille tent ferme.
> . . .
> Gelee est freide e si est dure,
> E mult estreite a desmesure
> Ewe corante si ferm lie
> Ke ne se put remuër mie,
> Coure de li ne departir,
> Plus ke dame de chambre issir
> Ke gelus tent en sa baillie
> E garde en prent par gelusie.
> Gelee terre mole endure,
> Cume cailloy eschet e dure
> E tant l'estreint par sun geler
> Ke buef ne le puet reverser;
> Dure e freide est asprement.
> Est li geluz est ensement:
> Par sa femme est refreidiz
> Durs est a granz e a petiz,
> A sa feme nomeement,
> Kar il la guaite estreitement;
> Enteins que lui fait un reguard

Le gelus tut se deive e art:
Ne put fere a sa feme ren,
N'il ne suffre qu'autre i ait ben,
Joie ne ben ne nul deduit;
Estreit la garde e jor e nuit
E mult espie sun afaire;
Trop li est durs e de mal eire.
Pur ço que il est durs e freiz,
E tent sa feme en granz destreiz,
E fermine la garde e tent
Cume gellee l'ewe prent
Par tel reisun tut a estrus
De gellee est nomé gelus.

(549–88)

He is called jealous from *gelee* 'frost' which holds soft water firm. . . .
Frost is cold and also cruel, and exceedingly restrictive. So tightly it binds
running water that it cannot move at all, leave, nor run away from him
any more than the lady can go out of her room whom the jealous man
has in his power and jealously keeps and guards. Frost turns the soft
earth hard and [?] as flint and so much binds it by his freezing that an
ox cannot turn it over. Bitterly cold and hard it is. And the jealous man
is like that. With regard to his wife he has grown cold and he is hard
to everyone, and particularly to his wife, for he watches her closely;
even if anyone glances at her, the jealous man gets furious and seethes:
he can't do anything for his wife, nor will he tolerate anyone else
gaining any benefit, pleasure or amusement. He guards her closely by
night and day and constantly pries into her business. He is too hard and
cruel to her. Because he is hard and cold and keeps his wife in such
misery, and keeps and guards her in confinement, just as frost holds the
water, for that very reason the jealous man is called after the frost.

As etymology, this is nonsense, but the associations upon which it
depends are revealing. The identification of coldness and hardness as
the semantic motivation of an alleged connection between jealousy
and frost, especially in the context of allegations of pleasure-denying
churlishness, reveal a contrast between *curteisie* and *vilainie* drawn in
terms of psychological differences. Whereas the *gentil* heart is sensitive and yielding, lack of natural warmth and hardness of heart are
characteristic of the *vilayn*. In the *Romaunt of the Rose*, instead of
being moved by the *pitous* song of the birds in spring, the
hard-hearted *cherle* goes out to trap them. In the fifteenth century,
Caxton's translation of the *Knight of the Tower* offers an appropriate
gloss to these psychological assumptions: 'by the corage and herte

ben the gentylmen knowen fro the other' (p. 128). Of course, it was recognized that the ideals of courtliness were a form of social control within the aristocratic household, and that, to some extent, they could be acquired from instruction in the social virtues, the manners, and the service proper to any well-run household. Yet the attitude illustrated in the passages above suggests that churlishness was often seen to be deep-rooted and connected with personal qualities which were innate and not easily subject to change by social circumstance. Conversely, the virtues of courtliness sprang also from an inalienable condition, and were inherent characteristics of the noble personality.

From the simple fact of membership of a body of household retainers, we have traced a process of idealization in the conception of courtliness, indicated first by the coinage of the abstract noun, *curtesie*, and then by a literature exemplifying social virtues or tracing the history of social custom through the invention of aetiological myths. Attention is now directed towards the qualities of the individual soul. The narcissism of the courtly world thus seeks to complement its history by a cogent hypothesis which will explain and reinforce its sense of its own superiority. The postulate is that external evidences of refinement arise from an inner nobility. Psychology is recruited to explore and validate a proposition that courtiers are not simply those people who occupy a particular role and station in life, but indeed are beings essentially and qualitatively different from ordinary and inferior people.

In literary representations, the internal drama which testifies to this special nature is developed as an explanatory gloss on the actions and motives of the heroes and heroines depicted, as they strive to match up to the ideal or fall short of it. As we have already seen, there is in formal literary descriptions an aesthetic value system implicit in the physical *effictio* and a system of moral values expressed in the *notatio*. Within the very process of narration, too, a third perspective on courtly values in literature makes its appearance: it is a covert appeal to a self-awareness presumed in the reader, which seeks to recapture personal emotional experience, linking it to contemporary theorizing about the nature of the refined soul and its emotional susceptibility. The courtly writer presumes a cooperative and sympathetic courtly audience. This appeal to a shared psychological insight was already apparent in Wace's exploitation of the erotic impression of Ronwen on Vortigern, which relies on the sympathy of the audience, but such an appeal may be made in other contexts too. Consider the *Romance of Horn*.

Here the youthful hero enters a crowded hall to serve before his lord for the first time. It is a moment of great significance in the career of any *valez*. The author records that he blushed, but retained his sense of *mesure* and self-control. Clearly such a moment would have been likely to stir a sympathetic response in the poem's original audience. Recognition of the significance of Horn's blush and its circumstances required no mediating explanation, for his change of colour spoke wordlessly of inward turbulence which some at least of the audience could have readily shared in reminiscence; and they clearly were expected to do so.

Hue de Rotelande, describing the re-union of the half-brothers Ipomedon and Capaneus, tells how they wept 'de joie e de pite' (10291) at their meeting. Audience participation in their mixed emotions is here confidently and explicitly demanded by the author:

> Il n'ad si felun quer el mund,
> Ki veïst la joie, k'il funt,
> Ki d'eus mut ne se rehetast
> E de la pité ne plurast.
>
> (10303–6)

There is no so unfeeling heart in the world who, seeing the joy that they felt, would not have rejoiced greatly with them, and wept for the pathos.

Such open appeals to audience response are by no means unusual in courtly literature, and no member of a courtly audience would be likely to admit, when called upon to do so, to a heart so *felun* as not to be affected by the story. Indeed, this particular motif of *pite* and *joie* accompanied by tears, often at the first issue from a period of suffering, or at reconciliation after estrangement and separation, became commonplace. It is found in works from the Anglo-Norman *Ami e Amilun* (489–90) in the late twelfth century to Chaucer (B.1114; E.1080; *TC*, IV, 683) and even Malory (II.6) at the close of the middle ages. The extent of this motif throughout the courtly literature of medieval England – and indeed represented too in that of France and Italy – testifies to the importance of emotional susceptibility in the notion of inward *curtesie*. It is in fact related to the increased emphasis on affectivity found in religion after the eleventh century, which derived from Patristic teachings on charity, and which found literary expression in the religious lyric. But emotional sensitivity could play an altogether different and quite fundamental role in the self-esteem of courtiers, quite distinct from ideals of Christian charity. The formulation of this role in detail is not the business of the literature of entertainment, and in such works its theoretical basis may be obscured, but it frequently underlies the unashamed proposition of superiority in terms of sensitivity accorded by courtly authors both to themselves and to that community which they shared with their audience. We may consider one final literary example of affective sensitivity before enquiring what lies behind it.

In the late twelfth-century *Guillaume de Palerne*, the author presents a scene in which the heroine, Melior, is so forcibly impressed by the sight of the hero, William, that she cannot erase his image from her mind. The English translator of the middle of the fourteenth century, in contrast to the usual procedure expected of English redactors, greatly expands upon the psychological struggle experienced by Melior. She is shown seeking help from her maid for the pain she feels, and explaining her predicament in analytic detail. Her pains, she says:

> it komses of a kene þouȝt þat ich have in hert
> of William, þat bold barn, þat alle burnes praisen;
> nis no man upon mold þat more worship winnes.
> Him so propirli have I peinted and portreide in herte,
> Þat me semes in mi siȝt he sittes ever meke.
> What man so ich mete wiþ or mele wiþ speche,
> me þinkes euerich þrowe þat barn is þat oþer.
> And fele times have ich fonded to flitte it fro þouȝt,
> but witerly al in wast þan worche ich ever.
>
> (616–24)

Melior's self-examination blames her troubles first upon her eyes, but, recognizing that 'mi siȝt is servant to mi hert, / and alle my noþer wolnk wittes, to wirchen his hest' (467–8) 'my sight and other proud senses are servant to my heart, to do its bidding', she comes to the conclusion that the trouble lies within her heart which, according to ancient tradition, is viewed as the centre of all sense experience. As the organ ultimately receiving the powerful visual impression which William has made upon her, it has been so altered by the powerful impact that, looking at any man, she now sees only his image.

These remarks about the relationship between the sense of sight and the heart, in circumstances which are foreshadowed in Dante (*Purgatorio*, 16, 17, 23) and repeated in Caxton's *Eneydos* (p. 48, 26–8), go well beyond the simple stigmatization of a heart as *felun*, confirming the conception of a psycho-physiological dimension to courtly theorizing on sensitivity and the tenderness of the heart. The importance of these ideas to courtliness in general makes them the subject of this chapter, where Democritean and Aristotelian notions of nobility in the soul are to be investigated. Our initial concern is with the relationship between perception and intellect, but tenderness of heart is important too to sympathy and love, and this aspect will be delayed for discussion in Chapter 9.

A medieval conspectus on the material with which we are now primarily concerned is provided by a curious fourteenth-century Spanish work, Huarte's *Examen de Ingenios*, which was translated into English in the sixteenth century. It states that the earliest thinkers had believed that the seat of the human soul, that is, the seat of all psychological processes, was situated in the heart, and that although Hippocrates and Plato had preferred the brain as the scene of such activity, Aristotle had upheld the older notion of the heart as the centre – a view endorsed by the Fathers of the Church. By the fourteenth century, however, no serious scientific or medical writer any longer believed that the heart was the centre of psychological activity; yet the older tradition flourished in literary texts, and indeed separate functions, such as perception and memory, located by physicians in the brain, were transferred to the heart by popular writers. It is therefore rare to find in vernacular literature anything other than the traditional belief that the heart is the centre of the life of the senses. References such as that by Chaucer to *the humour malencolyk* or *celle fantastyk* (*KnT*, I, 1378–9) are best regarded as consciously scientific in tone.[3]

The importance of the sensuous nature in the Aristotelian tradition of the thirteenth-century schools is expressed by the aphorism *non fit intellectio in nobis nisi per conversionem ad fantasmata*.[4] The intellect depends for its operation upon the data about the external world gathered by the senses. Although direct spiritual illumination of the intellect is possible, it is normally unable to engage with the details of the material world, solve problems or make decisions connected with them, except by the mediation of the senses. As a consequence of this dependence, subtlety of reasoning about any matter connected with life on earth required good sense data upon which to operate.

The model of sense perception which was universally accepted was a markedly materialistic one.[5] A visual image transmitted by the eyes was impressed upon the *imaginacioun*, which was situated either in the head or heart according to the tradition followed, and thought to be soft so as to be readily imprinted. Variations of this basic psychological model envisaged a common sense preceding the *imaginacioun*, and an estimative power – a simple faculty for 'thinking in pictures' – succeeding it. All versions placed memory as the final repository of the sense images, and assumed that it had a somewhat firmer consistency than the *imaginacioun*, since its function was long-term storage. It was acknowledged that powerful stimuli could result in temporary or even permanent damage to the recipient faculties, as for example when taste is impaired by very bitter flavours like that of aloe (*De Anima*, III.2, 426b; III.4, 429b and Bartholomew Anglicus, *On the Properties of Things*, 118.15). This is presumably what has befallen Melior, whose sensitive nature has been powerfully affected by her sight of William. A slightly different picture is painted in the *Book of the Duchess*, where an experienced man, disorientated by the loss of the woman who has helped to form his character, looks back to his youth, to a time before his sensitive powers had diminished:

> . . . malyce hadde my corage   'impairment' 'spirit'
> Not that tyme turned to nothyng
> Thorgh to mochel knowlechyng   'experience'
>
> (*BD*, 794–6)

It was a time when as a young man his power of discrimination was not developed, and, indeed, he exhibited that instability regarded as typical of his age:

> For al my werkes were flyttynge
> That tyme, and al my thoght varyinge.
> Al were to me ylyche good
> That I knew thoo . . .
>
> (801–4)

Because he was young, his heart was a *tabula rasa* ready to be imprinted by whatever came his way. It was love for a beautiful and good woman, which as Calcidius (see below, p. 86) noted, because it was a habit formed in early youth, has remained with him.[6] The implication is that experience has made him less susceptible. The idea that the sensitive power could be impaired by prolonged or over-use was denied by Aristotle, and by Huarte, but was popularly believed, and is a very plausible extension of medieval perception theory. It is asserted, for example, in a late fourteenth-century treatise on the *Fyve Wyttes* preserved in MS Harley 2398.

Medieval commentary upon Aristotle emphasized the importance of the sense of touch, perceiving it as that sense upon which all the others were founded. Aristotle himself was not entirely consistent on the matter, positing in different places first hearing (*De Sensu*, I 442b), then sight *(De Anima*, II.9 2; *Metaphysics*, I), and then touch (*De Anima*, II.9 2, 421a) as the most important of the senses underlying reasoning power. However, it is this last reference which is repeatedly quoted by medieval commentators, and it is supported from other works of Aristotle.

The intellectual superiority of mankind over other animals arises, it emerges, from his subtle sense of touch, as can be seen by the fact that hard-skinned individuals are duller in intellect than those with softer skins. The hearts, too, of animals of low sensibility are hard and dense in texture (*De Partibus Animalium*, III.4, 667a), and in mankind hardness of the receptive medium impedes impression and is associated with slow wits (*De Memoria et Reminiscentia*, 449b–450b). Thus the implication of Aristotelian psychology is that a hard and resistant consistency in either the flesh as the organ of the sense of touch, or in the heart as the centre for the receipt of sense data, results in intellectual impairment.

Medieval commentary on such passages supports this view, and the passage is mentioned by most commentators. Simplicius and Averroes merely note the relationship between human intelligence and soft flesh, contrasting humans with animals, but Aquinas's commentary on *De Anima* applies it to the human condition more particularly, stating that:

> Qui enim habent duram carnem, et per consequens habent malum tactum, sunt inepti secundum mentem: qui vero sunt molles carne, et per consequens boni tactus, sunt bene apti mente
>
> (Lectio, xix.483)

> Those who have hard flesh, and as a result a bad sense of touch, are not well adapted to mental activity: those who are soft-fleshed, and as a result have a good sense of touch, are intellectually able.

The possibility that the connection should have been made between sight and intellect rather than with touch is explicitly rejected by Aquinas, since touch is the fundamental sense distributed throughout the body on which all other senses are based:

aliquis habet meliorem tactum, sequitur quod simpliciter habet
meliorem sensitivam naturam, et per consequens, quod sit melioris
intellectus. Nam bonitas sensus est dispositio ad bonitatem intellectus.

(xix.484)

Whoever has a better sense of touch, it follows inevitably that he has a
better sensitive nature, and as a result, that he should be of better
intellect. Thus quality of sense powers is a disposition towards quality of
intellectual powers.

However, he goes on to explain that this is not simply a matter of
more tender flesh or heart, but that these are in turn dependent
upon the correct balance of humours in the body, that is upon the
complexion. This view is made explicit in his *Sentencia Libri de
Anima*:

ad bonam autem complexionem corporis sequitur nobilitas anime, quia
omnis forma est proportionata sue materie. Vnde sequitur quod qui sunt
boni tactus sunt nobilioris anime et perspicacioris mentis.

(II xix, quaestio 1)

Nobility of soul is consequent upon a good complexion of the body,
because form is proportionate to its matter. Whence it follows that
those who are good in sense are more noble of soul and sharpness of
mind.

The theory of the human complexion, which is analogous to
that of four elements in cosmology, is of very ancient origin.
Briefly, it was presumed that, just as matter was composed of the
four elements, earth, water, fire, and air in varying proportions, so
the well-constituted human body was composed of a balance between
the four humours. These are described in Trevisa's fourteenth-
century translation of Bartholomew's Encyclopaedia as Cholerik
(fire), Sangwyn (air), Phlegmatik (water), and Melancholik (earth).
The combination and proportions which these assumed in any
individual were known as his or her *complexio*, and theoretical
accounts of the effects of the predominance of one above the others
are common.

Albertus Magnus, commenting on *De Anima*, II.3, 23, states that
proper softness of flesh is a symptom of a more fundamental balance
in the constitution, arising from a balance between dry and humid
humours. This balance is exemplified also by fine hair and thin
nails, but most importantly by the subtlety of the *spiritus cordis* or
'vital spirit'. Although Albertus thought of the *spiritus cordis* as a

kind of fluid refined from the blood, its function was similar to that of the more recent conception of the nervous system: to transmit sense data to the recipient centre. Thus, neither the flesh as organ of sense, nor the *imaginacioun* as recipient and creator of images is the ultimate conditioning factor; behind these two were the *spiritus cordis* and the *complexio*.[7]

By situating the distinguishing quality of a person's perception in his *spiritus* and *complexio*, and regarding softness of flesh as an incidental symptom, certain awkward problems could be solved. The author of an anonymous thirteenth-century commentary on Aristotle's *De Anima* (ed. Steenberghen) points out that demonstrably intelligent people may have their hands hardened by labour, yet lose none of their intellectual skills, and by contrast others with quite soft hands may show little understanding. This would be puzzling if a simple equation existed as an exceptionless natural law between softness of flesh and subtlety of intellect. However, if softness is merely a symptom of other more fundamental characteristics, then the observable facts are more easily explained. A kind of softness may be posited which is unconnected with the ideal balance, one arising rather from an excess of phlegm, the moist humour, which while softening physical substance also thickens the *spiritus*, thus hindering its ability to transmit data. One manuscript exemplifying medieval clerical prejudice against female intelligence, suggests that this is true of the sex as a whole, a view already taken by Albertus Magnus (*Quaestiones super de animalibus*, xv). This permitted the maintenance of the inherited opinion about the irrationality of women while acknowledging the obvious impression of their softer flesh.

The Aristotelian psychology of the schools thus provided a scientific basis to justify the supposition of a quite superior kind of human being, one in whom intellectual adroitness was founded on outstanding sensitivity, and in whom these properties were accidentally accompanied by physical refinement and softness. This conception was worked out in detail by thirteenth-century Aristotelian commentators, but its essentials belong to no particular school. The Neoplatonist Calcidius (*Timaeus*, p. 247), as well as both Hippocrates and Galen, acknowledge that the senses are necessary to human perfection, that intelligence varies between individuals (pp. 244–8) and that Aristotle's view was that perfection of the soul depended upon perfection of the body (pp. 236–7). Thus, when Aquinas says that individuals may differ in understanding as the result of differences in intellect caused by the balance of their disposition (*Summa Theologiae*, 1a 85, 7), he is not stating a radical or unexpectedly elitist view, but endorsing established scientific tradition. It was simply accepted that by nature certain people may be in all respects superior to others. Indeed, it was an inescapable fact of life on earth, inherent in the very union of soul with body (Bartholomew Anglicus, III). The fourteenth-century author John Blund expresses this definitively when he asserts that, after death, when separated from his body and the encumbrance of perception *per conversionem ad phantasmata*, the soul of an idiot, receiving direct illumination of the intellect, will become better informed than the best earthbound philosopher. However, although acknowledging in principle the view that the refinement of the soul is essentially dependent on the nature of the body to which it is attached, he nevertheless retains the possibility of intrinsic superiority of soul when he states that, all things being equal, after his own death, the superiority of the philosopher will be restored. Even divested of the distinctions imposed on human beings by the contingencies of earthly existence, some will remain superior to others (Blund, *Tractatus de anima*, p. 372).

A fourteenth-century tract on the nobility of the soul brings these questions more firmly into the social sphere of courtly theory. After equating the nobility of princes with the nobility of the soul, the author enquires whether all men are noble by nature.[8] There are arguments for taking this view – for example their common descent from the same mother and father, Adam and Eve – but, he concludes, the Aristotelian psycho-physiological arguments are against it. A mother does not distribute her matter equally between her sons, but to those to whom it applies that they:

> corpus bene dispositum et temperatum et bene formatum existit animam habent expeditam nec malitia complexionis torquentur, immo naturaliter tendunt ad ea que sunt rationis et intellectus tamquam ad operationem propriam inclinari, unde tales dicuntur boni per se et primo *Politicorum* dicuntur domini per naturam. Alii vero quorum corpora dura rudia et inepta formantur habent multum animam impeditam et de facili ad rudem sensualitem declinant et deficientes ab operacione humana in operaciones bestiales labuntur et sunt viles et servi iudicantur naturaliter.
>
> (Colker, 'De Nobilitate Animi', pp. 67–8)

have a body well disposed, balanced, and well formed this gives rise to an unencumbered soul, not distorted by poorness of complexion; rather, they tend naturally to matters of reason and intellect, as if inclined to their own natural function, whence such are to be called intrinsically good, and in the first [book of Aristotle's] *Politics* (I, 5, 1254a–55a), they are called natural rulers. But others whose bodies are formed hard, rough, and clumsy have a very encumbered soul and easily sink into coarse sensuality; declining from human behaviour, they slip into that of animals, and are base and to be accounted as slaves by nature.

Such ideas were by no means restricted to Latin philosophizing. A mid-thirteenth-century French philosophical compilation intended for a courtly audience explains that a prince must be an example to his people: 'plus enseigniés, plus doctrinés, plus affaitiés, plus nes et plus courtois que tous ceuls qui desous vous seront' ('more educated, more learned, more accomplished, more pure and more courtly than all those who shall be beneath you'). All men are not equal, and the difference lies primarily in the body rather than the soul:

> L'ame si samble le candaille ou la lampe clere qui est mise dedens le lanterne et vous savés que, se le lanterne est obscure, que la lumiere qui est mise dedens si est enclose que elle ne peut sa clarté demonstrer, si ne tient mie en la lumiere qui est dedens, mais a l'oscurté de la lanterne, car c'est certaine cose que, se celle lumiere estoit en une clere lanterne, la clarté em parroit dehors. Tout ainsi est il de l'ame.
>
> (Thomasset, *Placides*, pp. 206–7)

> The soul resembles the candle or bright light which is placed inside a lantern and you know that, if the lantern is darkened, the light which has been placed therein is so contained that it cannot show its brightness; and it is not the light within which is at issue, but the darkness of the lantern, for it is certain that, if the light was in a clear lantern, its brightness would be apparent outside. Just so is it with the soul.

If the body is fleshy, its matter gross, memory resistant and coarse, the posterior cell of the brain restricted or hampered by melancholy, then the virtues of the soul are inhibited. The question now arises as to whether those who are *viles per naturam* can be ennobled by instruction or upbringing. This is denied by both the Latin and the French texts: the circumstances of birth negate nobility in a way which cannot be remedied by instruction.[9]

It is easy to slip into regarding this dichotomy between the noble and the base as one founded on moral worth, and indeed nobility is often construed in this way since morality is itself grounded on the rational faculties, but at present it is important to recognize that the authors here discussed are not primarily concerned with moral values. Rather, they are stating in terms of contemporary science an explanation of the inequality of man. The account given is not partisan or controversial in its major tenets and would be well-known as an opinion. Courtly literature in the vernacular appropriated a suitable image from Boethius (I, p. iv, 1–3) to illustrate the fatuousness of seeking to instruct the *vilain*. Thus in the *Donnei des Amantz*, it is expressed proverbially:

> Sun travail perd senz recovrer
> Cil qui aprent asne a harper.
> Autretel est de vus, vilein:
> Apris vus ai trestut en vein.
>
> (1149–52)

Whoever teaches an ass to play the harp uselessly wastes his effort. It is just so with you, vilein: I have taught you utterly in vain.

The same image is used by Pandarus to taunt the noble Troilus:

> 'What! slombrestow as in a litargie?
> Or artow lik an asse to the harpe,
> That hereth sown whan men the strynges plye,
> But in his mynde of that no melodie
> May sinken hym to gladen, for that he
> So dul ys of his bestialite?'
>
> (*TC*, I, 730–5)

Although there are those who by nature can never attain the refinement proper to courtliness, the commentator on nobility allows the existence of a third group who are hampered by their constitution: 'alii sunt in quibus non invenitur perfecta natura, immo invenitur impedita in aliquibus propter aliqualem intemperiem corporalem' (Colker, 'De Nobilitate Animi', p. 69). But such are capable of improvement by suitable instruction: 'Qui autem medio modo se habent indigent doctrina et possunt boni per alium, licet non per se perfecte.' This group is ultimately, of course, the largest and most important, and indeed the cause of much literature intended for self-improvement. Here one sometimes encounters in the vernacular the psychological theorizing more often expressed in Latin. Thus the Ashmole (mid-fifteenth-century) version of the *Secretum Secretorum* (see further, p. 94) alludes to this material in the guise of physiognomy:

Flesshe in plenti and harde, grosse witte and intellect it shewith. Light
flessh signifieth vpon good nature and vnderstandyng. The subtilte of
the body shewith moche delyuernesse and full many conceytes.

(p. 110)

This statement shows as many parallels with Plato's Timaeus 76c as
Albertus Magnus' Aristotelian commentary (*De partibus animalium* ix).
A fuller statement occurs in Huarte's Spanish text, first translated
into English in 1596 as *The Tryal of Wits*:

> of nine Temperaments found amongst Men, there is but one (as
> Galen [Problemata xiv. 5] affirms) that makes a person as Wise as
> Nature can herself. In which Temperament, the first qualities are so
> justly balanced, and so well proportioned, that neither the Heat exceeds
> the Cold, nor the Moist the Dry, but all is found Equal and
> Harmonious, as if really they were not Contraries, nor had any natural
> Opposition: Out of which arises an Instrument so well fitted and turned
> for the Operations of the Rational Soul; that the Man is provided with
> a perfect Memory for things past, and a strong Imagination to see what
> is to come, and a great Understanding to Distinguish, Infer, Argue,
> Judge and make Choice.

(xvi, p. 368)

In view of the importance of its role in the composition of
personality, it is not surprising that courtly literature lays heavy emphasis on emotional sensitivity. It is a symptom of the nobility of
both mind and body, and the measure of a man's status in society.
The man of *gentil* and *tendre* heart, through his perfection of
constitution, and on the authority of Plato as quoted by Albertus
Magnus, rose up the natural scale of being towards divinity, while
the hard-hearted, coarse-fleshed *vilain* slid down towards the
condition of the animals. Sensitivity and refinement, consciously
exhibited, therefore became the insignia of social and natural
eminence.

Use of the word *man* here raises a new question. Discussion so
far has dealt primarily with the *gentil herte* located in humankind as a
whole, but covertly in fact in a man. What of women? How do
women fit into the complex of elitist psychology underlying the
superiority of the courtly individual? Vernacular literature often emphasizes the tender-heartedness of women, their characteristic *pite*,
experienced in readiness of sympathy, and sometimes in inconstancy
as the result of easy impressionability. Technical literature goes into
the reasons for this, discussing differences between the sexes at some
length. Medieval Latin commentary recognized women as the softer

sex; indeed Isidore of Seville derived the etymology of the Latin word for 'woman' (*mulier*) from *mollities* 'softness'. They might therefore be expected to be more susceptible to sense impressions, but medieval clerks did not find it necessary to proceed to the apparently logical conclusion of a superior reasoning power in women. Rather, in women, softness of skin and flesh, which in a man was associated with subtlety of the *spiritus*, could indicate instead a different *complexio*, with a lack of natural warmth and excessive moisture (Albertus Magnus, *Quaestions super de animalibus*, xv, 9). Thus the softness of women is 'a sign of instability and inconstancy and a defect, and so women are more inconstant, changeable than men' (xiii, 3). The lack of warmth in the female *complexio* has serious consequences 'quia propter frigiditatem complexionis in muliere debilitantur vires sensitivae quia peioris tactus, et per consequens est debilioris intellectus' (because as a result of the coldness of *complexio*, the sensitive powers are weakened in a woman because of a worse sense of touch, and as a result she is of poorer intellect). In short, women are soft as the result of an imbalance of humours; like the *vilain*, but for different reasons, their sensitive powers, and thus their intellectual discrimination, are weaker than in the ideal man. For this reason Albertus Magnus will not allow prudential wisdom to a woman, arguing instead that the sex is capable only of astuteness in practical everyday matters:

> Complexio enim feminae magis humida quam maris sed humidi est enim de facili recipere et male retinere. Humidum est enim de facili mobile, et ideo mulieres sunt inconstantes et nova semper petentes . . . nulla fides est in muliere.
>
> (*De animalibus*, xv, 11)

> Indeed the *complexio* of a woman is more humid than that of a man, and humidity easily receives impression, but retains it badly. Humidity is easily changeable, and so women are inconstant and always seeking something new . . . there is no faith in a woman.

These traits, and their explanation, are acknowledged to be found sometimes in men, but they are regarded as characteristic of women, and the scientific explanation offered lent authority to the general accusation levelled in more popular literature that women were unstable, easily affected, and untrustworthy.

The tradition which Chaucer received when drawing the character of Criseyde represented her in this way. He concedes that she was tender-hearted, and consequently readily sympathetic, but also records that she was *slidynge of corage*, which may be interpreted as both changeable in affections and unstable of purpose. He shows her as well-intentioned, but weak, making excellent resolutions, but incapable of carrying them through into her actions. It may be argued that Criseyde is the victim of the paternalistic powers which shaped medieval society, lacking both security and freedom of action, but in several passages throughout the poem Chaucer very deliberately presents her taking decisions or striking moral postures which she proves unable to fulfil. The reason why she does not carry out her expressed intention of returning from the Greek camp is not that she is devious or a liar, nor because such a journey, although dangerous, would be a practical impossibility, but, as Chaucer emphasizes in an addition to his sources, that 'bothe Troilus and Troie town / Shal knotteles thorughout hire herte slide' (V, 768–9). One purpose is replaced by another in Criseyde's sliding, feminine heart. Chaucer respected the *données* of his story matter in the creation of Criseyde, but modified them so as to present his heroine in an attractive light. Instead of moral disapproval, which is the traditional attitude to feminine untrustworthiness, Chaucer substituted courtly aesthetic appreciation and emotional enthusiasm. Criseyde is consequently a highly romantic creation: morally flawed, yet aesthetically pleasing and easily lovable. As a defender of women, Chaucer did not contest the accusations brought against their nature, but outflanked them by a means which, according to tradition, at least one woman, Queen Anne, apparently found unacceptable, for, in the *Legend of Good Women*, Chaucer was given the task of directly refuting the clerkish slander of the moral weakness of women. Whether he in fact did so is disputable, since the portraits of women there given are practically as insupportable as that of patient Griselda in the *Clerk's Tale*, who is explicitly rejected as a model for contemporary womanhood. Earlier in his career, however, Chaucer, inspired by Machaut's *Remède de Fortune*, had depicted in his portrait of Blanche a woman at once lovable by a courtier and admirable to a clerk.

In describing the lady Blanche, Chaucer adapts his sources by considerably expanding on her moral constitution. Part of this expansion is in terms of the psychology of perception. Blanche, we are told:

> . . . had a wyt so general,
> So hool enclyned to alle goode,

That al hir wyt was set, by the rode,
Withoute malyce, upon gladnesse;
And therto I saugh never yet a lesse
Harmful than she was in doynge.
I sey nat that she ne had knowynge
What harm was; or elles she
Had koud no good, so thinketh me.

. . .

Therto she hadde the moste grace,
To have stedefaste perseveraunce,
And esy, atempre governaunce,
That ever I knew or wyste yit,
So pure suffraunt was hir wyt.
And reson gladly she understood;
Hyt folowed wel she koude good.

(990–1012)

This passage has been widely misunderstood and mispunctuated by editors. In it, Chaucer plays on the scholastic notion of knowledge by contraries in order to argue that Blanche's goodness and innocence arise from a conscious awareness. Her *wyt*, that is her sensitive nature, is called *general*, which seems to have the unusual sense of 'noble, perfect', so that as a consequence her soul tends towards goodness. Both this awareness and her 'stedefaste governaunce' are to be explained by the fact that this *wyt* was *so pure suffraunt*; another unusual phrase, which emphasizes the perfection of the receptive powers of the sensitive nature.[10] This, coupled with her ready rationality, inevitably results in her moral goodness. Chaucer has here faced directly the psycho-physiological account of woman's inadequacy to present the picture of a woman of true nobility.

Every action provokes an equal and opposite reaction, so that the scientific assertion of the inconstancy of women was countered by examples of women who belied this claim. In some cases, like that of Blanche, it was through their own virtue, but in many others by the grace of God remedying the defects of nature. Another kind of defence is an excuse not unlike that which modern critics bring to the aid of Criseyde. Lydgate's explanation of women's duplicity in a lyric on 'Doubleness' is that of a self-protective measure in an unjust society. By the fourteenth century, indeed, the courtly tradition was marked by a readiness to defend women against the psychological arguments which impugned them, and to argue their moral and intellectual equality with men. Indeed, although Latin psychology furnished an explanation of the inferiority of women, it did not assert that the dichotomy between the sexes was absolute. Boys, for example, although possessing the potential for nobility, were no more rational than women (*De animalibus*, VIII.1, 588b). Furthermore, since the softness associated with femininity arose from an imbalance of the humours, it could also be encountered in men, so that the superiority of men over women was considered to be a relative rather than absolute one.

This rather more liberal attitude to women suggests that a more fair-minded judgement of *vilains* may be available than that expressed by Walter Map and some other early authors. Courtly townsmen are conceivable in vernacular literature even in the twelfth century. Indeed, the moral philosophical tradition had distinguished between nobility of birth and of character long before the medieval period, and the medieval courtly emphasis upon the virtues of the individual helped to break down the assumed connection between birth and nobility. By the fourteenth century, the views on this expressed by Boethius, Cicero, and Seneca had become commonplace. Chaucer makes a distinction between *gentillesse*, which he perceives as signifying inner nobility, and *curteisie*, which tends to indicate various social skills and accomplishments. In his *Wife of Bath's Tale* and the short poem *Gentillesse* he asserts that *gentillesse* belongs to the individual and is not the gift of ancestry. This view is echoed by Gower, and Scogan makes it central to a *balade* of instruction written for the sons of Henry IV, whose education had been entrusted to his care. The *Secretum Secretorum* (Ashmole), also intended as a work of instruction to the nobly born, still asserts the link between refined judgement and bodily constitution, but notes that circumstances of birth do not determine the individual's talents or disposition: a man may be disposed to be a clerk although born in a weaver's house, and sometimes a king's son by birth might have made a better blacksmith (76.13). The change of tone can be summarized by the assertion that nobility *ought to be* rather than necessarily *is* the property of the courtier and aristocrat. In these circumstances, the old antinomy between *vilain* and *curteis*, which had originally been one between peasant and courtier, was re-aligned as one between the base and the noble, understood in terms of manners and behaviour. Emphasis fell upon the individual soul independent of circumstances of birth.

The *Secretum Secretorum*, traditionally composed for Alexander by his *mestre*, Aristotle, but widely read in the middle ages by many who thought that *gentillesse* lay within their grasp if given proper instruction, commences its treatment of physiognomy in the Ashmole version with an exemplary story about Hippocrates (p. 90). The disciples of Hippocrates had his picture painted. Taking the parchment to the physiognomist, Philemon, they asked him to 'considre this figure and juge vs the qualitees of his complexion'. Philemon, after some consideration, replied 'This man is lecherous, a bigiler and loveth venerien actes and deliteth þer-in'. Hippocrates' followers were incensed by this calumny of their revered teacher, but Philemon insists that these are the qualities that his art reveals in the man whom he yet acknowledges to be 'þe wise Ypocras'. On returning to Hippocrates and placing the matter before him, the followers are told:

> 'Certaynly, Philemon told you trouth and left behynd no lettre. Sothly, sithen Y saw and considred þe foule and reprouable disposicion, I ordeyned and stablisshed my soule to be kyng vpon my body and withdrew it fro the bad inclinacions, and Y had victorie and put resistence ayens my concupiscence.'

The purpose of learning, concludes the author, is to ensure the dominion of the rational and moral faculties over the evil desires which might arise from an unfavourable *complexio*. Thus the *Secretum Secretorum* may be said to be addressed to that middle condition of humankind who are neither destined by nature to be princes and judges, nor be all but barred from the human race by their defects, but who may profit from cultivation, attaining nobility through study.

Emphasis upon rational moral control and the possibility of attaining nobility through education places the role of the *mestre* in a new light. He is the moral mentor and guide, no longer simply the man who instructs the *valez* of the household in social proprieties, feats of arms, or accomplishments like chess and music. By the end of the fourteenth century this change to more clerkish values is complete, but it is evident much earlier. Already in the *Romance of Alexander*, the value of a classical education in forming *gentillesse* is asserted. Referring to Athens, Thomas of Kent remarks:

> La comencea honur primes e cortoisie,
> Doctrine e discipline e engin de clergie,
> De auturs de gramaire e de philosophie,
> Retorike, phisike, musike e geometrie;
> De tuz les set ars i ot la mestrie.

(2347–51)

There first began honour and courtliness, the teachings, discipline and skills of learning, the authors, grammar, philosophy, rhetoric, natural science, music, and geometry; they were pre-eminent in all the seven arts.

The close connection between the ideals of the courtier and the seven arts represents an assumption that such clerkly learning has a part to play in the formation of courtliness, an assumption echoed in the fourteenth century. Chaucer, Gower, and the author of *Mum and the Sothsegger* share a vision of the *sapiens* as the guide to a prince. The examples of Aristotle and Alexander, and of Seneca and Nero become part of courtly mythology.

The extent to which the targets of clerkly propaganda accepted instruction must have varied considerably. The adage *rex illiteratus asinus coronatus* 'an illiterate king is a crowned ass' belongs to the twelfth century, but Walter Map's description of Henry II is significant in this context:

> with no polite accomplishment was he unacquainted; he had skill of letters as far as was fitting or practically useful, and he had a knowledge of all the tongues used from the French sea to the Jordan, but spoke only Latin and French . . . [he was] . . . a great connoisseur of hounds and hawks, and most greedy of that vain sport.
>
> (*De Nugis Curialium*, Dist v, c. 6)

Although Map clearly admires Henry, his final remarks and the phrase 'as far as was fitting or useful' express adequately the attitude of the courtier to philosophy. In so far as *clergie* could offer practical instruction, it was of value; too rarely is it seen as the road to spiritual nobility. What is true for the nobility seems to have been true also for the peasants. Map laments that the peasants (*serui, rusticos*) 'vie with each other in bringing up their ignoble and degenerate offspring to those arts which are forbidden to them; not that they may shed vices, but that they may gather riches' (Dist I, c. 10). At least in the earlier period in England the situation seems to have fallen well short of the idealizing account given by Christine de Pizan of Jean, Duc de Berri:

> se delitte et aime gens soubtilz, soient clers ou aultres; beaulz livres des sciences morales et hystoires nottable des pollicies romaines ou d'autres louable enseignemens moult aime, et voulentiers en ot, tous ouvrages soubtilment fais et par maistrie beaulx et polis, aournemens riches, beaulz edefices, dont a fait faire maint en son pais, à Paris et ailleurs. Est

prince de doulce et humaine conversacion, sanz haultainété d'orgueil, benigne en parole et response, joyeux en conversacion, et en toutes choses tres traittable.

(*Fais et Bonnes Meurs du Sage Roy Charles V*, pp. 142–3)

He loved and took pleasure in intelligent people, whether clerks or lay; he loved. and eagerly collected fine books on moral science and important works on Roman political history and other worthy subjects; all works cunningly made and refined and polished by outstanding skill; rich ornaments, fine buildings, of which he had many built on his land, both in Paris and elsewhere. The prince was gentle and urbane in conversation, without any distant haughtiness, kindly in speech and reply, delighting in conversation, and in every way most approachable.

Christine's picture lifts us beyond the level of the ordinary courtly man to that of the prince, magnificent in his cultural achievements, and from the middle ages to the threshold of the Renaissance, but her emphasis is upon his skilled conversation and his easy approachableness, and indeed even her word *traittable* in this context has echoes in Chaucerian English. It seems that both in her conception and in the language she uses to express it, there are parallels with Chaucer, who found the Man in Black equally easy to talk to:

> Loo! how goodly spak thys knyght,
> As hit had be another wyght;
> He made hyt nouther tough ne queynte.
> And I saw that, and gan me aqueynte
> With hym, and fond hym so tretable
> Ryght wonder skylful and resonable.

(*BD*, 529–34)

Both authors seem to have in mind a common conception of some social virtue, an approachability and friendliness in attitude expressed through the mastery of conversational exchange. In the case of both men their grasp of the social use of language is the subject of admiration. Indeed, the relationship between courtliness and the use of language has been an undercurrent in this discussion for some time, and the time has come to investigate it more thoroughly.

NOTES

1. A contrast between the nobility of hounds and vulgarity of mastiffs is frequently made. The fourteenth-century *Weye of Paradys* figures well-intentioned reformers as gentlemen hunting with hounds, whose good work may be impeded by mastiffs: 'Alle tho that don soo ben gentelmen. But there be

many, as I trowe, that ben lik to mastyfes; tho ben churlysche howndes. ȝif
they se gentyl howndes rennen aftir here beest that they chace, they schul not
helpen hem to chace ne to take here beest, but thei schul rennen on hem and
byten hem and stranglen hem, ȝif they mow' (ed. Diekstra, *ME Weye of
Paradys*, p. 283). The *Master of Game* (p. 68) also testifies that 'þei byn of
cherlich nature and of foule shape' and that their 'nature his not to be tendirly
norshed' (i.e., *norissed*). See also Elliott, *Chaucer's English*, pp. 342–3.

2.   Duby, *Chivalrous Society*, pp. 182–3.

3.   On humours and the complexion, see below, p. 85 and *De Proprietatibus
Rerum*, I, iv. The *celle fantastyk* is one of the three chambers which medieval
physicians placed inside the brain and associated with the process of cognition.
According to Bartholomew Anglicus, the first, in which images are formed
from sense impressions, is the chamber of the *ymaginacioun*. The second,
which analyses and assesses these images, is the seat of *reason*, and the last, in
which concepts are stored, is the *mynde* or memory (*De Proprietatibus Rerum*, I,
v, 173–4). The *celle fantastyk* is synonymous with the chamber of the
imagination.

4.   'The function of intellect does not arise in us except through the mediation of
images'. Transcribed from BL MS Add. 19585 f.92r. I owe this reference to
my colleague, Brian Donaghey.

5.   For the broader functions of memory in medieval literate society, see the
book-length treatments by Yates (*Art of Memory*) and Carruthers (*Book of
Memory*). Although both are more concerned with artificial memory systems,
they also treat the general conception of memory.

6.   'Certumque illud expertus sum tenaciorem fore memoriam eorum quae in prima
aetate discuntur' Waszink, *Timaeus*, p. 18. But Chaucer may have have taken
the idea from the *Roman de la Rose* (12887–92), where it is attributed to Plato.

7.   A similar metabolism is discussed in Trevisa's translation of Bartholomew
Anglicus's *De Proprietatibus Rerum*. It is explained that a 'spirit' is a subtle
substance which stimulates the powers of the body to action. A spirit is
produced by heat acting on the blood and is refined in the liver to become the
spiritus naturalis. This stimulates the motion of the blood. It is further refined in
the heart, producing the *spiritus vitalis*, which gives life and pulse to the body.
Transmitted to the brain, it is refined in the foremost cell to become the
spiritus animalis, which empowers the common sense and imagination, and is
the bearer of sense information. It also carries commands for the motion of the
limbs. Bartholomew notes that, whatever the name drawn from its site at any
particular moment, this is essentially the same fluid extending around the body
(ed. Seymour, III, pp. 120–2).

8.   Compare Gerson, *De Nobilitate*, p. 478.

9.   Some constitutions resist instruction: 'the well-complexioned man is thus like
good land where nothing more is necessary than to sow the grain, but
whoever sows on poor land or on hard rock wastes his time' (Thomasset,
Placides, p. 207). Although produced in the thirteenth century, this text
survives in manuscripts of the fourteenth and fifteenth centuries, and in
numerous printed books of the sixteenth century.

10. In his translation of Boethius, and elsewhere in technical contexts, Chaucer
calls the sensitive nature the *suffraunce*.

Chapter 7

Courtliness and Language

Courtliness, at its simplest, was a condition recognizable from characteristic modes of behaviour or aspects of appearance, but such a judgement was made to appear superficial by the assertion that courtliness was in fact a kind of nobility whose sources lay deeper in a person's constitution. The following anecdote, taken from Caxton's fifteenth-century translation of the *Knight of the Tower*, illustrates this attitude:

> It hapned that I was in a companye of knyghtes and ladyes / And that a grete lady tooke of her hood and humbled her self curtoysly vnto a tayloure / And ther was a knyght that said to her / Madame why haue ye taken of youre hoode vnto a taylloure / And she answerd that she had leuer to take it of to hym, than to haue lefte it vnto a gentyll man / And that was reputed for ryght wel done / and as for the best tauȝt of all the other.
>
> (24–5)

The instructive nature of the anecdote lies in its need for interpretation: the assertion is that courtliness lies in the recognition that, despite his humble social status, the tailor may have possessed traits of nobility which, although hidden by his station in life, yet deserve acknowledgement. Both the content and also the language of this passage are significant. *Curteis* burgesses appear in French from the late twelfth century, but the fact that this story has been translated into English suggests that it is intended for a broader audience who could not claim nobility by birth. Furthermore, the words of approval of the lady's action (*best tauȝt*) draw further attention to courtliness as nurture rather than nature. It is, in other words, a story illustrative of the moral proposition that nobility is derived from sources other than simple inheritance.

The argument that true nobility resides in the soul naturally places a greater emphasis upon linguistic performance. Motivations, intentions and feelings are conveyed by speaking. If the noble soul received information from the material world by gathering data through a heightened sensitive nature, it communicated in return with the world external to it through the medium of language. Language, or more precisely speech, was the means by which the inward nobility of the individual could best and most surely be judged by outsiders, and generations of rhetorical theorists regarded it also as the means by which the noble soul could itself influence, direct, and improve the world around it.

Because of the complexity of courtly ideas, as well as that of language itself, the spoken word acts as a communicator of the courtly qualities of the individual in a large variety of distinct ways. It may reveal innate qualities of the soul, giving expression to the compassion and sympathy which arises from sensitivity, or it might express friendliness and approachability in the speaker. The *tretable* behaviour and speech of the Man in Black to the Dreamer in the *Book of the Duchess* (531–4) is an example. Indeed, affability and willingness to enter into conversation with a stranger often forms part of the idealizing description of courtliness. Writing on the topic of conversation in his encyclopaedia, *Li Tresor*, Brunetto Latini remarks:

> Et en tenir li mi doit on estre plaisant en parler, et en demorer avec les gens et en converser entre les homes, et k'il soit de bele compaignie et soit communaus as choses qui se covient et en maniere et en leu et en tans k'il covient. Et ceste conversation est samblable a amistié; mais tant i a de difference, k'en amistié covient avoir compassion et unité de corage, mais en conversation n'a nule compassion, car on puet bien converser avec .i. home que on ne connoist.
>
> (p. 196)

And in moderation one should be pleasant in speech, both in lingering with mixed groups and conversation between men, and that it is suitable to good company and related to things which are relevant, and suitable in manner, in place, and in time. And this conversation is like friendship; but there is this difference, that in friendship fellow feeling and mutuality of desires is required, but in conversation there is no fellow feeling because one can easily converse with a man whom one does not know.

Although lacking the emotional commitment of the latter, conversation is analogous to friendship: it is a means by which social contacts are made and maintained, and as such is the reflection of a disposition towards sociability which is highly valued. The establishment of contacts in a decorous way through verbal exchange forms an important scene in many narratives. Authors of more sophisticated romance rarely fail to mention that one character greets another (*salue*) and the second returns the greeting. Very often the words uttered are quoted, and nearly as often the greeting is said to be delivered *curteisly*. Among the advice on refined behaviour given to the new Lover in the *Romaunt of the Rose* is some which turns narrative into precept:

> And whanne thou comest there men are,
> Loke that thou have in custome ay
> First to salue hem, if thou may;
> And if it fall that of hem som
> Salue thee first, be not domm,
> But quyte hem curteisly anoon,
> Without abidyng, er they goon.
>
> (2216–22)

However, the use of language does not simply reveal the inherent nobility of the individual soul; for the man of the court, perhaps in actuality, and the noble man certainly in theory, is destined to be a lord and a leader of men. As a person of importance, he aspires also to be a man of influence, whether persuading his peers or exhorting his troops. In this sphere, linguistic skills perfected by study do not express sensitivity, but serve to complement wisdom and political judgement. It is not by chance that, in his *Confessio Amantis*, Gower placed the linguistic arts in a section (Book VII) on civil administration. In court circles, eloquence was valued and may be rewarded by promotion, and the ability to 'say fittingly what the mind wishes to express' was widely reckoned of practical value to a prince.

This tradition of eloquence in the leader drew quite consciously upon values descended from the classical past, and formed part of the clerkly interpretation of nobility. Those who set themselves to celebrate, record, and legislate the literate culture of monarchs and great men did so in full awareness of Imperial Roman traditions, where, although linguistic skills had been studied as an aid to efficacy in political and legal debate, yet a liberal education had been valued for its own worth, and evidence of personal refinement and quickness of wit had been respected as signs of a cultivated man.

Latin *urbanitas* underlay at least some attitudes to medieval courtliness, and as a quality of personal refinement distinct from the political use of rhetorical skills, is indeed part of monastic culture. The word itself is first recorded in one of Cicero's speeches, where it means elegance of manner, and in the Roman world it developed to connote many of the same aspects of refinement as were understood in medieval courtliness.[1] Its original purpose was to designate those features which were held to distinguish the citizens of Rome from the inhabitants of the surrounding countryside (*rusticitas*); the sophistication and refinement of the city-dweller by comparison with the peasant, a distinction closely related to that we have seen in Chapter 2 between *curialitas* and *villanus*. Early texts suggest a reference to features of the pronunciation of Latin, the city-dwellers favouring a higher, closer articulation and avoiding aspiration before a vowel,[2] but *urbanitas* quickly became associated with pre-eminence in the cultural ideals subsumed under the heading *humanitas*. Horace sees *urbanitas* as coinciding with literary interests, and it becomes associated also with eloquent, sophisticated and witty utterances. As befitted a rhetorician and educator, Quintilian couples *urbanitas* with formal skills such as appropriateness of expression and grammatical correctness to complement its acknowledged association with wit.

The clerkly medieval commentator, wishing at the same time to emphasize the importance of his own skills and to flatter the object of his eulogies with possession of the highest cultural values, tended to impose aspects of Latin *urbanitas* upon him. Walter Map's description of Henry II, with his limited practical grasp of languages and preference for hunting, contrasts with Aelred of Rievaulx's encomium of Walter Espec, which mentions both his imposing physical appearance and also his 'trumpet-like' voice, and his eloquence. Both volume and eloquence are put to good use before the Battle of the Standard, when Espec, a respected and prudent leader, delivers an inspiring oration before the battle, no doubt written for him in retrospect by Aelred, and in the late Latin tradition of 'comforting' the troops.[3] Although a Yorkshire baron is here conceived of by a clerkly author in Latin heroic terms, the degree of cultivation extended to him once again pales into insignificance when compared to that allotted by Christine de Pizan to a French dignitary of the early fifteenth century, Charles V of France. He, we learn, was skilled in eloquence 'par nature et aussi par science' (II, 34):

Ot belle aleure, voix d'homme de beau ton, et avec tout ce, certes, à sa belle parleure tant ordennée et par si belle arrenge, sanz aucune super-

fluité de parole, ne croy que rethoricien quelconques en lengue
francaise sceust riens amender.

(I, 49)

He had a good pace, a good, manly tone, and indeed, in addition,
with his good speech so ordered and with such a good style, lacking
any prolixity of words, that I do not think that any rhetorician
whatsoever in the French language would know how to improve it in
any way.

Such an account marks decisively the growing prestige of literate culture among the court community in the fifteenth century. In the
portraits painted by Christine de Pizan the clerkly ideal of the
accomplished monarch has developed to approach the humanist
conception of the philosopher-prince, linking ancient ideals with
those of the Renaissance. The English middle ages cannot match
Christine's fulsome portraits, but the contrast between her account
and that of Walter Map points to the direction of development.
Increasingly, values of clerkly accomplishment impose themselves
upon the ideals of courtliness, and with them more attention is
given to the skills of eloquence and of learning.

The association between courtliness in its widest sense and the
use of language may occur in many different ways. We shall consider four of them: that with courtliness understood as nobility of
birth; that with the nobility of soul; that with the holding of
important office; and that with personal refinement and
accomplishment.

The sociolinguistic situation as it appeared to an author writing
in London around 1300 is summed up at the beginning of *Arthour
and Merlin*: *Freynsche vse þis gentil man* 'noblemen use French'. William
of Nassyngton, writing his *Speculum Vitae* in the next generation,
confirms the association of French with the court, but acknowledges that many gentlemen are not familiar with it; a situation
which by 1400 could be true even for great noblemen.[4] But the
precise grasp which courtiers had of French does not concern us
here. Rather it is necessary to notice the social status which French
enjoyed during the middle ages. As the result of its association with
the noble descendants of the Conqueror's army, by its prestige as
the language of refined literature, and through its use as the
language of administration, it held a position of unchallenged social
supremacy throughout the period. It was spoken, at least on public
occasions, in the royal court until the end of the fourteenth
century, and was more commonly used than English in

administrative documents until the third decade of the fifteenth century. Moreover, scholars who learned and conducted their studies in Latin were, until the second half of the fourteenth century, likely to have learned French as a preliminary. Nor was this simply a rarified academic exercise, for even in the later fifteenth century Oxford schools produced advertisements for business training which promised to instruct boys in French as part of the preparation for a lucrative apprenticeship.[5] A grasp of French might therefore indicate noble birth, a good education, or an important job; at any rate it would indicate a position of some eminence in society. These desirable associations were not, however, restricted to the demonstration of a complete grasp and fluency in French: the occasional phrase, such as *grant mercy* or *par dieu* carried with them a certain cachet which made them attractive to some of Chaucer's pilgrims, who sprinkle their discourse with French phrases as the Pardoner 'saffrons' his sermons with Latin. Such phrases are common too in the earlier London romances. This raises the interesting question of which of the vast number of French loan words and phrases in fourteenth-century English would be recognized as such, and so share the social cachet of the French language. There is clear linguistic evidence that certain words were stylistically distinct from the common core of English forms. For example, the adjectives written inflected and often post-posed as in *goodes espirituels*, and derivational affixes such as *-el*, *-erie*, *-able*, and *-ous*, which combine in Middle English only with Romance base forms. However, the apparent implication of some awareness of French etymology may not be the full story. Such words and phrases were distinguished in use from the common core as much by their propriety to a slightly elevated stylistic level – that of learned and administrative discourse – as by their diverse linguistic origin. Words, word-formations, and phrases which were in fact of French origin had become most strongly associated with formal styles and elevated registers. Thus, when in the Wakefield Second Shepherds' Play, Mak adopts the role of a king's officer, he adopts not only the Southern forms of Middle English which are an overt cause of comment, but also some characteristic French-based phrasal patterns and abstract nouns which seem appropriate to the part. Because of their French origin, phrases such as *have mercy*, *have pitee*, *make joye*, or *make complaynte*, were felt to belong to a somewhat elevated kind of language. But the causal link would have been rather indirect; more directly, they were associated with discourses and situations which had arisen in those areas of life which had once been dependent upon the use of French: the situation, perhaps, of the lord and petitioner, or the literary representation of love which we shall examine in Chapter 9.

French influence on the use of English in the more elevated spheres of life may be both more subtle and more pervasive than the selection of particular words and phrases. It may, for example, be extended to a whole style of discourse, so that the very construction of the prose may be modelled on French precursors. Fifteenth-century authors tend to use in the prologues and epilogues to their works a form of prose which is deliberately artificial and elaborate, displaying their own skills in its construction and complementing the dedicatees by its learned elevation. The following is an example from Caxton's prologue to his translation of *Blanchardyin and Eglantine*, printed about 1489:

> Unto the right noble, puyssaunt and excellent pryncesse, my redoubted lady, my Lady Margarete, Duchesse of Somercete, moder unto our naturel and soverayn lord and most Crysten kynge, Henry the Seventh, by the grace of God Kyng of Englonde and of Fraunce, Lord of Yrelond etc., I Wyllyam Caxton, his most indygne, humble subgette and lytil servaunt, present this lytyl book unto the noble grace of my sayd lady; whiche boke I late receyved in Frenshe from her good grace, and her commaundement wythalle for to reduce and translate it into our maternal and Englysh tonge; whiche boke I had longe tofore solde to my sayd lady, and knewe wel that the storye of it was honeste and joyefull to vertuouse yong noble gentylmen and wymmen for to rede therin, as for their passe-tyme.

This kind of style, which is marked by its learned Romance vocabulary, by its lengthy sentences, and above all by the devices it uses to maintain coherence (*whiche* + noun, *sayd* + noun) has been called 'curial style', an expression formed on the noun *curia* 'court'.[6] The significance of the word *curia* here is to do with that aspect of the court as the centre of administration and law-making. For this purpose the necessity for unambiguous reference led to the development of techniques for handling coherence in complex and lengthy statements. Although based on Latin practice, this style flourished in French both in England and abroad, and extended itself to formal letters.[7] In this context, Chaucer refers to it as *heigh stile*, and uses it in parodic form in the *Squire's Tale* (102–59), but also as a serious means of presenting ordered information in his *Treatise on the Astrolabe*. Thus, curial style, originating in the world of state affairs, made a temporary transition to that of elevated literary expression, and was associated with courtliness interpreted as social elevation.

The association between recognizable features of style and social status lies behind the medieval understanding of the classical theory of three styles, which was stated by late twelfth- and early thirteenth-century rhetoricians in an overtly social framework. Each of the three levels of style was associated with vertically separated social levels, so that the high style was considered to be 'high' because it used words and references connected with the life of the nobility.[8] If such a formulation were to be interpreted in terms of medieval English usage, this would naturally imply the assembly of words and phrases, often of Romance origin, which, in one sphere or another, were associated with the world of important people. Although the very ability to speak French had earlier been counted as indicative of nobility, by the fifteenth century the association between English words and the concerns of the gentleman had become much more direct: no conscious association with French was necessary. Thus the language of the gentleman was to be identified with terms drawn from his presumed leisure interests: knowledge of the correct language to use in describing a horse, a greyhound, or a hawk. Malory remarks that one can discern a gentleman from a yeoman by the former's knowledge of hunting terms.

Viewed as a quality of the man of affairs, or of the gentleman of leisure, courtliness could be seen to be reflected in language as a characteristic style derived from typical occupations. But there is a more subtle connection between courtliness and language than these. It is concerned not with social status *per se* but rather with interpersonal relations. Here language use is considered to reveal something deeper about the personality of the speaker through his dealings with others.

In the B Prologue of *Piers Plowman*, a lunatic abruptly addresses the king:

> Thanne loked vp a lunatik, a leene þyng wiþ alle,
> And knelynge to þe kyng clergially he seide,
> 'Crist kepe þee, sire kyng, and þi kyngryche,
> And lene þee lede þi lond so leaute þee louye,
> And for þi riȝtful rulyng be rewarded in heuene'.

(B Prologue, 123–7)

The apparent approval of this speech expressed in the word *clergially* may well be derived from the sentiment contained in it, but there is a curious feature about its style which emerges by contrast with other addresses to the king found in the poem. The majority of these, including those by Mede, Conscience, and Reason, use the second person plural form of the pronoun, *ye*. The lunatic's address, then, is distinguished not only by its paradoxically good counsel, but also by its contrast with other forms of address used to the monarch in the poem.

Yet this lunatic is not alone in addressing kings in these abrupt terms. Use of the second person singular, and a more direct style, is the characteristic of those who set themselves to be the instructors of the great; clerks who adopt the role of *mestre* to the king. Thus Jean de Meun dedicated his translation of Boethius to Philip IV of France using the pronoun *tu*, and Chaucer's Prudence switches to *thow* to her lord, Melibee, when quoting the instruction of the ancients, even though she normally addresses him as *ye*, as a wife should in polite society. In France there is some evidence that address with *tu* became recognized as a feature of the *style clergial*, the style of clerks, by the early fifteenth century. It is certain that some learned men in Latin, French, and probably in English, insisted forcefully on the use of the singular form of address to single individuals whatever their status. Their protest was against what they saw as social vanity and linguistic illogicality: the development first in fifth-century Latin and subsequently in French, and in English from the mid-thirteenth century, of a form of address to a single individual using the plural form of the pronoun. At the time when Langland wrote, address to a king would normally be at the very least by the use of the plural of majesty, and more usually by some periphrastic title. Indeed, in formal situations, a complexity approaching that of Caxton's prologue might be expected. The lunatic is therefore using forms of speech which, whatever the value of the content of his speech, would have been unlikely to have availed him much in the real royal court.

Address in plural number was recommended by the masters of the *ars dictamen* as part of the art of writing formal letters, and by the end of the fourteenth century it was expected in speech also when one addressed a superior. Its use testified both to an acknowledgement of the status of the addressee and confirmed the *savoir faire* of the speaker. By the mutual benefit derived, its extension was therefore guaranteed. By the same principle which made a great lady doff her hood to an unknown tailor, *ye* was normally used to strangers, and to all those who were not obviously of an inferior status to the speaker. Thus, greeting and reply by the use of the plural form became a feature of courtly speech.

It should be emphasized that the distinction between *ye* and *thou* in Middle English was not a feature of earlier English, and in fact was modelled on French and Latin usage. It was socially motivated; a refinement adopted by those who were aware of polite manners, rejected by those who thought it an affectation, and unknown to those who were ignorant of courtly manners in general. Among those who recognized its desirability, its status is clarified by the way in which it tends to form a system of address, so that *dame*, *madame*, *lady*, *sire*, and *lord* are normally followed by *ye* in the poetry of Chaucer. Consciousness of the social compliment implied by the use of *madame* and *dame* is presented by Chaucer as a marked feature of bourgeoise aspirations to gentle status, valued by guildsmen's wives, a miller's wife, and the Wife of Bath alike (*GP*, 378; *RvT*, 3948; *WBProl*, 296). However, awareness of the associations of address by French-derived forms does not carry with it the implication of much knowledge of French. Less conspicuous distinctions of grammatical usage, such as that between the singular and plural forms of the imperative, have not been extensively adopted on the French model. Nevertheless, certain features of syntactical organization may be closely associated with courtliness in language. The following is the speech uttered by Aurelius in the *Franklin's Tale* when he comes to collect the debt which Dorigen has incurred:

> And whan he saw his tyme, anon-right he
> With dredful herte and with ful humble cheere
> Salued hath his souerayn lady deere.
> 'My righte lady,' quod this woful man,
> 'Whom I moost drede and loue as best I kan
> And lothest were of al this world displese,
> Nere it that I for yow haue swich disese
> That I moste dyen heer at youre foot anon,
> Noghte wolde I telle yow how me is wo bigon;
> But certes outher moste I dye or pleyne
> Ye sleen me giltlees for verray peyne.

(F., 1308–18)

The situation is that he is holding the faithful wife, Dorigen, against her will, to her rash promise to sleep with him if he can save her husband from danger. But this bleak reality is not acknowledged in his language. His speech is formal, commencing with a salutation and address and proceeding by an elaborately composed sentence to the suffering lover's traditional, veiled accusation of feelingless tyranny which will martyr an innocent.[9] The indirectness of the expression is notable; the sentence is framed in hypothetical conditions before coming to the euphemistic statement of her responsibility. Analysis of those speeches stated by Chaucer to have been uttered *curteisly* reveals that the grounding of a petition upon elaborated conditionals and subjunctives forms a recurrent feature of such courtly language. An expressed reluctance to displease the addressee is followed by often elaborate solicitude for his or her agreement to a suggested course of action. All these syntactical devices reflect professed concern not to impose in any way upon the individual freedom of the addressee. This conflict between personal interest and the courtly proprieties goes on to make Aurelius's speech a masterpiece of tortuous casuistry. Similarly evasive syntax, similar reluctance to impose upon the addressee, forms a marked feature of Harry Baily's famous request to the Prioress for a tale (*CT Sh-PrL*, 445–51) the speech of the royal tercel in the *Parliament of Fowls* (*PF*, 416–41) or Gawain's to Arthur for the doubtful honour of being decapitated by a monstrous green knight (343–61).

Contrast such speeches with those spoken in a manner condemned as *vileynye* such as that by the three riotours to the old man in the *Pardoner's Tale*:

> The proudeste of thise riotours thre
> Answerde agayn, 'What, carl with sory grace,
> Why artow al forwrapped saue thy face?
> Why lyuestow so longe in so greet age?'
>
> (C., 716–19)

or a greeting by the summoner to an old woman in the *Friar's Tale*:

> 'Com out,' quod he, 'thow olde viritrate,
> I trowe thow hast som frere or preest with thee.'
>
> (D., 1582–3)

In their address forms, their use of the pronoun *thou*, and their contempt for the feelings of the one addressed, such utterances are diametrically opposed to approved courtly speech. As in the Arthurian tradition, Sir Kay is opposed by his brusqueness to the courtly eloquence of Gawain, so such speeches form a contrast to idealized courtly address. They are never uttered by heroes, even under provocation, and indeed the assumption widespread in literary sources is that abusive language is self-reflexive, revealing the baseness of the user.

The elegant address forms and elaborate sentence constructions of courtly speech arise not from features of language which belong inherently to the concerns of any particular social group; rather, they are related to the illocutionary force of language. The forms symbolize the underlying attitudes of the speakers, thus representing something more fundamental than the mere adoption of the terms of hunting or of chess. They are related not to status or birth but to the more sophisticated notions of courtliness which associated it with the nature of the soul.

This close association between manner of speech and nature of personality is assumed by Guillaume de Lorris when he makes the God of Love accept the worthiness of the dreamer in the *Roman de la Rose* from his words alone. In Chaucer's rendering:

> . . . 'I love thee bothe and preise,
> Sen that thyn aunswar doth me ease,
> For thou answerid so curteisly.
> For now I wot wel uttirly,
> That thou art gentyll by thi speche.
> For though a man fer wolde seche,
> He shulde not fynden, in certeyn,
> No sich answer of no vileyn.
> For sich a word ne myghte nought
> Isse out of a vilayns thought.

(1983–92)

It was, apparently, an easy assumption in the middle ages, as still today, that the listener can make sound judgements about a speaker by his manner of speech. A gentleman uses the language associated with his class; a man displays his inner worth by the polite consideration which he shows to others, or, by his failure to master the complex coherence of his sentences and in mixing his metaphors, he displays the confusion of his thinking. All these propositions, medieval and modern, have an element of truth, but in discussing the relation of courtliness and language medieval authors were conscious of how misleading appearances might prove. Chaucer himself, when adopting the words and sentiments of *vileynie* in the course of his fictions elaborately heads off the possibility that the obloquy which such expressions might provoke should be adjudged to him. Verisimilitude requires the adoption of improper voices. Moreover, if the cultivated author of *Troilus and Criseyde* can adopt the language of churls in the *Canterbury Tales*, is it not conceivable that these churls might in turn appropriate the style of courtliness? If this were merely the use of the characteristic language of hunting or hawking, of refined love, or even of French by honest, simple folk who wish to be taken for greater than they are, it would be no more than an occasion for scorn of social climbing; but the assumption that language reflects the soul means that the adoption of courtly language may become a masquerade of quite a different order. It may become a means of manipulation and deception about fundamental motives.

Despite the pretence that courtliness sprang naturally from a superior constitution, in fact most of its defining accomplishments could be acquired by instruction or imitation, the effective use of language among them. The linguistic arts of the ancient world survived in medieval times as an instrument of persuasion appropriate in the ecclesiastical sphere to preachers, and among laymen to rulers and the secretariat which surrounded them. But, although the skills of eloquence were often admired in encomia of rulers, there is little evidence of them actually employing rhetorical skills, and when they did, as in formal letters, it is likely that the eloquence arose as much from the secretary as the correspondent himself. The administrative functions of important courts had given rise to subsidiary linguistic arts such as those of legal drafting and of the writing of formal letters, which, as we have already seen, affected the style of courtly speech and literature. Imitation rather than extended study was the essential route by which the strategies of learned discourse became incorporated into the courtly world. Narrative scenes are not uncommon, however, in which heroes display very clerkish and considered rhetorical skills. Jason, in Lydgate's *Troy Book* rehearses the delivery of a speech to King Cethes in which he hopes to secure his help in the quest for the Golden Fleece:

. . . Iason, or he his tale gan,	'before'
Ful wel avised, and cherid lyche a man,	'considered'
Conceyved hath and noted wonder wel	'punctuated'
From point to point his mater euerydel,	
And nat for-gat a word in al his speche;	
But evene lik as rethorik doth teche,	
He gan his tale so by crafte conveie	'dispatch, accompany'
To make þe kyng, to þat he wolde seie,	
Condescende, and rather to encline	
For tassent þat he myȝte fyne	'to agree', 'complete'
Of his comyng þe knyȝtly hiȝe emprise,	'noble purpose'
Þus worde by worde as I schal her deuise	

(I., 1397–408)

Jason here relies upon his own advocacy to advance his cause, but a similar use of linguistic skills is frequently admired in messengers bearing the words of some employer. In the *Romance of Horn*, two Saracen kings send a message to King Hunlaf:

> Or s'en vont envers lui cist enveié message:
> Mut sunt bien cunreié e si sunt de parage,
> Si sunt bien enparlé, chescun en sun langage.
> Latimiers ont od eus pur mustrer lor corage,
> Qui de plusurs latins sunt escolé e sage.
> Dreit al rei sunt venu a sun mestre masage;
> Li portiers les guiad, cum esteit costumage,
> Sus al haut solier, ki fud fait par estage.
> Iloc i ont trové le rei od sun barnage.
> Primes l'ont salué, si cum iert dreit usage,
> Pus dient tuz les moz – ke n'i funt retaillage –
> Cum l'orent komandé cil ki vindrent a nage.

(1348–59)

Then these envoys make their way to him [Hunlaf]: they are very well arrayed and equally of high rank and just as eloquent, each in his own language. To reveal their intention, they have with them interpreters who are wise and learned in several languages. They make their way straight to the king in his principal dwelling. The porter escorted them, as was customary, up to the high chamber, which was storeyed. There they found the king with his barons. First they gave him greeting according to the proper custom, then they uttered their entire message without any curtailment as those who had arrived by sea had ordered them.

In a similar scene in the *Roman de Toute Chevalerie*, messengers bring not a verbal message alone, but also a letter:

> Cortoisement l'aresonent li estrange messager,
> Si li baillent le bref, le seel font briser:
> Saluz e amisté envoit al roy premer.

(6955–7)

The foreign messengers addressed him courteously, and gave him the letter, breaking the seal: greetings and friendship she sent to the king initially.

Here the message is in fact delivered by a combination of the skills of the messengers and a letter. Such scenes, which place messengers in a context of courtly ceremony, emphasize the importance of their role in court society; at their most elevated they are as much ambassadors as messengers. The letter, whose seal they appear to break before reading, serves as an instrument of credit. Yet not all messengers necessarily met this high expectation, and growing literacy tended to undermine the responsibility of their position. There is some evidence that letters may serve as an aid to memory, for messengers were unhappily not always so skilled as those pictured in romance. Conrad van Mure, writing in 1275, included in his manual of letter-writing, a brief paragraph on 'why the letter was invented':

> Epistola tribus de causis precipue fuit inuenta, scilicet ut secreta per ipsam celentur uel ocultentur, et ut inpericia seu rusticitas portitoris seu exhibitoris literaram non noceat mittentis intentioni, et ut localis corporum sequestratio seu distantia non inpediat comodum seu colloquium amicorum. unde uersus:firmat amiciciam, secretorum grauitatem celat, et excusat latoris rusticitatem. multotiens enim per uiles et rusticos latores litere magni nominis, magni negotii, magni secreti trans-mittuntur.
>
> (ed. Rockinger, *De arte prosandi*, p. 420)

> The letter was invented principally for three reasons, which are that through it secrets may be concealed and kept hidden, that the inexperience or incompetence of the bearer or deliverer of letters shall not jeopardize the intention of the sender, and that the separation or distance of place or person shall not hinder the pleasantry or conversation of friends. Whence the verse: 'it strengthens friendship, conceals the importance of secrets, and excuses the ignorance of the bearer'. Indeed, on many occasions, great affairs and great secrets of great importance have been transmitted in a letter by base and ignorant messengers.

The author of the *Secretum Secretorum* is dismissive of messengers when discussing the choice of servants; messengers are ideally honest but dim: 'And þou fynde hym noȝt scharp of wytt, but only truwe, make hym a masenger to ber letteris' (p. 193).

The strange knight who delivers a verbal message to the court of Kyng Cambyuskan in Chaucer's *Squire's Tale*, however, cannot be faulted. Like the messengers in the *Romance of Horn*, he obeys all the rules of courtly protocol, but like the later, fifteenth-century ideal exemplified by Lydgate's Jason or Christine de Pizan's accounts of the rhetorical mastery of men of affairs, he demonstrates all the skills of consciously acquired eloquence:

This straunge knyght that cam thus sodeynly
Al armed saue his heed ful richely
Salueth kyng and queene and lordes alle
By ordre as they seten in the halle
With so heigh reuerence and obeisaunces
As wel in his speche as in his contenaunces
That Gawayn with his olde curteisye,
Thogh he were come agayn out of fairye,
Ne koude hym nat amende with a word.
And after this biforn the hye bord
He with a manly voys seyde his message
After the forme vsed in his langage
Withouten vice of silable or of lettre.
And for his tale sholde seme the bettre,
Acordant to his wordes was his cheere
As techeth art of speche hem that it leere.
Al be that I kan nat sowne his style
Ne kan nat clymben ouer so heigh a style,
Yet seye I this that as to commune entente
Thus muche amounteth al that euere he mente.

(F., 89–108)

The 'art of speche' to which Chaucer here refers by his allusions to tone of voice and demeanour is that part of rhetorical teaching known as *pronuntiatio*. Vices of syllable and letter are fundamental to any contemporary teaching of Latin composition. Thus Chaucer's messenger, far from the *rusticitas* of Conrad's account, is imagined, not without a touch of irony, to be a clerically educated knight. His rhetorical prowess is at once demonstrated by Chaucer's admittedly inadequate account of his performance, which is in fact a verse pastiche of the kind of official letter in curial style which at this period would normally have been written in French. Chaucer himself employed curial prose for technical purposes, where he wished to write clear instructions, and some features of it are also to be found in his *Tale of Melibee*, but its relative absence from his works may suggest that, unlike Lydgate or Christine de Pizan and her circle, he did not regard curial style as suitable for creative writing. It was a fashion which developed in the decades after his death.

The acquired linguistic skills of the messenger were undeniably useful and positive ones, whose contribution was validated by the letters which he might carry. But Jason's speech to King Cethes, as represented by Lydgate, had a purpose beyond the revelation of unvarnished facts. It was calculated 'to make þe kyng, to þat he wolde seie, / Condescende'; in other words to persuade as well as instruct. As Gower remarks:

> Fair speche hath ofte brought above
> Ful many a man, as it is knowe,
> Which elles scholde have be riht lowe
> And failed mochel of his wille.
>
> (*CA*, III. 604–7)

Christine de Pizan makes no bones about stating that the persuasive power of eloquence is necessary in a ruler *car a peine est il si grande durté de coraige que belle parolle n'amolisse* 'for there is hardly such great hardness of heart that it may not be softened by fine speech' (*Livre du Corps de Policie*, 82). Such persuasive power for the good of the state or in order to improve the moral constitution of humankind are defensible uses of persuasive eloquence; but the end of persuasion may not always be so laudable.[10] This moral ambiguity in eloquence is represented in Middle English by the contrast between the phrases *curteis speche* and *faire speche*, both of which are courtly accomplishments.

The association between the word *curteis* and the act of speaking is very rarely pejorative; *curteis* speech, whether by its form, content, or implication is generally to be approved. The phrase *faire speche* may have identical significance, but in addition, often carries the implication of illusion or deception. The phrase may refer to utterances which are stylistically elegant, or superficially in accord with courtly ideals in terms of their content, but which are ultimately damaging: either intentionally deceptive or self-deluding. Again, Gower puts the deceptive capacity of *faire speche* succinctly:

> Of Falssemblant it nedeth noght
> To telle of olde ensamples oght;
> For al dai in experience
> A man mai se thilke evidence
> Of faire wordes whiche he hiereth;
> Bot yit the barge Envie stiereth
>
> (*CA*, II. 1897–902)

Because eloquence is a skill distinct from the intention of the speaker, fair speaking is a potentially dangerous art, possibly coercive to undesirable purposes, and capable of concealing the truth. It was therefore subject to the censure of moralists.

On the road to Canterbury, Chaucer's pilgrims are overtaken by

an ill-assorted couple, a Canon and his servant, and together they
address the pilgrims in proper courtly fashion:

> 'God saue,' quod he, 'this ioly compaignye.
> Faste haue I priked,' quod he, 'for youre sake
> By cause that I wolde yow atake
> To riden in som myrie compaignye.'
> His yeman eek was ful of curteisye
> And seyde: 'Sires, now in the morwe-tyde
> Out of youre hostelrie I saugh yow ryde
> And warned heer my lord and my souerayn
> Which to ryden with yow is ful fayn
> For his desport; he loueth daliaunce.'

(G, 583–92)

Daliaunce, like *faire speche*, could attract moral condemnation as
triviality ending in sexual licence, and it is in this sense that dances
– the scene of *daliaunces* – are avoided by Virginia in the *Physician's
Tale* (66). But this is certainly not the implication here. Rather,
daliaunce is simply a less serious kind of conversation, whiling away
the time in inconsequential chat. This may also be the skill of
Chaucer's Friar who is noted as expert in 'daliaunce and fair langage',
but the reputation of friars as masters of the art of seduction as
much as subtle conversation supports the promptings of the context
to understand it otherwise. When it becomes known to the
inhabitants of Bertilak's castle that the famous Arthurian Sir Gawain
is among them, like those who in Wace's *Brut* flocked to hear the
courtesies of Bran (p. 26), they eagerly look forward to witnessing
the fabled skills in polite conversation of this 'fyne fader of nurture',
and to learn of the 'teccheles termes of talkyng noble'. They also
immediately assume that much of Gawain's conversational skill will
take the form of *luf-talkyng*. It is important to the plot, of course,
that it should do so, and the most striking central scenes of the
poem consist of the conversational duel between the knight and the
lady of the castle. The adoption of rhetorical roles, the extended
expansion of the metaphors of captive and gaoler, mistress and
servant, teacher and pupil, and the interplay of initiatives and
implications in the contest have often been noted, so that anything
more than allusion is unnecessary here. Yet this scene, which fully
exploits the implicational, figurative and ambiguous aspects of
linguistic communication captures a crucial aspect of the subtler
kind of courtly *daliaunce*, in which indirectness is taken to extreme
limits. Understanding of what is to be communicated depends upon

the addressee reading the alternative or hidden meanings and responding to them appropriately and cooperatively. Gawain, playing for high stakes, accepts the lady's proffered imagery, but expands it to his own advantage.[11]

A less widely recognized example of this kind of courtly conversation occurs in the somewhat unexpected context of Chaucer's *Shipman's Tale*, where a personable monk, the friend of a conscientious merchant, has borrowed money from him and secretly used it to seduce the merchant's wife. On the day of repayment of the loan the following scene takes place when the merchant returns to town:

> And whan that he was come into the town,
> For greet chiertee and greet affeccioun
> Vnto daun Iohn he first goth hym to pleye
> Nat for to axe or borwe of hym moneye,
> But for to wite and seen of his welfare
> And for to tellen hym of his chaffare
> As freendes doon whan they been met yfeere.
> Daun Iohn hym maketh feste and murye cheere.
> And he hym tolde agayn ful specially
> How he hadde wel yboght and graciously,
> Thanked be god, al hool his marchandise
> Saue that he moste in alle maner wyse
> Maken a cheuyssance as for his beste
> And thanne he sholde been in ioye and reste.
> Daun Iohn answerde: 'Certes I am fayn
> That ye in heele ar comen hom agayn.
> And if that I were riche, as haue I blisse
> Of twenty thousand sheeld sholde ye nat mysse.
> For ye so kyndely this oother day
> Lente me gold; and as I kan and may
> I thanke yow by god and by seint Iame.
> But nathelees I took vnto oure dame,
> Yowre wyf at hom, the same gold agayn.'
>
> (B^2., 1525–47)

The passage commences with the information that the returning merchant visits his friend the monk out of a sense of companionability, to share with him the events of his business trip. Although he tells the monk that he himself will now have to borrow to complete his business satisfactorily, the implication that he might be there to request the return of a loan is specifically denied by the narrator. This denial, however, is superseded by the later complaint of the merchant to his wife (B². , 1575–82) that her lack of book-keeping has caused him to embarrass his friend by mentioning the loan which had already been repaid. At any rate, the monk understands the allusion immediately, and answers it as if it were a request for repayment. The context of this exchange is not that in which we might expect to find courtly sensibilities, nor the respect accorded to them by the indirect allusiveness of courtly speech; nevertheless the principles are the same, and the monk's reply is the model of a coldly polite refusal to comply with the suggestion put to him, even, to the forms *kan and may*, drawn from high-style discourse. In fact, by the closing decades of the fourteenth century, wealthy merchant circles were just as capable of adopting the values of courtliness as provincial courts, and applying them to their own world.

The perspective from which courtliness is viewed may radically affect what is considered to be courtly language. In the court, different skills might be expected of the great nobleman from those of the messenger or those of the page boy. The nobleman may exercise wit and creativity in his speech, becoming an example and the envy of others. He may, the Knight of the Tower warns, employ these skills less than charitably to defeat others in altercation. Do not, the Knight advises, enter into contention with those who are 'langageurs and full of wordes', and he gives the salutary story of a lady who tried to get the better in this respect of the Marshal of Clermont and:

> said to hym tofore alle the peple: 'Clermont, in good faythe ye ought to gyue grete guerdon ['thanks'] vnto God, for ye be a good knyght and semely ynough, and ye knowe many and conne many merueyles, and were parfit ynough yf your mockyng ne were and youre euyll tonge, which somtyme can not be stylle'. 'Now, madame, is this the worst tatche ['fault'] that I haue?' She sayd 'Ye'. 'And I shalle saye yow wherfore ye haue me repreuyd and tolde me the worst tatche that I haue after youre aduys ['opinion'], and I haue not said the worst tatche that I know in you? What wrong haue I doo thenne, madame? I am not so swyfte of my speche as ye are'. The lady helde her pees thenne, and wold that she had not stryuen ne spoken to hym.
>
> (p. 41; punctuation modernized)

Such sharpness of tongue allied to wit is found in anecdotes of court life at least from Walter Map onwards, but always among the mighty. The lesser fry have to be more careful. In *William of Palerne*, the Emperor encounters a child in the forest who is distinguished by the beauty of his appearance and the natural refinement of his demeanour:

> Þe child comes him agayn and curtesliche him gretes.
> In hast þemperour hendely his gretyng him   'graciously'
>   ȝeldes,   'returns'
> and anon riȝttes after askes his name,   'straight afterwards'
> and of what kin he were kome komanded   'descended from'
>   him telle.
>
>   (233–6)

Following this characteristically courtly introduction, it transpires that the child is not the natural son of the cow-herd with whom he lives, and, despite the misgivings of his foster-father, the Emperor decides to take him into the court. As he leaves, the cow-herd offers some advice:

> . . . þou swete sone, seþþe þou schalt hennes wende,
> whanne þou komest to kourt, among þe kete   'bold'
>   lordes,
> and knowest alle þe kuþþes þat to kourt   'skills'
>   langes,   'belongs'
> bere þe boxumly and bonure, þat ich burn   'meek and mildly'
>   þe love;
> be meke and mesurabul, nouȝt of many   'moderate'
>   wordes;
> be no tellere of talis, but trewe to þi lord;
> and prestely for pore men profer þe ever   'readily'
> for hem to rekene wiþ þe riche in riȝt and in   'deal with'
>   skille.
> Be feiþtful and fre and ever of faire speche,
> and servisabul to þe simple so as to þe riche,
> and felawe in faire manere, as falles for þi state;
> so schaltow gete Goddes love and alle gode mennes.
> Leve sone, þis lessoun me lerde my fader,
> Þat knew of kourt þe þewes, for kourteour   'customs'
>   was he long.
>
>   (329–42)

Clearly this advice is far removed from the world of Clermont, of Christine de Pizan's ideal nobles, or even of Gower's conception of the role of language in courtesy. The advice is limited to being of *faire speche*, not bearing tales, and avoiding unnecessary prolixity. This is no recipe for political eloquence, even if it has some practical value. With its heavy emphasis on loyalty, serviceability, morality, and knowing one's place in the court, its perspective is very different from the ideals we have been discussing. Indeed, this point is made by the reaction of the Emperor, who 'had god game of þat gomes ['fellow's'] lore' (346), and who afterwards laughs also at the quaintly rustic names of the new page's playfellows. The requirements of courtesy for the two are quite different, and the advice given by the father to his son is that appropriate to servants of the court rather than its masters. It is, however, a salutary reminder that courtliness and 'kourteours' may be quite different in kind and status.

NOTES

1. *litteris eorum et urbanitate Chrysogonus ducitur* 'their culture and elegant manners are so attractive to Chrysogonus' (*Pro Roscio Amerino*, 120).

2. Ramage, *Urbanitas*, p. 69.

3. Burnley, 'Comforting the Troops'.

4. The Cambridge University Library copy of the *Speculum Vitae* in MS Ff.4.9 adds a significant couplet to the passage usually quoted in histories of English, in which it states that English is the native language in England: '. . . Englysch that men vsen mast / For that is owre kynde langage / That we haue here most off vsage' (f.1ra).

5. Meyer, 'Manuscrits français', p. 56. Meyer prints the text of a dialogue in French composed as a testimony to the benefits of William Kyngesmylle's school, where he has learned to 'escrire, enditer, acompter, et ffraunceys parler'. Indeed, he goes on to claim ability in three languages, English, French and 'good Norman'. These abilities will facilitate his apprenticeship to a London merchant. See further, Legge, 'William of Kingsmill' and Richardson, 'Business Training'.

6. Caxton uses the word *curious* (which can be regarded as an equivalent of *curial*) to describe elaborated style, but this seems to refer more to its subtlety and complexity than to its connection with the *curia*. Occasionally, in some contexts, that association may have been possible.

7. For more detailed definitions of this style, see Bornstein, 'French Influence' and 'Tale of Melibee' and Burnley, 'Curial Prose'.

8. The schematic representation of the three stylistic levels in association with social orders of knights, farmers, and shepherds, three corresponding genres of Virgil's poetry, and specimen terms appropriate to each level is best illustrated by the diagram in John of Garlande's *Parisiana Poetria* (ed. Lawler).

9. On the use of *thou* and *ye* forms, and their implications for characterization in the *Franklin's Tale*, see Pearsall, 'The Franklin's Tale'. An interesting social perspective on the use of *madame* is offered by the alliterative *Wars of Alexander* (228–33) in which Anectanabus, speaking *maisterlike* to Olympadas, maintains his kingly status in spite of his clerkly appearance, by avoiding the *madame* form of address: 'deyned him na daynte "madame" hire to call.' This assertiveness is strikingly at odds with usual courtly custom.

10. These improving roles of rhetoric are stated by Gower (*CA*, 7, 1505), and in the French translation of the *Ad Herennium*.
11. Burnley, 'Style, Meaning and Communication'.

Chapter 8

Courtly Literature

In 1974 the International Courtly Literature Society was formed. That an international body should be founded to study a phenomenon distinguishable by the use of capital letters would imply that its founding members had a clear idea of their object of study. Yet, introducing a collection of essays from the Society's second triennial congress, the editors admit that 'the coining of the expressions *courtly love* and *courtly literature* has caused nothing but trouble' (Smith and Snow, p. 3). The former is a notorious cause of scholarly debate and re-assessment, and will form the subject of the next chapter, but the latter, which is further described as 'multi-hued and capable of subtle shape-shifting' (Smith and Snow, p. 3), is an equally indefinite concept and must be considered now.

Scholars of medieval literature use the word 'courtly' to refer to a wide range of works and authors. We confidently describe authors like Marie de France, Chaucer or Gower as courtly, but should we then add Geoffrey of Monmouth, Hoccleve or Lydgate? What of texts like the Harley lyrics or the *Secretum Secretorum*? There may be dissenters, but none of these would be foreign to the activities of the International Courtly Literature Society. Yet this list consists of works of very different kinds. They are written in three languages by court functionaries, a monk, an important cleric, and a relatively humble secretary. The content and genre of their works vary from a prose legendary history and a didactic treatise to brief, highly worked lyrics. Some works are concerned with the subtleties of the human heart, others with the practicalities of government. Without further investigation, it is apparent that whatever it is that we accept as qualifying literature for the designation 'courtly', the matter is likely to be quite complex. Many characteristics are potentially involved, but it requires only a sub-set of these constituents to permit the designation.

The simplest and most uncompromising approach to definition would be through narrow social history, countenancing only that literature which can be shown to have been written by or for some member of the royal court; in effect literature associated with a small social group in the London area. But this would exclude poems like *Sir Gawain and the Green Knight*, for which no certain connection with the royal court can be assumed. An alternative mode of definition might be through content, as those works whose main purpose it is to give instruction on 'nurture' or the customs and manners specifically appropriate to court life. But even this might seem too exclusive. References to 'courtly wit' reflect an aspect of courtliness discussed in Chapter 7, which might independently justify the use of the word 'courtly' with literature that exhibits it. So it seems that a rather different, but equally acceptable conception of courtliness may lie in the manner of execution of the work itself: a certain subtlety in conceptualization and the exploitation of linguistic ambiguities for showy effect, might justify the designation courtly. However, this last, like the expectation that a certain elevation in style will be used, would be insufficient in itself, without some coincidence with appropriate content. That content we should expect to be secular in nature, but, as we shall see, religious works were not barred from the his- torical courtly circle. From its inception the concept of courtliness possessed the ability to change its apparent substance in response to prevailing values, perspectives and circumstances, and courtly literature inherited a similar chameleon quality. We must therefore expect the justification for calling any particular work of literature 'courtly' to be a complex one. As with other aspects of this phenom- enon, courtliness in literature may be better characterized than defined. But we may begin with a review of the kind of literature known to have been associated with court society.

Works which originate in the court (even the extended view of the court) are much more readily identifiable in French than in English. A key issue here is the existence of patronage. There is evidence that before the end of the twelfth century many of the baronial class had adopted English as their first language, but many also retained the ability to understand and read French, and from the mid-thirteenth century efforts were made to maintain this ability.[1] The aristocracy, and especially those closest to the royal court, could not only speak and write letters in French, but could compose literature in that language until the close of the fourteenth century. French poets were welcome at the court of Richard II, and Froissart writes not only of his successful meeting with the king, but affectionately in memory of the Duchess Blanche, who is the central figure in Chaucer's *Book of the Duchess*. Chaucer himself admired the poetry of Granson, and was the recipient of praise from Eustache Deschamps for his work in translating into English the prototypical text on the ideals of courtliness, the *Roman de la Rose*. Associates of Chaucer at the royal court seem to have composed French poetry, as did his acquaintance John Gower, and the Duchess Blanche's uncle had himself been the author of a work in French. Although the high prestige of French in England descended from an aristocratic tradition of francophony, the French literary milieu in the English royal court at the close of the fourteenth century was a reflection of the prestige of contemporary France rather than the evolution of a native Anglo-Norman literary tradition. The native flowering of French literary production then lay many years in the past.

At the court of Henry II, probably in the 1170s, an author by the name of Denis Piramus wrote the following lines, which he attaches to an opening passage where he has renounced his arts as a courtly writer of love epistles and lyrics. Now, he says, he intends to write a truly improving work, which he contrasts with the limitations of the work of other authors popular in the court.

> Cil ki *Partonopé* trova
> E ki les vers fist e rima
> Mult se pena de bien dire,
> Si dist il bien de cele matire;
> Cume de fable e de menceonge
> La matire resemble sounge,
> Kar iceo ne put unkes estre.
> Si est il tenu pur bon mestre
> E les vers sunt mult amez
> E en ces riches curz loëz.
> E dame Marie autresi,
> Ki en rime fist e basti
> E compassa les vers de lais,
> Ke ne sunt pas del tut verais;
> E si en est ele mult loée
> E la rime par tut amée,
> Kar mult l'aiment, si l'unt mult cher
> Cunt, barun e chivaler;
> E si enaiment mult l'escrit
> E lire le funt, si unt delit,
> E si les funt sovent retreire.
> Les lais solent as dames pleire,
> De joie les oient e de gré,

Qu'il sunt sulum lur volenté.
Li rei, li prince e licourtur,
Cunte, barun e vavasur
Aiment cuntes, chanceuns e fables
E bons diz, qui sunt dilitables,
Kar il hostent e gettent puer
Doel, enui e travail de quer,
E si funt ires ublïer
E del quer hostent le penser.

(Vie Seint Edmund, 25–56)

That one who composed *Partenope* and who versified and rhymed its
lines took great pains to achieve eloquence, and he presented the
subject matter very well; [but] like the subject matter of a frivolous or
lying tale, it resembles a dream because it could never happen. And he
is considered a good model and the lines are much loved and praised in
fine courts. And the lady Marie likewise, who made and composed in
rhyme and planned out the lines of *lais* which are not at all true; and
yet she is greatly praised for it, and the rhyme loved by one and all, for
counts, barons, knights love it greatly and hold it dear, and they like
the writing very much and get someone to read it and take pleasure in
it so that they often cause them to be related. *Lais* customarily please
ladies, who hear them with pleasure and a good will, since they are
according to their wishes. Kings, princes and courtiers, counts, barons,
and vavassours like *contes*, *chansons* and *fables*, and good *dits*, which are
enjoyable, because they take away and overthrow fear, depression,
agitation and heartsickness, and they cause anger to be forgotten and
cast out troublesome thoughts from the heart.[2]

Both the author of *Partenope* and Marie (de France) were the
authors of engaging stories of the supernatural, and although
Marie's *lais* have been classified into those with supernatural and
those with pyschological interests, the division is somewhat
artificial. Seen purely in terms of narrative, they remain idealizing
fantasies whose adventures, although rooted in the values and
manners of the contemporary world, are equally as unlikely as their
accounts of enchantments. Piramus acknowledges the recreational
function of such poetry, but regrets its popularity by comparison
with work which he feels might have a more fundamental value.
For our purposes, however, what is striking about his remarks is the
way in which they reflect his sense of a literary community. He
himself has written in the past to fulfil the demands of the court,
and he is familiar with – and implicitly critical of – other authors
serving the same public. Later in his work, he mentions (2925) an
earlier author who had dealt with his own story matter, Geoffrey

Gaimar, whose work has been quoted above, and who himself employed aristocratic contacts in North Yorkshire to supply him with a copy of Geoffrey of Monmouth's *Historia* when composing his *Estorie des Engleis*.[3] These references are not unique. Anglo-Norman authors seem surprisingly frequently to know of each other's works, to have opinions about them, often to use them in the composition of their own poems. Not all these authors were directly connected with the royal court, but such personal reference would have been pointless unless all belonged to a network of acquaint-anceship, literary or personal, a network which extends to the court.

Probably the earliest work identifiable with this post-Conquest court milieu is the Anglo-Norman *Voyage of St Brendan*, which seems to have been produced in versions dedicated firstly to Henry I's queen, Maud, and then subsequently to her successor, Adeliza. We have William of Malmesbury's evidence (*Gesta Regum*, ii, 494) that for two decades after her marriage in 1100 Maud patronized poets in her court at Westminster, and it is M.D. Legge's judgement that this patronage affected Benedeit's handling of his task of composition. When he re-wrote his originally Latin work in French 'with a courtly audience in mind',[4] by comparison with the Latin text, he reduced material of interest only to clerks and emphasized the sensuous richness of descriptions. Adeliza, Henry's second wife, although of less scholarly tastes than Maud, continued to offer patronage to writers, and Philippe de Thaon's *Bestiary*, a translation of the Latin *Physiologus*, which seems to have found a public in continental France, is dedicated to her. The *Romance of Horn* was probably connected with the court of Henry II, and Marie's *Lais* were written in honour of the king. The twelfth century, then, saw in the English court and in more extended aristocratic circles, the flourishing of patronized literature in Anglo-Norman, which although by no means all courtly if judged by its content, was nevertheless courtly in terms of its origin and destination, and in its sense of a refined literary community.

After the end of the twelfth century this sense of an extended court network vanishes in England. Although some works, such as *Gui de Warwic, Fulke Fitzwarin*, and the *Histoire de Guillaume le Maréchal*, seem to be connected with provincial aristocratic families, there is no suggestion of patronage by the royal court. With a few exceptions, such as the Chandos Herald's biography of the Black Prince, both the sponsoring and production of literature in Anglo-Norman passed to provincial or religious households. Yet, even if the production of extensive works in French declined in the royal court, the vacuum was not at once filled by works in English. The French literature of the past was re-copied and, through bequests, was to form the staple content of both royal and aristocratic libraries for generations. Elizabeth Salter remarks that 'the linguistic habits and literary tastes of the English aristocracy during the fourteenth century appear conservative. . . . The prestige of literature written in French seems to have gone unquestioned by them'.[5] Ian Doyle supports this, casting doubt on the role of the royal court in the production of books in English. Edward III cannot be shown to have possessed any books written in English, and this same deficiency is shown by library inventories and wills to be continued into the fifteenth century.[6] However, a study of the book holdings of the Stafford family shows great variation from individual to individual, and this is echoed by the variety among noble families in the degree of their bookishness. Traditions of bibliophily existed in the Beauchamps, who were also literary patrons, but less markedly in the Staffords, with whom possession of about 150 books can be associated during the century. The language of many books is uncertain, but those in Latin seem to have outnumbered the French or English by two to one. This is because many books were objects of intrinsic value, illuminated hours or psalters, and many were of a religious, ethical or informational character, but there are also a substantial number of works of entertainment. Higden's *Polychronicon* in Latin, the *Roman de la Rose* in French, the *Canterbury Tales*, and Lydgate's *Fall of Princes* are among works which recur in the listings. Thomas of Woodstock, Duke of Gloucester, who was murdered in 1397, had the most varied library, including beside the *Polychronicon*, a copy of Brunetto Latini's *Livre dou Tresor*, a French romance of Alexander, a copy of the *Roman de la Rose* obtained from the estate of Richard II's chamber knight Sir Richard Stury, and a Wycliffite Bible in English.[7]

In seeking to sum up the evidence for court literature understood in its locational sense, a number of problems present themselves which are likely to distort our view. Much of the evidence comes from inventories and wills, but in relation to these it is worth taking into account the relative status of the French and English written languages in England during the later middle ages. French began to be used as an alternative to Latin for administrative and commemorative purposes in the final decades of the fourteenth century. It is therefore often difficult to assess with certainty the language of texts mentioned in wills and inventories, which are likely to be given titles in French or Latin whatever the language of the original. Social prestige, too, cannot be ignored as a factor in book listings. Throughout the medieval period, French had had much greater prestige than English in literature and in society. Moreover, it is striking how many wills mention religious or morally improving texts, and how relatively infrequent is reference to secular works of entertainment. This infrequency may indeed represent a true balance of proportions of works in their owners' possession, but it may also reflect the relative monetary value and social kudos of certain kinds of literary production as compared with others. Cheaply produced romances in English presented as a bequest indicated neither the same esteem for the legatee nor the same credit on the donor as did some prestigious French or Latin work. Bequests, especially, require interpreting with considerable scepticism, since they are a public declaration of taste, and in the memorial context of a will works are likely to be mentioned which reflect well on the memory of the deceased. Nevertheless, despite this warning, it must be admitted that the evidence points to an ossification of court literature accompanying the progressive decline of spoken French in England throughout the thirteenth and fourteenth centuries. Court literature in French had become more an inheritance than a living force, and although translation in the fifteenth century partially remedies this situation, the English nobility, even in the Renaissance, made substantial purchases of French-produced work.[8] Many of the book possessions of both the king and the aristocracy were not works which we would readily describe as 'courtly' in any sense other than that of association with the status of their owners. After the close of the fourteenth century, literature promoting the values of courtliness became more widely available in English. Some of it originated from the court milieu, but its readership was by no means restricted to the court. Concluding her survey of 120 fifteenth-century manuscripts containing lyrics of courtly love, Julia Boffey remarks that 'the reading of English courtly lyrics was not an activity confined to the literally "courtly" sector of society; it was apparently enjoyed . . . by all classes of cultivated reader' (p. 140). Courtliness in literature had broadened beyond the court and even the aristocracy; copies of Chaucer's poetry may be owned as well by country gentlemen or clergy as by members of the court circle. Although courtly poems in English could be found there, the libraries of courtiers, even at the end of the middle ages, tended to contain mostly French and Latin works of a religious, ethical or allegedly functional kind.

The particular functions which were popular among the aristocracy were those served by books which purported to educate the courtier in the principles of military conduct, legal procedure, government, or protocol. Aegidius Romanus and Vegetius figure among authors represented in the Stafford materials. There were, however, two other genres which appear rarely in inventories or wills, but which claim to be handbooks of court behaviour, giving guidance on the conduct of a courtier's life: these are the manuals of courtesy and of hunting. The former type are often brief works of a few pages or even a few lines represented by texts such as the Latin *Facetus: Cum Nihil Utilius* (which commences 'Because nothing is more useful to human wellbeing . . .'), the Anglo-Norman *Petit Traitise de Nurture*, and the English *Babees Book*. These works were produced in Latin from the twelfth century onwards, but the majority of English examples are from the broadening of interest in these topics which took place in the fifteenth century. As is apparent from their titles, many, such as *Stans Puer ad Mensam* ('a boy standing at the table . . .'), a thirteenth-century Latin work with three fifteenth-century English versions, were intended as guides in instructing children in appropriate manners. A few seem to have been intended for older, but still inexperienced, members of court society.[9]

The purpose of these works is ostensibly to teach their readers how to flourish as members of a large household, and their teaching varies very little. Few seek to instruct at any more than a superficial level, putting their faith in inculcating good manners rather than forming the personality at any deeper level. Almost all are organized thematically, devoting time to circumstances such as arrival in the hall, meetings, leave-takings, and especially behaviour around the dinner table. They give more general precepts on conduct towards others: do not interrupt, do not speak too long or pointlessly, look people in the eye, do not fidget, try to look cheerful. *Urbanitatis*, somewhat unusually, advises self-respect, suggesting that although one should respect those who obviously deserve it, no credit is to be gained from obsequiousness to people whose status is unknown. Table etiquette falls into two main categories: advice given on demeanour as a diner, and that offered to those serving the meal. Advice on manners at table varies from the obvious to the downright recondite. One should not reach greedily for food, neither should one take a bite then return the food to the communal dish. Picking your nose or wiping it on the table cloth should be avoided and breaking wind should be done with discretion. Both throwing bones on to the floor and picking your teeth with a knife are frowned on (*The Young Children's Book*. Ashmole 61). More subtly, you should not take the largest or choicest piece on a dish, nor dip too deep into broth. Pick up food only between the thumb and two fingers, and always use the left hand. When drinking you should avoid transferring grease from food to the rim of a glass. A variant version of the *Book of Curtesye*, printed by Caxton, in 1477, exists in Oriel College, Oxford MS lxxix, which remarks: 'Ensoyle not youre cuppe, but kepe hit clenely, / Lete no fatte ferthyng of your lippe be sen' (*Babees Book*, 185–6), echoing both Chaucer's description of the Prioress who 'peyned hire to countrefete chiere / Of court' (*CT*, 1, *GP*, 139–40) and also the French *Roman de la Rose*.

The second category of manual, directed towards those who were to serve in the hall, gives advice on providing four-day-old bread for trenchers, the provision of water and towels for the diners before and after the meal, and warnings about difficulties which might be encountered in carving ('Crabbe is a slutt to kerve'). Advice on service gave rise to larger and more specialized works such as Wynkyn de Worde's *Boke of Keruynge* (1508), designed as a manual for all those intending service at table, not only carvers. It contains advice on wine for butlers, instruction on the duties of a chamberlain, and a number of useful recipes. The role of the marshal of the hall receives separate treatment. He is the figure who is called *seneschal* in earlier romance, and the essence of his duties lies in his knowledge of the rank and status of all present, so that they may be treated with due deference and seated and lodged according to their position. Chaucer's Harry Baily, who seemed suited to the task (*CT*, 1, 754), shows something of the appropriate skill in his intention of selecting pilgrim storytellers in order according to their rank until interrupted by the anarchic Miller. This function of the marshal gave rise to a specialized type of work known as the 'book of precedence', which not only listed the relative merit of various estates, but also gave details of the order to be adopted in processions on state occasions and the appropriate complement of the household of each estate. More idiosyncratic, it seems to us, such works listed the rights of costume, and who could appropriately bear the train of each estate. Thus a duchess's train may be borne by a baroness, and a countess's by a gentleman, but no baron should wash before dinner with an earl, except by invitation. Such regulations may seem petty, and even hard to credit, but they served to define relative status in society and were therefore treated with the greatest seriousness by whoever felt they had a position to maintain. Chaucer notes the opinion of the wives of successful City traders that:

> It is ful fair to been yclepyd madame
> And goon to vigilies al bifore
> And haue a mantel realliche ybore.

(*CT*, 1, *GP*, 378–80)

Such symbols of status assumed great importance, and indeed a squabble over relative precedence in Parliament between the Earl of Norfolk, Earl Marshal of England, and the Earl of Warwick occupies most of the English language records of business transacted in the national Parliament during the year 1425.

The audience to which these books of good conduct was addressed extended far beyond the court, or even those who were likely to form a part of the court. It has been suggested that the shorter Latin works may be associated with the schools, and indeed the *Facetus* was considered to be a supplement to the popular school text, the *Disticha Catonis*, 'the Distiches of Cato'.[10] The breadth of interest in the practices of refined conduct extended also to the Church. Monastic communities had incorporated into their rules instructions on table manners and aspects of more general demeanour which contributed to amenity as much as holiness. The Dominican friars even had at their disposal a French manual of conversation which gave hints on behaviour at table when away from the convent visiting the houses of the gentry, as well as topics for uplifting conversation.[11] But the majority of these works seem to have been directed towards the socialization of children who were envisaged by the author as *valez* or pages in a large household. Their duties shaded into the role of other household servants of various ranks, and it was to these latter that most of the longer works were directed. The courtesy text in MS BL Sloane 1896 is a rather uneven compilation of three books, the first of which seems to be aimed at the more adult visitor to a great house and spends some time on the details of procedures on arrival. The second book echoes the teaching and the religious concerns of works such as the *Young Children's Book*, and the third outlines the duties of various office-holders in the court. John Russell, who claims to have been marshal in the hall of Duke Humphrey of Gloucester (d. 1447), at one time the most powerful nobleman in England, compiled the compendious *Boke of Nurture* apparently in his retirement. More than any other, it reflects the concerns of a single viewpoint, that of the career court servant, containing advice on a range of things from looking out for moths in the master's clothes, making sure that clean garments are laid out, and taking care of fires and candles, to preparing a medicinal bath. Sample menus aim above such mundane matters, and the suggested courses are adorned with 'subtleties', decorative devices such as the angel Gabriel greeting the Virgin Mary at the Annunciation, or an image of a gallant young man piping and singing, representing the season of spring. These menus are unified by developing such devices into a narrative of the advent of Christ on the one hand and a complex reference to the four seasons combined with the four ages and four complexions of man on the other. This may be a book for a servant, but such suggestions for serving go some way beyond the homespun advice offered by the father to his son departing for court in *William of Palerne*, quoted at the end of the previous chapter.

If the courtesy books were often for children and court servants, manuals on the courtly sport of hunting were for young adults, more elevated servants and gentlemen. These are also found in the three languages of medieval England, and the earliest vernacular treatise on hunting is a short work by William Twiti, huntsman to Edward II, which survives in Anglo-Norman and Middle English versions. Of the four extant Middle English treatises on hunting which have been counted by the latest surveyor of this field, the *Master of Game* is the most substantial and originates most demonstrably from the court milieu, since it was written between 1406 and 1413 by Edward, second Duke of York, who was Master of Game to his cousin Henry IV. The book is a translation and adaptation, with omissions and additions to suit English conditions, of Gaston Phoebus, Count of Foix's *Livre de Chasse* (*c.* 1388). Few books could therefore have a better pedigree as a courtly product. Although the book has no clear structure, the contents in the version in MS Cotton Vespasian B.xii may be divided into four main topics: first, an account of the nature of the quarry animals (hare, red deer, fallow deer, roe deer, wild boar, wolf, fox, badger, wild cat, and otter), followed by advice on the characteristics and management of hounds, then information about the *queste*, the finding and determination of a quarry, and finally a brief account of the conduct of the actual chase, which is managed in narrative mode and forms an addition to the original.

At least some of the courtesy books, the works on precedence, and the hunting manuals such as the *Master of Game* constitute literature of the court, but are they courtly literature? The question might be re-phrased in another form: are they practical manuals for the activities which they describe, and if so, is that all they are? Anne Rooney, in her survey of hunting manuals, remarks that the French versions of such works tend to be more noticeably practical than the English.[12] Duke Edward, for example, suppressed from his translation all details of utilitarian trapping in favour of the exciting chase, and after faithfully following his original in including the otter and wild cat, he adds a note[13] disclaiming extensive knowledge of the otter, and referring the curious reader to the king's otter hunter. He denies that anyone would contemplate hunting cats, polecats, martens or rabbits except to keep down vermin or for their fur. In Edward's view, real hunting is not for the control of vermin, but for sport or venison. Knowledge of the terms of hunting figures large in the *Master of Game*, as in every other English treatment of the subject. Many of these are of French origin; indeed, the successful huntsman apparently addresses his hounds predominantly in that language:

> Whan þe door is oppenede he shalle say loude, 'Ho, ho, arere' ['back!'], for cause þat his houndis wold come out to hastely; and whan he vncoupleþ ['unleashes'] his houndis he schal say to hem in to þe tyme þat he is comyn in to þe felde, 'Sto, moun amy, sto, atrete'. And whan he is commen forþ in to þe felde he shalle blow iii moot ['notes'] and vncouple his houndis. Than shalle he twyes speke to his houndes in þis wise, 'Hors de couple, auaunt cy auaunt', and þus shal he shay thries, 'So how', and no moor. And afterward he shall saye lowde, 'Sa say cy auaunt', and thann, 'Sa cy auaunt, sa cy auaunt, sohow'; and if he se his houndes drawe fast fro hym and wolden fayn renne he shalle say þus to hem here, 'How amy, how amy', and þus he shal say, 'Swef, moun amy, swef', for to make hem goo softly, and ay among blowe iii moot. And if eny of his houndes fynde and grete ['give tongue'] of þe hare where he haþ be, he shall say to hem in þis wise, 'Oiez a Beamond la vailaunt', or what þe hounde highte.
>
> (p. 103; re-punctuated)

This passage gives a very good impression of the style of those chapters which the author composed himself. This is not text-book material. Behind it is the visualization of an excursion, and a delight in the event and its technicalities which seeks to reconstitute it for the reader in a way not so different from the deer hunt evoked by the author of *Sir Gawain and the Green Knight*. Indeed, the word *queste*, used by the *Gawain*-poet in the description of the deer and boar hunts (1150; 1421) was rather unusual in Middle English. *MED* records two early uses prior to the *Master of Game*, but the others are from the *Awntyrs off Arthure*, *Ipomadon*, *St Erkenwald* and

Malory, texts later than the treatise. Duke Edward liked the word, and deliberately sought to introduce it into English hunting terminology, explicitly preferring it to the English *serchyng* (pp. 6, 86). His reasons for this preference are its fairness and brevity, but this rationalization does not stand comparison with his rejection of the French term *pace* for English *goynges* (p. 74). In this latter case, he says, he felt that knowledge if not use of current French hunting terminology was desirable in the English huntsman. It is apparent that the practice of hunting was to be accompanied by a body of theoretical knowledge, a mystique, which would set the informed huntsman apart from the mere practitioner. It is interesting that a sharp distinction is repeatedly made between these 'English' hunting terms and those used across the water. Although this specialist terminology is evidently derived from French, that fact is not recognized. Their origin is here ascribed neither to French nor to Tristran, but to the ancient sport of hunting the hare, which is regarded as the noblest of quarries. Part of the mystique of the business of hunting is its antiquity and imponderable origin.

To know these things, however, does not help very greatly in actually catching a hare. In fact, the information given here is not really the material of a practical manual; it is too much engaged with the peripheries of the hunt. The interspersed *exempla* of noble hounds in an idealized past which guarded or avenged their dead masters belong rather to the world of sentimental and moral story. The appended virtues of the huntsman, who should be 'wel avised of his speche and of his termys and euer glad to lerne and þat he be no boostour ne jangelere' (p. 69), sound very much like literary treatments of a courtly hero. The *Master of Game* sometimes calls upon the courtly conception of life for imagery and narrative procedures. At rutting time stags sing 'as a man þat louethe para-mour' (regrettably, the author's involvement with technical terms causes him to add that this is known in England as 'bellowing'). The picture given of the huntsman venturing out on a May morning enlivened by the bird song, the sunshine, and the dew on the leaves, is reminiscent of the opening of a dream vision. Both the *Master of Game* and Russell's *Boke of Nurture* have this kind of literary prologue. In the latter, Russell meets a young man in a sylvan setting who, it transpires, wishes to become a carver at table; and so the usual flow of dream vision information is reversed when the poet becomes the teacher of his chance encounter.

These more elaborate books, whose background is the court, are not practical manuals, nor are they fully courtly literature, but they may occasionally come very close to such literature. Indeed, they may deliberately echo it in literary procedures, dedications and prologues, and the *Master of Game* even quotes a newly fashionable court poet in English when it alludes to Chaucer's *Legend of Good Women*. If we were to try to find a modern analogy for the possible role of these works in medieval society, we might turn to magazines such as *The Field, Country Life, The Lady, The Tatler*, to find publications which to some extent participate in the world whose lifestyle they record, and which may even offer a route into that world, but whose readership far exceeds those who either participate or ever hope to do so. They offer a window into a way of life which holds a fascination for their readers. So, in the fifteenth century, courtesy books and hunting manuals had a limited practicality, but must have appealed as entertainment to a class of people not of noble birth nor of francophone descent, but nevertheless eager to understand the customs and practices of gentility. These could be encountered in the idealized and escapist stories of older romances, of course, but to a harder headed generation, books purporting to be practical manuals had the fascination of the real. The *Master of Game* was, after all, by the man himself, the *Boke of Nurture* was by the marshal of a ducal hall, and, just as Caxton's prologues rarely fail to mention when the work has been suggested by a member of the nobility, the reader could feel in contact with the taste of the contemporary great.

So, what is it that enables us to call literature courtly? It seems that it may be defined by origin and by destination, by style and by content, or, more usually, by some combination of these things. In fact, since courtly literature is the reflection of the world and values of the court, any one of these defining features tends to be interconnected with one or more of the others. At first, this seems a workably simple formulation upon which we could build, but in practice it often proves difficult to apply. Even the simple matter of origin may require interpretation. *Sir Gawain and the Green Knight* is an anonymous work which has no demonstrable court origin, but we may be ready to accept it as courtly on grounds of its content, its sophistication, and its elevated style. If we do accept it as courtly, is *Pearl*, or even *Patience* to be considered courtly also because they are by the same author, and are therefore of the same origin? Neither has a very secular subject matter, but we may wish to make a distinction in this respect between *Pearl*, which exploits ideas associated with courtliness (although for a non-courtly purpose) and *Patience*, which is much more narrowly religious in outlook. Let us consider another case of a work whose origin seems more certain. Sir John Clanvowe, a knight of the chamber of Richard II, is credited with the composition of two works: a love vision, *The Cuckoo and the Nightingale*, and a religious treatise, *The Two Ways*. The former would unhesitatingly be described as courtly both by its content and origin; the latter expresses no ideas which could be associated with courtly culture. Nevertheless, it was produced by a courtier in a court milieu. It is not an isolated case. Indeed, there is ample evidence of the fashionability in court circles in the fifteenth century of moral and religious writings, some of which, by their sympathy with Lollard doctrines, even risked charges of heresy. If we are to consider *The Two Ways* as courtly because of its strong association with the court, should we then consider all the works of the *Gawain*-poet as courtly because they were produced by an author who demonstrably understood courtly values, and because we cannot prove that they were *not* produced in some courtly milieu? It begins to appear that origin in the court may paradoxically be incidental to whether we perceive a work as courtly. Court origin is simply a historical accident without necessary connection to the quintessential courtliness of a work. If we resist the idea of *Patience* or *The Two Ways* as courtly works, we are in fact adopting the view that courtliness in literature is not necessarily a function of the author or the historical circumstances of composition, but more essentially of the subject matter and/or style. Such a view is easily justifiable. Gervase Mathew opened his book on the international court culture of the middle ages with the words 'court life was a factor in the society of western Europe from the late fourteenth-century until the early twentieth century'.[14] To be a factor in society implies that the values of the court were very much more widespread than that very restricted group who formed the court proper. Indeed, the court itself was never a very stable and fixed entity. True, there were long-serving members of the royal household, but the offices of state were filled by a succession of people. Successful court servants retired to country estates and were replaced by new ones recruited from the ranks of the gentry or nobility; new petitioners arrived from the country and passed through; the children of the nobility came to complete their education. The court, viewed not as the assembly currently in the household but as a network of retainers and dependants, past and present, who had had court experience, was quite large and extensive, even disregarding those with aspirations to courtly demeanour but no connections to the court. Hence it is at least arguable that attempts to limit the use of the epithet 'courtly' to those works actually composed within any definable court is a trivialization of the issue, limiting what was the expression of a transcendent culture to works from a single geographical location.

If we seek to define courtly literature as that which shares the values of the court rather than that actually produced within the court, the definition may be more satisfactory, but raises new difficulties. Assuming that a work shows awareness of courtly values, to what extent does it need to understand or promote them, in order to be considered courtly? The question becomes more difficult still in the case of works of the earlier and mid-fourteenth century which may be translations from courtly French originals and may therefore carry over part of the courtly trappings of their source. *William of Palerne* is the translation, produced at the request of a nobleman, of a French courtly romance, and it contains much of the courtly content of the original. Yet critics have been reluctant to admit it as courtly in terms of its destination, largely on an aesthetic judgement as to its value.[15] It is not regarded as sufficiently subtle and accomplished to justify the epithet 'courtly'. This introduces questions of degree of courtliness and also of literary merit into the ultimate judgement as to whether a work is courtly, and thus considerably complicates the issue. This problem arises with most English adaptations of French courtly romance. The romances of the Auchinleck manuscript, which tend to emphasize chivalry over courtesy, although they are written in some cases by authors with consciously literary aspirations, nevertheless do not seem to be *fully* courtly. Is *Kyng Alisaunder* a courtly poem? It is quite an accomplished literary work, reflecting some of the values of courtliness, but it is lacking in psychological subtlety and strong in military activity, and might therefore be rejected. But what of *Sir Tristrem*? It is arguable that here courtly subject matter (mutual love and conflicting loyalties) has been so attenuated that a courtly work is no longer to be considered such. In this book, we have repeatedly used the *Brut* of Wace to illustrate aspects of courtliness, but no one would consider Layamon's *Brut* a courtly poem. Yet it is a close adaptation of Wace's poem. Consider, for example, Layamon's handling of the familiar *wassail* episode:

Hængest eode in-to þan inne; þer wunede Rouwenne.
he heo lette scruden; mid vnimete prude.
al þat scrud þe heo hafde on; heo weoren swiðe wel ibon.
heo weoren mid þan bezste; ibrusted mid golde.

Heo bar an hire honde; ane guldene bolle.
i-uulled mid wine; þe wes wunder ane god.
Hæʒe iborenne men; heo lædden to hallen.
biuoren þan kinge; fairest alre þinge.
Reowen sæt a cneowe; & cleopede to þan kinge.
& þus ærest sæide; in Ænglene londe.
Lauerd king wæs hæil; For þine kime ich æm uæin.
Þe king þis ihærde; & nuste what heo seide.
þe king Vortigerne; fræinede his cnihtes sone.
what weoren þat speche; þe þat maide spilede.
Þa andswarede Keredic; a cniht swiðe sellic.
he wes þe bezste latimer; þat ær com her.
Lust me nu lauerd king; & ich þe wulle cuðen.
whæt seið Rouwenne; fæirest wimmonnen.
Hit beoð tiðende; inne Sæxe-londe.
whær-swa æi duʒeðe gladieð of drenche;   .
þat freond sæiðe to freonde; mid fæire loten hende.
Leofue freond wæs hail; Þe oðer sæið Drinc hail.
Þe ilke þat halt þene nap; he hine drinkeð up.
o[ð]er uuel me þider fareð; & bi-thecheð his iueren.
þenne þat uul beoð icumen; þenne cusseoð heo þreoien.
Þis beoð sele laʒen; inne Saxe-londe.
& inne Alemaine; heo beoð ihalden aðele.
Þis iherde Uortiger; of alche[n] uuele he wes war.
& seide hit an Bruttisc; ne cuðe he nan Ænglisc.
Maiden Rouwenne; drinc bluðeliche þenne.
Þat maide dronc up þat win; & lette don oðer þer-in.
& bi-tæhten þan kinge; & þrien hine custe.
& þurh þa ilke leoden; þa laʒen comen to þissen londe.
wæs-hail & drinc-hæil. moni mon þer-of is fain;
Rouwenne þe hende; sat bi þan kinge.
þe king heo ʒeorne biheold; heo was him an heorte leof.
ofte he heo custe; ofte he heo clupte.
al his mod & his main; hælde to þan mæidene.
Þe Wurse wes þer ful neh; þe in ælche gomene is ful ræh.
þe Wurse ne dude næuere god; he mæingde þas kinges mod.
he murnede ful swiðe; to habben þat mæidene to wiue.
Þat wes swi[ð]e ladlic þing; þat e Cristine king.
luuede þat haðene maide; leoden to hærme.

(Laʒamon Caligula, 7131–73)

Hengest went into the lodging where Rouwen was living. He had had
her clothed with lavish ostentation; all the clothing she had on became
her very well. She was all embroidered most richly with gold and she
bore in her hand a golden bowl filled with the finest wine. Nobly born
men led her, the fairest of all, into the hall before the king. Rouwen

knelt and called to the king and thus said first in England 'Lord king, wassail! I am glad at your coming'. The king heard this but did not know what she said. King Vortigern quickly asked his knights what that speech could be that the maid uttered. Then Keredic, a very remarkable knight, answered. He was the best interpreter that ever came here. 'Listen to me, lord king, and I shall inform you what Rouwen, the fairest of women, says. It is the custom in the land of the Saxons that whenever the knights enjoy a drink, the one friend says to the other, with fair and gracious demeanour "Dear friend, wassail"; and the other says "Drinkhail". The one who is holding the cup drinks it up. Another cup is brought and presented to his companion. When the cup has come, then they kiss three times. These are the good customs in the land of the Saxons and in Germany. They are highly esteemed.' Vortigern heard this (he was versed in every wickedness) and said it in British (he knew no English) 'Maiden Rouwen, drink heartily then'. The girl drank up the wine and had it refilled and gave it to the king and kissed him three times. And through these folk the customs came to this land of wassail and drinkhail, to the satisfaction of many a man. The gracious Rouwen sat beside the king, and the king eagerly gazed on her and she was dear to his heart. Often he kissed her and embraced her. All his force and inclination was directed to that maiden. The Devil, who in every amorous play is most fierce, was close by. The Devil never did any good. He stirred up the king's passions, and he greatly longed to have that maiden as a wife. That was an evil thing that the Christian king loved that heathen girl to the detriment of his people.

Although dependent on Wace's *Brut*, Layamon's handling of this scene is significantly different from that of his source, and in some respects moves away from Wace's treatment back towards the perspective of pseudo-Nennius. The narrative perspective has changed and the impact of Rouwen's entrance has been undermined by the behind-the-scenes details of her preparation. Hengest's scheming is foregrounded, and Rouwen becomes merely her father's instrument, led into the hall rather than making an appearance. Layamon's interest is not in the effect of Rouwen's appearance on Vortigern. He does mention the gold, but the description lacks sensuous appeal, and is implicitly critical of ostentation. Rather than elaborate the desire of Vortigern for the girl, he repeats sententious warnings against the Devil, and especially, he expands on the details of the custom of wassailing. Layamon is clearly not in sympathy with those aspects of courtliness which are associated with sensuousness or sexual relationships. What is arguable here, however, is that Layamon, compelled by his clerkish and heroic outlook, is quite deliberately turning his back on the attractions of French courtliness and its morally ambiguous aspects. Certainly, deliberate clerkish renunciation must also be the case in the contemporary *Ancrene Wisse*, which was written for three ladies of elevated background, but which turns to courtly ideas simply to achieve more forceful illustration of the religious and moral teaching that is its central purpose. It seems, therefore, that the designation of a work as courtly, may involve not only the various features associated with courtliness, nor even the degree to which those features in themselves are evident in a work. The absence of courtliness in English works may not always be constrained by the resources of the author. Rather it may be the result of the adoption of an authorial mode, and the extent to which the courtly mode is realized may vary according to the degree of sympathy as much as the understanding possessed by the author. Popular literature in English, even those romances based upon courtly originals, probably often lack understanding of the psychological subtleties, social refinements, and richness of context of the originals. However, more sophisticated English writings of a clerkish or religious outlook may simply lack sympathy with the courtly ideal.

In the royal court at the end of the fourteenth century, Chaucer offered a new kind of secular yet sophisticated writing, composed in English, but in close contact with the French-based courtly tradition. He was sufficiently distanced by social position and by inclination not to accept the inherited values of courtly literature without question, nevertheless he had considerable sympathy with and understanding of the values of courtliness. He was praised by his contemporaries as an orator, a poet of love, but also as a philosopher, and so it is appropriate that he does not emphasize in a crude and simple way the unquestioned virtue of wealth or noble birth. Falling in with a widespread opinion in his time, he adopts the traditional moralist's view that true nobility springs from individual virtue. Regard for the experience of human love and for depth of feeling, appreciation of both sensuous attraction and courtly accomplishments, and quickness of wit and eloquence can all be found in Chaucer's works. Moreover, he worked in close collaboration with members of the royal court, serving various members of the royal family. Nevertheless, his poetry demonstrates effectively the broadening of the values of courtliness to a wider community. Despite a continuing pretence of insensitivity, of failure to comprehend, expressed in his narrators, the fundamental lesson of his outlook is the extension of the values of courtliness to all humanity who were able to adopt and profit from it. His poem

Gentillesse expresses most concisely the reconciliation of elements of courtly, religious, and philosophical idealism, deriving virtue from the example of Christ, and nobility from virtue. Chaucer, along with other English writers of the last half of the fourteenth century, substituted the word *gentillesse* for *curteisie* when referring to the more fundamental and determinate qualities of personality, and reserved the latter for the more external accomplishments and acquired aspects of refinement. *Gentillesse* was a multi-facetted concept, applicable in various ways. Linking together moral worth, refinement and nobility, it could be employed as a justification of secular power; or, in contrast, it could be developed as a consolation by locating virtue independently of wealth and status (the view which Chaucer investigates in the *Franklin's Tale* and states flatly through the mouth of the Wife of Bath. Developing this division between the possession of power and nobility, a contemporary of Chaucer, Henry Scogan, adopts the words of the Wife, and borrows the entire text of *Gentillesse* in his *Moral Balade* (ed. Skeat, *Works of Chaucer*, vii), addressed about 1406 to the royal princes. His role is that of *mestre*, or instructor of princes, a role which philosophically inclined authors such as Chaucer, Gower, or Christine de Pizan tended to adopt unbidden, but in which Scogan seems genuinely to have been employed. His purpose in the poem is to acknowledge the breach between nobility of birth and inward *gentillesse*, but to argue the necessity of their reconciliation in those in power. Scogan's poem represents a court poem written in the philosophical mode for an audience from the court, but its earnestness may restrain us from considering it prototypically courtly. For court poetry written in the courtly mode, and with courtly sympathies, we must turn to Chaucer.

Chaucer began his poetic career perhaps by composing in those genres often known by the collective phrase 'balades, rondels and virelayes', and it has been suggested that some extant French verses in MS Pennsylvania French 15 may be the poet's earliest works.[16] His translation of the *texte sacré* of courtliness, the *Roman de la Rose*, also belongs to his early poetic activities, but the earliest work which can be dated is the *Book of the Duchess* (*c.* 1369), a work which fully exploits many of the traditions of French courtly poetry. A brief resumé serves to illustrate the courtliness of the *Book of the Duchess*. In it, the narrator, suffering from melancholy and unable to sleep, prefers reading a romance to playing at chess or tables. The story is a version of a tale from Ovid's *Metamorphoses*, a tale of love and separation. In a dream induced by reading this story, the narrator finds himself in a chamber painted with the text and commentary on the *Roman de la Rose*, is aware of the springtime song of the birds, and wanders out into the forest to seek solace for his melancholy. He encounters a hunt, not forgetting to provide his reader with a certain amount of technical detail and appropriate terminology and, led by a small dog, he wanders through the verdant forest until he becomes aware of a man in black standing beneath an oak tree. This gentleman has all the appearance of suffering, and is composing a poem upon the death of his lady. He is almost fainting as the narrator doffs his hood and introduces himself, but eventually replies with such courtesy that the reader is invited to take note of his example. There follows the extended account of a love affair and of its idealized object, amplified by considerable psychological technicalities, before the revelation of its ending in separation by death.

Many of the accomplishments, values and attitudes of courtliness are exhibited in the *Book of the Duchess* without the questioning or scepticism apparent in most later works. Not only is it courtly in content, and perhaps also in the associations of its octosyllabic versification, but also in its historical associations. It is traditionally associated with the death of the duchess Blanche, first wife of John of Gaunt. The poem has its interpretative difficulties, but they do not compromise this essential courtliness. But even here, although most of the indications of courtliness are present, and there is some word-play, it does not exhibit the subtlety of wit which we would customarily associate with courtliness. If the *Book of the Duchess* can stand as one example of courtly literature, we may end with the analysis of a brief poem which possesses this wit, and well illustrates the subtle shape-shifting of courtly poetry noted at the beginning of this chapter.

> Ma dame ye ben of al beaute shryne
> As fer as cercled is the mapamonde
> For as the Cristall glorious ye shyne
> And lyke Ruby ben your chekys rounde
> Therwyth ye ben so mery and so iocunde
> That at a Reuell whan that I se you dance
> It is an oynement vnto my wounde
> Thogh ye to me ne do no daliance
>
> For thogh I wepe of teres ful a tyne
> Yet may that wo myn herte nat confounde
> Your semy voys That ye so small out twyne
> Makyth my thoght in ioy and blys habounde

So curtaysly I go wyth loue bounde
That to my self I sey in my penaunce
Suffyseth me to loue you Rosemounde
Thogh ye to me ne do no daliance

Nas neuer Pyk walwed in galauntyne
As I in loue am walwed and iwounde
For whych ful ofte I of myself deuyne
That I am trew tristam the secunde
My loue may not refreyde nor affounde
I Brenne ay in an amorouse plesaunce
Do what you lyst I wyl your thral be founde
Thogh ye to me ne do no daliance

The balade *Rosemounde* is found only in the late fifteenth-century
Troilus and Criseyde manuscript, Bodleian Rawlinson Poetry 163. Like
Troilus in the same manuscript, it is signed 'tregentil Chaucer'. There is
no further evidence of its authorship. The absence of certain
context makes the poem hard to judge. Is it an artful *folie*, or is it a
botched attempt at the courtly treatment of love? Attribution to
Chaucer prejudges the question, so let us consider the stylistic
choices in the text itself. There are some unusual images, such as
that of the pike in aspic jelly, or the claim to sensitivity made in the
reference to having wept a bucketful of tears, but courtly poetry is
not without unusual images, so let us first consider less prominent
detail in the use of the word *thral*. It is, in Middle English, an
emotionally charged word with rather different associations from
the word *servant*. It is relatively rarely used in reference to love, but
in Chaucer's *Legend of Good Women* (1313) Dido is considered to
have humiliated herself by promising to be Aeneas's *thral* or 'servant
in the leste degree', and in *Troilus and Criseyde* (I, 235 and II, 773)
thralldom is opposed to liberty. In the *Franklin's Tale* (6, 61)
thralldom is reckoned incompatible with true love, and in the
Romaunt of the Rose (5807) is associated with prostitution. At the
best, it seems to imply unreasonable excess in the lover (*BD*, 767).

The lexical context of the term furnishes an objective means of
assessing its stylistic associations, and it is revealing that among the
commonest collocations with the word *thral* in fourteenth-century
English are terms like *God, synne, free, cherle, lord*, and *servant*. A *thral*
implies a servant totally subjugated, and in both Chaucer's and Gower's
works is often used metaphorically to imply subjection to sin. The
phrase *thral of God* occurs very rarely, and only in special rhetorical
contexts. By contrast, the lexical accompaniment of *servant* includes
God, lord, lady, kyng, grace, humble, trewe, blisse, herte, and *wise* (as

well as *synne*). The contrast between *thral* and *servant* is apparent. Whereas servants may occupy a respected position in society and discharge duties of responsibility and trust, the thrall was by definition of low esteem, owing no loyalty, but merely absolute submission, to his master. The desire to be Rosemounde's *thral*, therefore, strikes a discordant note. It is that status normally regarded as most undesirable to a free man. From whatever aspect it is viewed it casts no credit on the speaker. But if *thral* is dubious, much the same can be said for the refrain word *daliaunce*. Although usable in polite society, its most frequent occurrence in the works of Chaucer is to describe the conversations of clerks. It is in fact never used to describe the behaviour of aristocratic figures, and is associated with words like *desport, plesaunce, amorouse,* and *beaute,* as well as *dance, singe,* and *pleye.* Its associations are perhaps not far removed from those of the *reuell* at which Rosemounde dances. Revels usually imply boisterous entertainment, which may be condoned in certain circumstances – for example wedding feasts – but which can also be viewed with suspicion. In merchant circles revels are considered dangerous, irresponsible, and probably costly. The apprentice of the *Cook's Tale* (1, 4389–94) finds revels a short way to Newgate, and the merchant's wife in the *Shipman's Tale* (10, 3–7) poses a threat to her husband's purse. The serious-minded heroine of the *Physician's Tale* on occasions even feigns sickness:

> For that she wolde fleen the compaignye
> Where likly was to treten of folye
> As is at festes, reuels, and at daunces
> That been occasions of daliaunces.
>
> (*CT*, 9, 63–6)

Reuell, daliaunce, and *thral* are at least potentially inappropriate words in a serious courtly context, and their inappropriateness is complemented by some verbal choices in the description of the lady, most obviously the description of her cheeks as round as rubies. The conventions of feminine description have here become dis-jointed. Rubies are not particularly round, and ladies' cheeks are not normally mentioned in courtly description. On the other hand, breasts are mentioned four times in Chaucer's poetry, and on three of these four occasions are described as *rounde* (*RvT*, 1, 3967; *BD*, 819; *TC*, III, 1250). It is tempting to assume that the word *ruby* has been shifted from a description of the lips, but this collocation seems rare before the time of Shakespeare. Nevertheless, there does seem to be an element of the preposterous in the description of

Rosemounde. This extends to the imagery. The idea of a woman shining bright as crystal, the concept of the ointment of love's wound, and the kitchen imagery of the pike in aspic may all seem curious; although all three have parallels in Gower or the *Roman de la Rose.* Shortly before the close of the latter poem the lover is advised to seek experience by going into the kitchen and tasting all the dishes – including galantyne. This kitchen imagery had a lengthy tradition as the grounds for comic comparison in medieval literature. But why does the speaker compare himself to a pike, a word which Chaucer uses only twice elsewhere? One of these instances is in *Troilus and Criseyde*, in which a statement is made about the nature of the comic in poetry:

> 'Ne iompre ek no discordant thyng y-feere,
> As thus, to vsen termes of Phisik
> In loues termes; hold of thi matere
> The forme alwey and do that it be lik;
> ffor if a peyntour wolde peynte a pyk
> With asses feet and hedde it as an ape,
> It cordeth naught, so nere it but a iape.'

(II, 1037–43)

The source is Horace's *Ars Poetica*, re-interpreted to refer to lexical incongruity and the comic effect of inappropriate verbal choice. This is a pointer to the genre of *Rosemounde*, which appears to belong to a type of lyric represented less subtly by Hoccleve's poem *To His Ugly Mistress*, an exercise in comic incongruity which depends upon grotesque description and the inappropriate ordering of conventional epithets in description.[17]

Such inappropriateness seems a feature of *Rosemounde* and occurs also in an example which medieval rhetoricians would have deplored as the vice of style, *acyrologia*. The line 'I brenne ay in an amorouse plesaunce' is problematic. In Chaucerian usage one may burn with love, lust, or even covetousness, but what all such burning passions have in common is their anguish or intensity. A burning *plesance* is either a vice of style pure and simple or a conventional, but awkward, courtly paradox which fails to capture the proper extremity of the predicament of the courtly lover. Instead of intensity of feeling we have a sort of detachment, savouring the situation, an intellectualized posturing in the role of lover. This is clearly apparent in the self-comparison with Tristran; but this self-reflexivity is perhaps most noticeable in the unusual collocation *I go curteisly*. Normally, the adverb qualifies specific actions, but here it qualifies a verb which means little more than 'to live'. The tone of self-congratulation seems unmistakable. It is by the subtle use of verbal choice that Chaucer insinuates dramatic attitudes which cause this poem to surpass others in a similar genre which depend simply on the re-distribution of epithets in physical description. The Chaucerian lyricist consciously wallows, like the Miller's Absolon, in the conventionalities of his situation. Through his self-centred consciousness his feeling is diffused, but his expression remains hyperbolic, culminating in the extreme subjection implied by the choice of the word *thral*. The word might be justified as the expression of extreme commitment in love or in religion, but that language of excess is inappropriate to the self-centred fantasizing of the poem's speaker. This is the culminating incongruity of a poem fashioned from inappropriateness and incongruity.

This chapter has found many different justifications for applying the epithet 'courtly' to literature. It origins and destination, its concern with the values and ideals of courtliness, but especially its awareness, understanding and sympathy with those ideals. Not least among these are the ways that such understanding and sympathy make themselves felt in stylistic choices and linguistic strategies mentioned also in the last chapter. Among them is the eloquent and witty use of language. There is, perhaps, no need to conclude that in *Rosemounde* we have a brief comic poem by an author well aware of the preoccupations of courtliness, and capable of employing the familiar literary procedures in order to subvert them. In some sense, this poem reflects the warnings issued in Chapter 7 not to under-estimate men who possess skill in the use of words. But as well as looking back to Chapters 6 and 7 it looks forwards to the next chapter and the courtly experience of love.

NOTES

1.   Baugh, 'Walter of Bibbesworth', pp. 21–33; Rothwell, 'Teaching of French' and 'Role of French'.
2.   For an extended treatment of the conception of literature as therapeutic, see Olson, *Literature as Recreation*.
3.   In fact one of the providers of material for Gaimar was the lord of Helmesley, Yorks, Walter Espec, whose eulogistic portrait by Aelred of Rievaulx is discussed in Chapter 3 (above).
4.   Legge, *Anglo-Norman Literature*, p. 13.
5.   Salter, *Fourteenth-Century English Poetry*, p. 34.
6.   Doyle, 'English Books'.
7.   Urquhart, 'Fifteenth-century literary culture'.
8.   Boffey, *Manuscripts of English Courtly Love Lyrics*, p. 138.

9. Nicholls, *Matter of Courtesy*, pp. 57–74. As well as a study of their content, Nicholls provides useful appendices listing the texts and reviewing their authorship.

10. Nicholls, *Matter of Courtesy*, p. 66.

11. Philippe of Ferrara's fourteenth-century work, *Liber de introductione loquendi*, draws stories from the *Historia romanum*, *Alphabetum narrationum*, *Legenda aurea* and Vincent of Beauvais suitable for talk at table, before the fire, on a journey, at times of bereavement, and so on. Nearly half the work is devoted to table talk.

12. Rooney, *Hunting in Middle English Literature*, pp. 7–20.

13. *Master of Game*, pp. 40–1.

14. Mathew, *Court of Richard II*, p. 1.

15. Pearsall, *Old and Middle English Poetry* (p. 157) suggests that the translation was the product of an importunate clerk, and was perhaps 'intended for the kitchen staff'. The suggestion is an extension of Turville-Petre's suspicion ('Humphrey de Bohun') that it was produced for members of the household rather than Humphrey de Bohun himself, who is associated with 'sumptious illustrated MSS'. However, part of the problem of assessing the courtliness of literature is that a taste for luxury items is no guide to the limits of a patron's literary taste.

16. Wimsatt, *Chaucer and the Poems of 'Ch'*.

17. Stemmler, 'My Fair Lady'.

Chapter 9

Courtly Love

In 1883 the French journal *Romania* published an article of incalculable importance to the development of the criticism of medieval poetry.[1] In it, the eminent medieval scholar and critic Gaston Paris stated concisely his analysis of the representation of love in Chrétien de Troyes' *Lancelot* (*Li Chevalier de la Charrette*) and in a number of other shorter poems.

The principle characteristics of love thus understood are the following:

1. It is illicit and furtive. Similar relations between man and wife are inconceivable; the lover's constant fear of losing his mistress, of not being worthy of her, of displeasing her in anything whatsoever, cannot be reconciled with tranquil and open possession. It is to this ever-retractable gift of herself, to the immense sacrifice that she has made, to the risk that she continuously runs, that the lady owes the superiority that the lover acknowledges in her.

2. Because of this, the lover is always in a position of inferiority before his lady, in trepidation which nothing can reassure, in a constant tremble, although he may nevertheless in every encounter be the bravest of warriors. She, by contrast, whilst truly loving him, behaves capriciously towards him; often unjust, haughty and disdainful, she makes him feel all the time that he may lose her and that, at the slightest breach of the code of love, he will in fact lose her.

3. In order to be worthy of the affection he seeks or has already received, he fulfils every feat of prowess imaginable, and she for her part dreams always of making him a better man, of making him more 'worthy'. Her apparent arbitrariness, her fleeting moments of harshness, normally have this end, and are no more than the means of either refining his love, or exalting his courage.

4. Finally, and this sums up all the rest, love is an art, a science, a virtue which has its rules just like chivalry or courtliness, rules which are grasped and applied better the more progress has been made, and from which there must be no default on pain of being deemed unworthy.

This *courtly* love (amour *courtois*), so it seems to me, appears in no French work prior to the *Chevalier de la Charrette*.

His formulation was widely adopted in France and within a few years we find Joseph Bédier re-phrasing Paris's ideas, emphasizing the quasi-religious aspects of such love and the claim often made by poets that love in itself promotes nobility:

> What is characteristic of it is the conception of love as a religious cult directed upon an outstanding object, and founded, like Christian love, upon the utter disproportion between merit and desire; as a necessary school for honour which refines the lover and transmutes the base into the courtly; as a willing servitude which conceals an ennobling power, and finds in suffering the dignity and beauty of its emotion.[2]

These ideas were introduced into English studies in an influential book-length essay by C.S. Lewis, *The Allegory of Love* (1936), in which he defined what he translated into English as 'courtly love', a love 'whose characteristics may be enumerated as Humility, Courtesy, Adultery, and the Religion of Love'.[3] The use of the word 'religion' implied not only something about the way this love was conceptualized by its practitioners, but also about the imagery in which it was expressed: the description of the relationship between men and women in love borrowed from the languages of religion and of feudalism to express ideas of generosity, loyalty, and dedication.

It is significant that Paris spoke of an itemized 'code of love' and stressed the importance of conformity to its stipulations. His article itself could be read as a rule-book, and tended to be interpreted as such by scholars during the first half of this century. The italicization of *courtois* in the French text, which emphasized its role as qualifier of the word *amour*, was lost in translation, and the phrase 'courtly love' quickly became an unanalysable label for a sharply defined set of beliefs about love in medieval literature rather than simply meaning that kind of love characteristic of courtly contexts. Just as the manuals of rhetoric provided a useful checklist against which medieval literature could be compared, allegedly revealing the principles behind its composition, so 'courtly love' furnished a strategy of apparent historical validity by which modern critics could interpret medieval authors. The latter could be seen as promulgating in their narratives a uniform code of courtly love. Lewis's suggestion that Chaucer's *Troilus and Criseyde* was written within this tradition encouraged T.A. Kirby to devote an entire book to the poem as a study in courtly love.[4] But, by the middle of the 1950s, misgivings were felt about this conception of a generalized code of love behaviour. Although love may be described as *cortese* in medieval Italian literature, and *cortes' amor* occurs in the Provençal poetry of Peire d'Auvergne and the romance of *Flamenca*, the phrase 'courtly love' (*amour courtois*) is absent in English and Northern French. Gower refers to Gawain as *courtois d'amour* (*Traité*, xvii, 13) and fickle, and the very rare occurrences in continental sources do not seem to refer to the code adopted by earlier scholars, but rather to an easy, and dangerous, fluency in love-talking. In addition, not only the phrase 'courtly love', but also a literature illustrating full compliance with the code described by Paris and Lewis turns out, upon cool reflection, to be absent from England before the end of the fourteenth century. The behaviour described in literature belonged essentially to the late middle ages in England.[5] The stipulation that love must be adulterous is scarcely to be met with at all. Indeed, the misconception about adultery (now largely abandoned) seems, among English scholars at any rate, to have arisen largely from C.S. Lewis's interpretation of medieval statements about the incompatibility of love with marriage, which involved a conception of adultery which equated pre-marital and extra-marital affairs.

Courtly love was assembled both as a critical concept and a phrase by Gaston Paris, and transmitted to the world of English studies largely by C.S. Lewis, where it is still widely disseminated outside the ranks of professional medievalists. Although it has been in many respects discredited in earlier English texts, it would be wrong to assume that it was originally concocted simply from the fruits of misreading vernacular literature. The medieval codification which seemed to give it justification could be found in a late twelfth-century Latin work, the *De amore* of Andreas Capellanus.[6] True, Andreas did not mention *amor curialis*, but he did discuss love at great length in a manner modelled on the *Ars amoris* and *Remedia amoris* of Ovid, and did treat love as a field of learning, a subject for extensive debate. He claimed knowledge of a code observed and enforced by quasi-legal proceedings at the contemporary court of Champagne, where he says he was chaplain. He stated regulations for amatory behaviour, and quoted the judgements of Marie de Champagne on a number of doubtful questions. Among these *dicta* was the notorious judgement that love was incompatible with marriage. To an earlier generation of scholars, Andreas seemed to provide the handbook and the theoretical background to what could be observed in literature. The court of Champagne was envisaged as engaged in the pursuit of love and refinement, and diverted by assemblies which discussed love cases in a pastiche of parliamentary procedure. Historical scholarship has since cast doubt on the actuality of this,[7] and has even demonstrated notable examples of loving marriages,[8] but the concept of 'courtly love' has not been abandoned as a literary fiction with possible repercussions on actual behaviour.

Whatever the reliability of Andreas as historical evidence, it should be recognized that he is no more satisfactory as a theoretician of the literary representation of 'courtly love' defined by Gaston Paris and his followers. His perspective is too ironic. He is clerkly rather than courtly; intellectual rather than sensual. He is not inspired by the springtime any more than by wealth (although he mentions the importance of *largesse*). He does not automatically esteem physical beauty, or even claim attachment to any particular lady or any particular convictions. Rather, his interest is in casuistry. His work is a compendium of conflicting views on love theory drawn from philosophical teachings and courtly adages. He comes to few conclusions, taking pleasure in the tensions revealed. He makes much of the challenge to natural order represented by attraction between persons of different social classes, and provides a series of specimen dialogues discussing these circumstances. He imagines a burgess arguing the now-familiar view that excellence of character ennobles more than inheritance. Yet although this philosophical contention is discussed at length, it does not prove finally convincing to the addressee. Although not so forthright on this matter as Walter Map (see p. 73), Andreas is no idealist with egalitarian views: the rigidity of class structure is repeatedly asserted, and a lady of the higher nobility reminds her plebeian suitor that virtue may be all very well, but it cannot repair a fundamental difference in rank (I. 6, 138). One can detect a certain mischievous pleasure in the process of turning the assurances of philosophical and courtly belief against one another. Marriage can be proved to be incompatible with love by using widespread definitions of love itself. Love requires freedom of will on both sides, and love consists of awareness of a desire for something not possessed. But the obligations of marriage defeat both of these characteristics; *ergo*, love cannot exist in marriage (I. 6, 367–72; 6, 397–400). The wryness of Andreas's treatment of his subject is equally apparent in his division of society into *plebeius*, *nobilis*, *nobilior*, and, as an afterthought, *nobilissimus*. This final group, the most noble of all, he defines as clerics like himself, but this high virtue does not prevent him from going on to ponder with deliberate disregard of both morality and canon law the relative merit of love affairs with nuns. Although he raises the possibility of what he calls *amor purus* (which resembles a legendary test of chastity imposed on unwilling Fathers of the Church), his idea of intense sexual titillation without ultimate fulfilment is at once dismissed as nonsense by the lady in the dialogue, who believes that *amor mixtus* (which includes physical satisfaction) is more likely to be encountered in the world of actuality (I. 6, 470–5). Andreas's work in general shows a marked lack of reticence about the sexual intention driving love discussions, and his explicitness in this respect goes far beyond what is encount-ered in serious vernacular literature of entertainment in his time. In this he is matched not by works we should normally consider courtly, but rather in the deliberately anti-courtly *fabliau* genre. The *De amore* is not therefore the sought-for text-book of courtly love, but a relatively sophisticated intellectual entertainment for those who could read Latin and appreciate its artful subversion of its sources. Known medieval responses to it varied from mirth to outright condemnation from the pulpit.[9]

Even before historians questioned reports of early 'courts of love', the near absence of the phrase *amour courtois* or its English equivalent 'courtly love' from medieval sources caused disquiet among literary scholars. One solution to the problem seemed to be in adopting some other qualifying adjective for love, which might have greater currency in medieval languages. D.S. Brewer, noting that the 'term "courtly love" has . . . acquired associations that are far too rigid and precise' suggested that the collocation *fine amor*, which seemed to refer to a concept not unlike that of 'courtly love', might be a satisfactory substitute.[10] He did, however, point out that in Chaucer's *Legend of Good Women* (F. 544) the phrase 'craft of fyn lovynge' explicitly refers to love and loyalty within marriage, so that the received concept of courtly love would require some adjustment if it were to be designated by *fine amor*. The passage in the *Legend of Good Women* is unique in Chaucer's works, but the proposal to refer to medieval love as *fine amor* had the advantage that it was at least a genuinely medieval phrase, representing a medieval conception. It resembled the phrase *fin' amors* by which Provençal lyric poets referred to ideals like those described by the phrase 'courtly love', and indeed the phrase was used in this way by Chaucer's contemporary, John Gower, in a sequence of French lyric *Balades*: the greatest delight in May-time is *fine amor* (xxxvii, 2); in *fine amor* the lover's heart, body, and reason are all submitted to his lady (xxi), and all his devotion is set on her (xxiv, 6). Whoever embarks on an affair according to the dictates of *fine amor* must be indifferent to fortune, must love, serve and cherish his lady (xlvii, 15). Just as the body is nourished by food and drink, so the heart is sustained by *fine amor* (xlvii, 1–2). The parallel between Gower's usage and the *fin' amors* of the troubadours seems close; and in this context the phrase *fine amor* seems a suitable substitute for 'courtly love'.[11] But Gower's is a somewhat special case, and we should be wary of assuming equivalence on this evidence alone. The *Balades* were written in French, and in the French lyric tradition which drew upon the lyric tradition of the south. It has been shown that it is not possible to equate the use of the phrase *fin' amors* in the lyric tradition of Provence with the *fine amor* of the northern narrative romance tradition. Quite different conceptions are likely to attach to the phrase.[12] Nevertheless, the fact remains that *fine amor* is used in England of the love relationship between men and women. In Thomas of Kent's *Roman de Toute Chevalerie*, written in England probably in the last quarter of the twelfth century, we hear that Alexander and Candace 'vont desur le lit parler d'amur fine' (7735). In the Middle English *Seven Sages of Rome* (MS CUL Ff.ii.38: 2989) Alexander again exchanges letters with his lady which 'spak of loue fyne'. The adjective *fin* also occurs frequently in adverbials describing love. In *Ipomedon*, the hero decides to leave the court of La Fiere in order to conceal his love:

> Kar ki eyme si finement
> Ne se puit covrir longement
> Se il pres de s'amye meint
>
> (*Ipomedon*, 1209–11)

For whoever loves so intensely cannot hide it for long, if he stays close by his beloved.

There is no hint of authorial disapproval of Alexander or Ipomedon's love, but the English romance *Arthour and Merlin* holds an interesting commentary on an event in English legendary history with which we are now very familiar.

> Angys hadde verrament
> A douhter boþe fair and gent
> (Ac sche was heþen Sarraȝin)
> And Fortiger for loue fin
> Hir tok to fere and to wiue –
> And was cursed in al his liue
> For he lete Cristen wedde haþen
> And meynt our blod as flesche and maþen.
>
> (*Arthour and Merlin*, 474–81)

The author of *Arthour and Merlin* takes the older, disapproving, view of the relationship between Vortigern and Ronwen: that it is the product of lustful desire, and a national disaster. The country, he continues, went to the devil because of this liaison between a Christian and a pagan. The phrase *loue fin* refers here to sexual love, but does not treat it sympathetically. In the Old French *fabliau Des Tresces* (55), the phrase occurs in a context even less easily reconcilable with 'courtly love', when *fine amor* constrains the lover to attempt to sleep with his lady in the very room in which her husband is present. What these last three examples have in common is the perception of *fine amor* as an overwhelming passion which compels actions which are ill-advised, scandalous, or disastrous.

Passages occur, however, in which the phrase denotes quite a different conception. Although Gower used *fine amor* to refer to something like 'courtly love' in his *Balades*, in the *Mirour del Omme* (14635) he uses it in quite a different context in the phrase *foy et fine amor*, where it has religious significance. The C-text of *Piers Plowman* echoes this phrase in translation in a similarly religious context:

> And as wex and weke and warm fuyr togyderes   'wick'
> Fostren forth a flaume and a feyr lye   'light'
> That serueth this swynkares to se by a nyhtes,
> So doth þe sire and þe sone and seynt spirit togyderes
> Fostren forth amonges folke fyn loue and bileue
> That alle kyne cristene clanseth of synne.
>
> (*Piers Plowman*, C-text XIX, 166–71)

In the Vernon version of the *Castle of Love* the reference is to the love of God for humankind:

> þat wiþ his blod he vs washed of sinne
> And brouȝt vs out of wo to winne –
> Neuer ffader for no childe
> Of fyn loue nas so freo ne mylde.
>
> (1397–1400)

Although the literal reference here is to the love of God, the figurative dimension exploits the traditional image of God as father and a comparison is made to the affection of a father for his child. It is not, apparently, felt to be inappropriate to use *fyn loue* of this relationship. Some irony or at least some shift from a more 'normal' secular meaning might be suspected, but in fact, in terms of frequency of occurrence in Middle English, the association between *loue fin* and Christian charity is very strong. Indeed, it has been claimed that this last is the sole significance of the phrase in Middle English.[13] Although this is not strictly true, it is a significance which can easily be matched from French sources written in England as well as on the Continent. Unlike Bishop Tempier of Paris, who condemned the teachings of Andreas Capellanus, the thirteenth-century Bishop of Lincoln, Robert Grosseteste, heartily approved of *fine amor*, which he interpreted as charity:

> Se il vit en humilite
> En droiture e en charite
> Kar dampnedeu n'ad rien tant chier
> Cume fin amor de quer entier
>
> (*Carmen de Creacione Mundi*, 993–6)

> So he lived in humility, righteousness and charity, for the Lord God holds nothing so dear as whole-hearted *fine amor*.

Nothing could be clearer than that the *fine amor* praised by Robert Grosseteste is quite distinct from 'courtly love'. No medieval Bishop of Lincoln, Chancellor of Oxford University, would be likely to claim that the God he served was enthusiastic about the adulterous courtly love described by late nineteenth-century scholars of medieval literature.

The phrase *fine amor* – as opposed to its translation *loue fin* – is unusual in Middle English, but the Auchinleck manuscript, which belongs to the London of the generation before Chaucer, contains three occurrences, and these are quoted below:

> Þemperour and his wif
> Þat he louede als his lif
> In chaumbre to gidere þai sete
> Gladliche þai dronke and ete.
> 'Sire, ʒhe saide, gentil emperour
> I þe loue wiʒ fin amour
> And þou nowt me sikeli.'
>
> (*Seven Sages of Rome*, 255–61)

> Þo spak Clarice to Blauncheflour
> Wordes ful of fin amour:
> 'Ne doute þou nammore wiþalle
> Þan to miself hit hadde bifalle.
> Wite þe wel witerli
> Þat hele ich wille þoure boþer druri.'
>
> (*Floriz and Blauncheflour*, 951–6)

'Ac no for þan,' þe fendes sede,
ʒif þou wilt do bi our rede,
For þou art ous leue and dere,
We schul þe bring wiþ fine amour
þer þou com in fram þe priour,
Wiþ our felawes yfere;

(*St Patrick's Purgatory*, 337–42)

It is apparent that none of these matches very well the Lewisian specifications for 'courtly love'. In the first passage a wife is accusing her husband of not reciprocating the loyalty which she feels for him; in the second, one young woman is offering support to her female friend in keeping the latter's love secret; in the last a troop of devils is ironically declaring their regard and offering sympathetic refuge in Hell to the knight Owein. Not only is it difficult to reconcile these different uses of the phrase *fine amor* with the meaning usually attributed to the phrase 'courtly love', but they seem difficult to reconcile with one another. On investigation, the truly medieval phrase *fine amor* and its Middle English equivalent *fine loue* give as much cause for disquiet as did the modern coinage 'courtly love'.

We find ourselves in an interpretative dilemma: the phrase *fine amor* may refer to Christian charity, but it can also refer to sexual and even adulterous love. It can refer to the affection between a father and child or to that between female friends. It can also be shown to have been used of the purely political regard existing between heads of state.[14] How can we reconcile such diversity in usage? Béroul's account of the Tristran legend can help us. In his poem the very same love between Tristran and Isolde is variously referred to as *fine amor* by the lovers on the one hand, and *amor commune*, *amor de putée*, *amor vilaine*, and *fol amor* by Isolde's husband, King Mark, and other members of the royal court on the other. Now, if many different kinds of love, from parental affection to Christian charity, and from sexual desire to simple friendship, can be designated by the phrase *fine amor*, yet at the same time that very same love can be denoted by such antithetical phrasing as *fine amor* and *amor de putée*, then we must assume that this phrase *fine amor* is referentially more or less empty. That is, that *fine amor* does not have a fixed and specific meaning which is independent of the circumstances of its use. As a phrase, it is much more like some such modern expression as 'good conduct' than a phrase with specific reference like 'Jumbo jet'. Moreover, that it *is* a phrase, and not a relatively opaque compound like the modern word 'holiday', means not only that it is capable of re-interpretation according to context and user, but that it consists of recognizable parts which are each usable individually in other contexts. This means that other contexts can be considered, and it can usefully be analysed in terms of the significance of these constituent parts.

The breadth of circumstances in which the phrase may be used derives largely from the semantic breadth of the word *love/amor* in medieval languages. Indeed, the simplex *love* covers much the same field of meaning as it does in combination with *fin*, and this needs no further discussion at present, since we have already gained sufficient impression of the range of circumstances to which it is appropriate. The modifier *fin* is etymologically derived from the Latin past participle *finitum*, which can denote that which is completed, to which nothing can be added by way of improvement. The word was especially used by Latin writers on rhetoric and composition to refer to a well 'finished' or 'perfected' piece of writing. Like the word 'perfect', which originally also meant 'completed', it seems very quickly to have developed strong qualitative associations.

In Old French the word first occurs in the *Chanson de Roland* in the phrase *or fin* 'pure gold'. Early scholars indeed derived the expression *fine amor* from the Latin *aurum finum*.[15] Although this may be fanciful, the association is a persistent one. The perception of a connection between something at once pure and valuable encouraged the thirteenth-century poet John of Hoveden to exploit it for didactic word-play:

> Jhesu, des sainz joie enterine
> Ma chanzounete qui termine
> T'envoie un salu d'amor fine;
> Preng la, doz ami, et l'affine.
> Et quant mort me ferra finer,
> Facet amours por moi finer
> Et me voillez si affiner
> Que soie o toi sanz diffiner

Jesus, the perfect joy of the saints, my sonnet which is coming to an end I send thee, a salutation of true love; take it sweet friend, and refine it. And when death causes my end, cause love to make a fine for me, and refine me so that I may be with thee without end

(Legge, *Anglo-Norman Literature*, p. 234)

Hoveden's word-play can be paralleled from later sources. It is in no way strained, since *fin* and its associated verb are used in technical contexts to refer to refining and purifying metals throughout the middle ages. In 1423, for example, Parliament took measures to restrain unscrupulous silversmiths from hallmarking with the leopard's head any silver products which were not of the correct standard of purity; the technical term used is *fyn*:

> And if it may be proved, that the forsed ['foresaid'] Keper of the touche ['punch'] afore seid, touche ony such Hernois ['ware'] wyth the Liberdisheed ['Leopard's head'], but it be as fyn in alay ['alloy'] as the sterlyng, that thenne the forseid Keper of the tuche, for every thyng so proved nowght so good in alay as the sterlyng, forfet double the valu to the Kyng.
>
> (*Parliament Rolls*, IV, 257)

Gold and silver are more valuable the purer they are, and the association between purity and value which attaches to the combination of the adjective *fin* with precious metals may be extended to its combination with base metals too. Chaucer mentions lead and iron (*HF*, 1431), the stanzaic *Guy of Warwick* a *gode swerd of stiel fine* (stanza 187), foreshadowing Gower's reference to a mail coat of *fin acier* (*Mirour del Omme*, 883). More intriguing is the statement in the *Seven Sages of Rome* that Virgil created a colossal statue made of *fin latoun* (1988). *Latoun*, of course, is notorious as the metal of the cross carried by the Pardoner (*CT*, 1, 701) and from which the helmet of Sir Thopas is inappropriately made (*CT*, 10, 877). Criticism has made some play of the contrast between *latoun* and precious gold or functional steel, yet here it is treated with respect. However, although it is debatable whether steel can be considered pure, whatever its functional value, there is no sense in which *latoun* can be considered a pure metal. Like brass, it is in fact an alloy (probably in this case of copper and tin). Thus, although associations of value and purity are appropriately combined when *fin* is applied to gold, the criterion of value can on occasions eclipse the association with purity when applied to other metals. The many combinations of *fin* with precious stones of all kinds, with pearls and with coral, while perhaps retaining some sense of flawlessness, also testify to a semantic shift from 'purity' towards 'value'. According to context, *fin* can therefore denote a combination of purity and value, or either of the two alone. The metaphorical connection with the human soul is never far away. Gower, when discussing the extraction of minerals, employs the verb *fine* (*CA*, IV, 2554), but imagines the process of separating the metal from the dross as purification of the ore from what he calls 'vices'.

In the Middle English *Ywain and Gawain*, the two eponymous

heroes are normally the greatest of friends, but, failing to recognize each other, they find themselves opponents in a single combat. The narrator remarks:

> Now was þis a grete selly   'wonder'
> þat trew luf and so grete envy,
> Als bitwix þam twa was þan,
> Might bath be in a man.

(Ywain and Gawain, 3521–4)

Although he finds it worthy of note that a single human being should at the same moment experience two such opposed emotions as love and malice, he is not very involved in the psychological implications and makes no particular comment a little later when he refers in passing to the conventional mixture of *joy and pete* (3618, 3712) which both knights feel when their identities are revealed. This short passage on mixed emotions is all that remains in the English poem of a very extensive psychological discussion in Chrétien's French original. There, Chrétien rhetorically develops the opposition into a long debate. Do Yvain and Gawain love one another, he asks; then in the words of Abelard, he answers 'Yes, and No'. One would lay down his life for the other: 'N'est ce amors antiere et fine?' (6013). But at the same time they wish to slay each other: is this not hate? How can these two contraries, *Amor et Haïne mortel*, co-exist in a single vessel? A pseudo-scientific allegory is offered in answer in which hate and love are pictured as occupants of the same house concealed from one another in different rooms, each as blind as the other. The two emotions occupy different areas of consciousness.

This question of mixed emotions is equally as prominent in Thomas's *Tristran*. There the author raises the question of Tristan's motives in marrying Ysolt aux Blanches Mains and accepts that love may be mixed with anger or resentment. By marrying, he hopes to share better the feelings of an unfaithful spouse, but perhaps also to hurt Queen Ysolt. Thomas remarks that these motives reveal a mixture of love and resentment in Tristran. He would not have married the girl for her beauty alone had she not also borne the queen's name. But neither would he have married her if she had lacked physical attraction. If Tristran's motivation had been resentment alone, the name of Ysolt would have held no appeal for him; but if his love for the queen had been pure and unmixed, the sensuous beauty of the maiden would have made no impression. Thomas sums up:

Pur ço dei jo, m'est avis, dire
Que ço ne fut amur ne ire;
Car si iço fin amur fust,
La meschine amé ne oüst
Cuntre [la] volunté s'amie.

(Tristran, 370–4)

Therefore I feel that I ought to conclude that this was neither love nor animosity. If it had been pure love, he would not have desired the maiden against his lady's will.

Discussion of the implication that true love is measured by adherence to the beloved's will is important, but must be delayed. What concerns us at present is Thomas's continuing discussion of the mixture of love and hate which he diagnoses in Tristran. He discusses the two emotions, comparing pure love, which he calls *fin' amur*, and pure hatred, which he calls *dreite haür*. He concludes this discussion with the view that, had Tristran regarded the queen with a pure and unmixed affection, he could not have married her namesake. This combination of love and hate is examined by Aquinas (*ST*, 1a.2ae 28, 4) in his discussion of jealousy. However, unlike Thomas, he does not consider that both contrary feelings can simultaneously be directed towards the same object.[16]

Fin, implying unmingled purity and intensity, is frequently found as a modifier of other psychological categories than love or hate. It combines with other emotions such as *fin hope*, *ioie fin*, and with desires in variants of the phrase *wille and talent fin*. In some contexts, the conception of purity is masked so that intensity alone is emphasized. Expressions indicating great force are especially frequent: *fin force*, *fin miȝt*, *main fin*, and *fin vigour*. The adverb, *finement*, can often be used simply as an intensifier, as in Gower's *Balades* 'Lors sui d'amour si finement espris / Dont maintenant m'estoet soeffrir la peine' ('When I am so fiercely seized by love, whose pain I am now compelled to suffer') (xiv, 5–6). A similarly intensifying usage is frequently found in adverbial phrases in which the adjective qualifies the word 'heart'; for example, in *Arthour and Merlin*, the British hew on the Saracens *wiþ god wille and hert fin* (6020). Since the heart was considered by medieval authors to be the centre of emotional life, the common phrase *with herte fin* is often no more than a specialized intensifier of feelings. Prayers are often offered with wholehearted devotion using this expression. However, even if the central function is intensification, the phrase will often draw upon the other senses for its associations; upon the 'purity' sense for notions of unmixed motives, of complete commitment, and hence sometimes loyalty; and upon the 'value' sense in contexts where the special quality of the heart is at issue. Thus, Jean Créton tells us in his account of the deposition of Richard II that the Count of Salisbury 'fu loyal iusqua la fin / Tant aima le roy de cuer fin' ('was true to the end, so greatly did he love the king with a pure heart') (386). This contrasts with the Duke of York, 'Qui navoit pas le cuer trop fin / Vers son nepveu le roy richart' ('who hadn't too *fin* a heart towards his nephew, King Richard') (386). Association of the phrase with love is such that *hert fin* can sometimes even form part of a construction with a verbal operator to indicate loving commitment, thus:

> Ac ich ʒou telle þat Merlin
> To Aurilis Brosias hadde hert fin
> And loued better his litel to
> Þan al þat oþer bodi þo,
>
> (*Arthour and Merlin*, 2054–7)

When qualities are attributed to the heart beyond the semantically depleted use as an intensifier, interpretation may become difficult. On some occasions, the focus may be more specifically upon the nature of the heart itself than upon the manner of loving, and its own inherent qualities are emphasized. One such contextual sense is that of unswerving loyalty in either a religious or secular context. In Simund de Freine's *Vie de Saint George*, the saint's virtues derive from the superior nature of his heart:

> Mult li fist hom peine e mal
> E tut tens out quer leal;
> Fin quer out, ferme e fort
>
> (15–17)

Great pain and suffering were inflicted upon him and he always had a true heart; his heart was true, stable, and steadfast.

The author of the *Gest Hystoriale of the Destruction of Troye* finds similar quality in the heart of Troilus in loving Bresaide:

> ffor Bresaide the bright vnblithe was his chere;
> ffor he louit hir full lelly, no lesse þan hymseluyn,
> With all the faithe and affection of hys fyn hert.
>
> (8029–31)

In his encyclopaedia, Brunetto Latini identifies the origins of Christian charity in a virtuous human heart of a nature suited for that purpose. It is *naist de fin cuer et de droite conscience et non de fausse foi* ('born of a *fin* heart and correct feeling and not of false faith') (*Trésor*, p. 285). The statement is rather a bold one, locating the origin of charity not in faith but in human nature, and specifically the heart capable of feeling. It puts into words in a slightly different context a claim which is repeatedly made by French lyricists and the authors of courtly *dits*, that *fine amor* is the product of the *fin cuer*; the quality of the heart determines the quality of the love.

To summarize what we have discovered so far, it appears that the phrase *fine amor* is not co-extensive with the 'courtly love' of earlier critics, which begins to appear highly specialized by comparison. However, neither is it completely remote from that conception. In certain contexts the two phrases may indeed be synonymous. But *fine amor* will be found in many contexts where it would be impossible to speak of 'courtly love'. It carries with it associations of purity (in the special sense of being unmixed with other emotions or intentions), worth, intensity, and constancy, but it may refer to love of a very wide range of kinds. In any particular context, the interpretation of the phrase may not be obvious, and the essential ambiguity which attaches to it can be well illustrated from two parallel uses with very distinct significances. In *Ipomedon*, the king refrains from loving La Fiere *trop de fin quer* (2292) on account of the closeness of their blood relationship. This implies control of a sexual interest, but this implication is denied by a similar use of the phrase in *Ami e Amilun*, where Amis's wife loves his leper friend *de fin quer* (*c*-text, 1060), 'as if she were his sister'. These two contexts seem to require quite separate interpretation, but what they have in common is the *fin quer* of the protagonists, the sensitive heart which predisposes them to love either intensely or nobly, either in passion or in charity.

As C.S. Lewis noted, after the millennium medieval authors wrote extensively on the subject of love, and they wrote at various levels of technicality. The subject had long been of critical importance in the Christian theology of redemption and in the concept of an ecclesiastical community united in charity. The major change which emerged after the millennium was a parallel importance in secular relations between human beings. Serious theorists treated love in an abstract manner as a psychological phenomenon, and they turned for their ideas about it to Classical writers, especially to Aristotle, and Cicero. The latter's *De amicitia* was a quarry of aphoristic

definitions of the kinds of love to which they returned again and
again. These Classical sources were supported on the one hand by
the writings of the Church Fathers, especially Augustine and Ambrose,
and on the other by recourse to the narrower concerns of Ovid's
Ars amatoria. General recourse to the same sources meant frequent
repetition of the same teachings. This is not the place to analyse in detail
these various treatments of love in medieval sources, but certain repeated doctrines require notice.

The *Trésor* of Brunetto Latini was produced in the middle of the
thirteenth century as a compendium of philosophical knowledge which
might prove of interest to an educated lay audience. As we have
seen, it was still of sufficient interest at the close of the fourteenth
century to be numbered among the possessions of Thomas of Gloucester,
and it also served as one of the sources of Gower's *Confessio
Amantis*.[17] It contains two distinct sections, both of which deal with
the subjects of love and friendship. The briefer is compiled from
the *Moralium dogma philosophorum*, a twelfth-century collection of
philosophical aphorisms dubiously attributed to William of Conches.
But the major treatment of the subject occurs in the translation of a
condensed Latin version of Aristotle's *Nichomachean Ethics* which
forms the first half of Book 2. The advantage of tracing the details
of the philosophical treatment of love in the works of Brunetto
Latini is that we shall be dealing not only with a work distributed
in the courtly milieu, but one which discusses these questions in the
vernacular, in the same language as they often emerge in courtly
literature. Moreover, this is not a specialized treatise on love, but an
encyclopaedia which may be expected to reflect more general
knowledge.

A word of warning is necessary before beginning: Brunetto, like
all medieval writers on the subject, does not systematically make the
modern distinction between love and friendship. As already noted,
the medieval application of the word love (*amor*) was extremely
wide and included friendship (*amistié*). Friends *love* one another. We
are dealing with a somewhat abstract psychological conception
where both *amor* and *amistié* can be synonymous nominalizations of
the verb *aimer*, with all its breadth of use. Friendship, Brunetto
begins, is important in all walks of life, and to the well-regulated
state. If the people were ruled by feelings of friendship and love
towards one another, the administration of justice would be unnecessary. The foundation of this friendship is Christian charity (II.
43, 3) and arises in the 'fin cuer et de droite conscience' (II. 101, 1).
The meaning which Latini evidently attributes to this francization

of the Latin word *conscientia* is worthy of note, since its traditional meaning had been that of a rational faculty which distinguishes good from evil. Here, however, it seems to have adopted a sense which emerged in the later medieval period, and which referred rather to the sensitive nature.[18] Chaucer, in his description of the Prioress in the *General Prologue*, is the first to introduce this courtly 'sensibility' sense into English.

There are various kinds of friendship (*amistié*), which may be distinguished by the benefits deriving from them. These benefits may include personal gain (*proufit*), pleasure (*delit*) or disinterested good (*bien*). Older people tend to make friends for the benefits derivable, and the young love for pleasure, but neither of these is true friendship:

> la droite amistié bonne et complie est entre les homes bons, ki sont sensibles en vertus et s'entraiment et welent bien par la samblance des vertus ki entr'aus est
>
> (*Trésor*, II. 43, 5)

> True, good, and perfect friendship is between good people, who are susceptible to virtue and who love one another and desire good through the similarity of the virtues which they share.

Such friendship is divine and is restricted to those capable of experiencing it. Friendship based on *proufit* can occur between far less worthy people: indeed, vultures will make common cause with crows for profit (II. 103, 105). This can cause dissension when the partners feel that the benefits they have derived have been distributed unfairly. These self-interested friendships, which are easily dissolved, can cause social disruption in the case of failed business alliances. In relationships between men and women:

> Quant li amis ayme s'amie par son delit et ele ayme lui por son profit, non ayme li uns l'autre par droite amour, certes cele amours sera tost desevree
>
> (*Trésor*, II. 18, 19)

> When the lover loves his girlfriend for his own pleasure, and she loves him for what she can get out of it, they do not love each other with true love and that love will certainly soon break up.

It must be acknowledged, however, that love founded on pleasure alone may endure for some time, becoming so intense that such people who love *folement* may be driven to commit all kinds of crimes (II. 106, 106). By contrast, true friendship, which is based upon no hope of tangible gain, but on regard for character, can last for ever, and is not disturbed by misfortunes (II. 43, 7). True lovers desire only love for love.[19] In this it is quite distinct from love for profit, for if a man sings a song in the expectation of payment, he feels cheated when he is paid only by a song in return.

The origins of love lie in shared interests and social environment, and also some kind of perceived similarity in personality. This similarity (*samblance*; cf. Latin *similitudo*) may lie in upbringing as well as the virtuous nature of the soul, so that:

> L'amor des freres est autel comme l'amour des campaignons, pour çou k'il sont vescu et norri ensamble et ont samblance de passion.
>
> (*Trésor*, II.44, 6)

> Love between brothers is like the love between members of the same household, because they have grown up and been educated together and share a similarity in feeling.

Such similarity is cited by many authors, along with mutual regard for virtue, as one of the fundamental requirements for the awakening of true love. Because discrepancies in the status of friends or lovers militate against such a disinterested relationship, equality of social status, as well as age, and various other qualities, are also regarded as a requisite for true love. True lovers receive reciprocal benefit of a non-tangible kind from an equal relationship:

> li un aiment l'autre, non mie por passion, mais pour abis. Et chascuns des amis ayme son bien, et li uns fet gueredons a l'autre par sa bone volenté, selonc ygaillance; et cele est veraie amistié.
>
> (*Trésor*, II. 43, 8)
>
> One loves the other not at all through feeling but through disposition. And each one of the friends loves his good, and quite freely reciprocates to the other on the basis of equality, and that is true friendship.

The mention of *passion* and *abis* here requires some comment, since Brunetto is using technical terminology. Other authors, including Andreas Capellanus in the opening words of his treatise, note that love is a *passio*, that is a motion of the sensitive part of the soul brought about by the effect of a stimulus to the external senses, or perhaps by the impression of the soul from the intellect.[20] The effect on the soul of such impressions may be quite temporary; in modern terms, a feeling brought about by some experience. However, such feelings may become established and habitual so that they become a more permanent part of the personality. These dispositions of personality, medieval philosophers, following Aristotle, called *habitus*. Brunetto is therefore at pains to assert that the elevated sort of friendship which he is discussing rises above the momentary passion to become an enduring part of personal disposition; that is, what he calls *abis*.

Love may be discussed as affective, to do with the feelings, or appetitive, and concerned with desires. Human beings are unique among creation in possessing a faculty which belongs more to intellect than feeling, but which is essentially a kind of desire to pursue the good. In English texts this desire for good is called the *wille*, and in Latin and French *voluntas* and *volunté* respectively. Although love may originate in sense perception, the tendency to become established into a disposition and the assumption that true love seeks out goodness of personality equal to itself, naturally mean that love is definable in terms of the *wille*. It is very commonly asserted that the similarity between personalities which is the occasion of the commencement of love becomes, as love develops, a kind of unity. This may be expressed either in affective or appetitive terms. In the former, love is a unity of feeling, in the latter a unity of desires. Brunetto does not expand much on this commonplace, but says that it is proverbial 'k'entre amis est uns sans et une ame, et ont toutes chose communes selonc droit' ('between friends there is only one mind and one soul, and they possess everything in common as far as is proper') (II. 45, 7). To St Thomas Aquinas, who produced his massive *Summa Theologiae* contemporaneously with the *Trésor*, the kinds of love could be divided into two, which he called *amor concupiscentiae* and *amor amicitiae*. The division is not identical, of course, with those made by Brunetto, but *amor concupiscentiae*, which seeks benefits for itself, compares well with love for *profit*, and *amor amicitiae*, which seeks good for another, compares well with love for *bienz*. Although both kinds of love may spring from a perception of a *similitudo*, in the case of *amor concupiscentiae* the similarity is potential – that is, there is a perception that the friendship will bring about similarity – whereas in *amor amicitiae* the similarity is actual. Thus, although the former kind of love is less noble than the latter, it may still be just and rational, since it is possible to strike up a friendship in the hope of acquiring virtues from the beloved, ennobling oneself by association with a superior. *Amor amicitiae* is reciprocal, between equals, and leads to union of feeling. Quoting Aristotle, Aquinas remarks that it is the characteristic of friends that they have a common will and take pleasure and pain from the same things (I. 28, 2). Gower sums up, quoting from St Ambrose: 'Ambroise dist en son decré / "Mon bon amy est l'autre je" ' ('Ambrose says in his authoritative writings: "My good friend is my other self" ', *MO*, 13729).

The importance of the heart in these discussions of love, both by serious Latin authors and in more popularized vernacular treatments, is striking. It is the nature of the heart, viewed as the centre of sensibility, which permits compassion and which facilitates the function of the intellect. In the words of Thomas Aquinas:

> Unde cordis congelatio vel duritia est dispositio repugnans amori. Sed liquefactio importat quandam mollificationem cordis, qua exhibet se cor habile ut amatum in ipsum subintret
>
> (*ST*, 1a 2ae 28, 5)

> Coldness or hardness of heart is therefore a state incompatible with love; whereas 'melting' or warmth suggests a certain softness which means that the heart will be quick to let the object loved enter it.

The love theorist, Richard de Fournival, quotes as a commonplace that the good heart cannot turn away love. With such references to the good heart we have come full circle to our point of departure in this discussion of medieval theorizing on love. Aquinas's words recall the fanciful etymology of the word *gelus* offered in the *Donnei des Amantz* in Chapter 6. Although it is probably justified now to assume that the *fin cuer* is that heart which by its nature is accessible to love, and that same heart which we discussed earlier as part of the constitution of the nobleman, we should not now jump to the conclusion that *fine amor* is equivalent to *amor amicitiae* or *amistié*. The ideal of love and friendship which we have traced depends on virtue, union of feeling, concord of will, similarity of personality and outlook, reciprocity of love and equality of status, and a relationship not marred by self-seeking motives. These character-istics may well be ascribed to *fine amor* in contexts where the adjective can be interpreted with evaluative senses, but on many occasions, and especially where *fin* operates as an intensifier, the equation would be quite unjustified. Neither is it necessary to add that this investigation of medieval love theory does not supply a very satisfactory referent for the phrase 'courtly love'.

Yet, although there is no absolute congruence between 'courtly love', *fine amor*, and the doctrines on friendship derived by monastic culture from the ancient world,[21] nevertheless many of these doctrines emerge piecemeal in vernacular literature of entertainment which was produced for, and sometimes by, those alleged to possess a *fin cuer*. When emphasizing the credentials of the love which he shared with 'goode, faire White', the Man in Black asserts that his *wille* was drawn to her as something superlatively good (1078), and goes on to represent the love of two people who share similar personalities and feel the same emotions:

> Therwyth she was alway so trewe
> Our joye was ever ylyche newe;   'unchangingly'
> Oure hertes wern so evene a payre   'well-matched'
> That never nas that oon contrayre
> To that other for no woo.
> For sothe, ylyche they suffred thoo   'in the same way'
> Oo blysse and eke oo sorwe bothe;
> Ylyche they were bothe glad and wrothe;
> Al was us oon, withoute were.   'denial'
> And thus we lyved ful many a yere
>
> (*BD*, 1287–96)

Shared will is at issue in the discussion between the lady and Gawain in the bedchamber (1495–500), but here, as often in poetic references, equivalence of wills is the result of imposition of one will over another. This situation is explicit in *Anelida and Arcite* (128) and the *Squire's Tale*:

> And shortly so ferforth this thyng is went
> That my wyl was his willes instrument,
> This is to seyn my wyl obeyed his wil.
>
> (*CT*, 4, 557–61)

The importance of equality between lovers is thematic in the *Franklin's Tale*, and the effects of love between those who are socially unequal, and where the dominant partner treats his wife as a possession, are explored at length in the *Clerk's Tale*. The *Wife of Bath's Tale* is a story of enchantment, dependent on the assertion that moral virtue subordinates beauty as the justification for virtuous love. It is tempting to suppose that Chaucer was consciously exploiting the teachings of *amor amicitiae*, but if so, he does not exploit it as an integrated concept. His borrowings of ideas are piecemeal, drawn from the bran-tub of medieval doctrine, and his handling of love is eclectic. It is perhaps significant that in *Troilus and Criseyde* he uses the expressions *frendes loue*, *loue of frendes*, and *loue of frendshipe* five times, but it is always in contexts which implicitly contrast it with sexual love. The significance is that of modern English; there is no suggestion that it has any of the technical significance of *amor amicitiae*.

Literary authors do not work within the strict definition of *amor amicitiae* to be found in the clerkly tradition, but they borrow suggestions from it. They often use the phrase *fine amor/loue fin*, but reinterpret its significance, within the limits discussed above, to suit their requirements. They treat the experience of love in ways which do not derive solely from the monastic tradition, and which may be far more realized in terms of recognizable human experience. Yet the conventionality of their treatment is declared both by their hyperbolic mode and by the repetitive similarities in approach encountered in different authors. Love is a literary theme in which the love affair has a predictable course, for which literary experience and compositional skills provide the techniques of realization. Yet the theorists and the practitioners of courtly verse had this in common, that they regarded the lover as an exceptional person. The noble heart (*fin cuer*) was the unquestioned necessity for the beginnings of love, as it was for courtly refinement; and the same personality would be inclined to idealized friendship as to whole-hearted love.

Because the refined heart was sensitive, its owner would be likely to be overwhelmed by passion. The sight of Criseyde, glimpsed among the crowd at the feast of the Palladion, overwhelms Troilus, who like Meliors in *William of Palerne* and many heroes and heroines of French romance, retires to the privacy of his own chamber to ponder on what has befallen him. The disturbance of the equilibrium of his soul is reflected in his changes of colour and frequent sighs. He is torn between the demands of responsibility and his desire. He becomes helpless, falling into what popular English works call *love-longing*, and he hovers on the edge of that love sickness which can develop, if no help is at hand, into the eventually fatal condition which Chaucer calls, borrowing from medical sources, the 'loueris maladye of Hereos' (*CT*, 1, 1376).[22] From Troilus's first glimpse of Criseyde to their union in Book III takes more than 3700 lines, nearly half the entire poem. There is nothing particularly notable in this, however, except its predictability. Far more unusual is the attention which Chaucer pays to the dissolution of the affair. But extended celebration of tranquil enjoyment of the relationship would have been unprecedented. Medieval authors, like modern song writers, spent far more ink on the pains of love-longing and parting than on any other aspect of love.

These, and especially the former, are psychologically the most interesting stages of any affair.

It has been argued, with some justification, that medieval authors derived their skills at treating the onset of love from reading Ovid's *Ars amatoria*, but the trauma of love, and even such well-used imagery as that of the sickness of love, for which the longed-for lady is the physician, need not be derived entirely from this source. Peter Dronke brought evidence to suggest that not only the psychological experience of frustrated love, but also the literary response to it, including the idealization of the lady, and even the metaphor of sickness and the physician, were extremely widespread phenomena. Something like a psychological universal of reaction to first love seems to have been elaborated metaphorically in much the same way in widely different times and cultures. He quotes from an Egyptian poem of around 1300 BC. Its account of love-sickness, apart from a certain note of disingenuousness, prefigures the imagery of medieval England:

> I shall lie down at home
> as though I were ill.
> Then my neighbours will come in to see me,
> and my beloved will be with them.
> She will make the doctors unnecessary,
> for she knows my malady.[23]

Inaccessibility of the desired lover and love-sickness, remoteness and idealization are causally related phenomena which are fully exploited in lyric poetry and in those stages of narrative which deal with the onset of love. Love-sickness is the penalty of refined feeling, idealization may or may not be actual experience, but is fully compatible with the theoretical explanation that love seeks what it considers to be good. The process of *delectatio* is one of rehearsing and pondering on the good of the object of desire. Both love-longing and idealization therefore flow from the essential inaccessibility of the beloved. In real terms, authors manage this inaccessibility by placing the lady in a socially elevated position by comparison with the lover, or more unusually, by ensuring that she is married. In either case the necessary inaccessibility is achieved, which functions to preserve that state of affairs in which the refined heart becomes the arena of suffering and the field of conflict between powerful emotions and rational restraint. That part of a love affair most fraught with conflicting feelings was privileged in literary treatment since it gave clearest demonstration of the nobility of personality and best illustrated the grounds for the assertion that those who were truly courtly must also be lovers, and vice versa. Thus, adultery, which since 1883 has traditionally been considered part of the essential description of 'courtly love', is perhaps better seen as simply an incidental narrative device to maintain such tensions. What was identified by earlier critics as a code of 'courtly love' is really a complex of philosophical doctrines, social aspirations, and literary techniques. Authors like Andreas Capellanus or Richard de Fournival compiled such material into treatises which had just as much authority as their readers were prepared to lend them. This may sound dismissive, but it is apparent that such codifications do not represent the essential circumstances in which the ideals of courtliness and of love were united. This lay in the interrelation of the refinement of the heart, sensitivity and love, the sense of a community of the *gentil*: all were deeply held medieval beliefs which were often held in defiance of demonstrable reality.

Contemporary writers were well aware that such ideals invited deception. That the illusion of a *fin cuer* could be maintained by those with baser motives becomes in itself a frequent theme of later medieval poetry: it is common in Chaucer, Machaut, Lydgate, and is a warning issued by a wife to her daughters when her husband conventionally eulogizes the benefits of loving *par amour*.[24] Like much else about courtliness and love, it is expressed fully in the *Romaunt of the Rose*:

And somme haue also this manere	'custom'
To feynen hem for loue seke	'pretend', 'sick'
Sich love I preise not at a leke	
For paramours they do but feyne	
To love truly they disdeyne	
They falsen ladies traitoursly	
And swerne hem othes vtterly	
With many a lesyng and many a fable	'lie'
And all they fynden deceyvable	'untrustworthy'
And whanne they han her lust geten	
The hoote ernes they al foryeten.	'pledge'

(4828–38)

Young men may have exploited the behavioural patterns of refined love to achieve their purposes, but their deception was no more than the individualization of a deception institutionalized in literature. The courtly lyric was founded on the pretence of over-abundant and sincere feeling, yet authors who expressed themselves in this mode were equally capable of adopting quite different perspectives when writing on other occasions. Gower's *Balades* adopt in full the assumptions and expression of courtly love:

> El Mois de Maii la plus joiouse chose
> C'est fin amour . . .
>
> (*Balades*, xxxvii, 1–2)

The most joyful thing in May is true love.

> celle q'ad dessoubtz sa discipline
> Mon coer, mon corps, mes sens et ma resoun
> Par fin amour trestout a sa bandoun
>
> (*Balades*, xxi, 3–5)

she who has under her control my heart, my body, my mind and my reason, completely at her disposal through true love.

But in his *Traité*, he adopts a different mode, and a different interpretation of idealized love.[25] Viewed in the perspective of his poetic career, Gower's change of heart could actually or fictionally be attributed to cooling passions and the wisdom of advancing years. Indeed, literary authors from Denis Piramus to Chaucer habitually retracted the folly of their youth when they adopted a different mode of expression with a different set of values.

A more generalized perspective on the perceived discrepancy between social ideals and contemporary actuality was to invoke the deplorable decline of modern morals from some imagined golden age. The ideals of courtliness, and the behaviour of courtly lovers, were the supreme example of this. At some long past epoch men and women had observed in their everyday life what now remained only as a literary ideal.

> Trouthe is putte doun; resoun is holden fable.
> Vertu hath now no domynacion.
> Pite exiled no man is merciable.
> Thorugh couetise is blent discrescioun   'blinded'
> The worlde hath made a permutacion
> Fro right to wrong fro trought to fikelnesse   'truth', 'treachery'
> That al is lost for lak of stedfastnesse
>
> (*Lack of Steadfastness*, 15–21)

This conviction of the decline from an ideal is apparent as soon as courtly ideals are expressed in English. Even in the *Ancrene Wisse*, written about 1225, the days when knights rode out dedicating their service to the honour of a lady is considered to belong to the remote past. In the world of everyday responsibilities courtly ideas are likely to lead to trouble.

The values of courtliness and the literary fantasy of the love which courtliness inspired had a powerful grip on the medieval imagination. In the later middle ages there were a number of attempts to remedy the perceived decline and emulate the supposed ideals of a former age. Literature began to be imitated by life. In the reign of Edward III, within a decade of the foundation of the Order of the Garter, a Round Table was constructed on the model of that around which Arthur and his knights had sat. In France at the turn of the century, Christine de Pizan sought to create an Order of the Rose to counter what she and her supporters saw as the scandalous cynicism and indecency of the *Roman de la Rose* and to protect women against exploitation. The knightly order of the Green Shield was founded by Marshal Boucicaut, and a court of love was established in Paris in 1400, with claimed jurisdiction over those who would slander women. This court was to function also as a kind of *puy* at which competitions for love poetry written from true feeling rather than as an exercise in craftsmanship were to be read.[26] The English court boasted no such provisions, but Chaucer's *Legend of Good Women* as well as an anonymous fifteenth-century poem, refer to the amatory orders of the Flower and the Leaf. The medieval period drew to a close with the heads of two of the most powerful nations in Europe facing each other garbed as medieval knights in a tournament at the Field of the Cloth of Gold (1520).

Love among courtly people, that is courtly love, was conditioned by complex factors. Fundamentally, it depended upon the supposition that a particular class of people were defined and united by certain characteristics of their inherent nature, and in particular by their possession of an exalted moral and physical constitution. This nobility pervaded their senses, feelings, and intellectual capacities, and influenced their ability to feel compassion, charity, and love. The noble heart was the essence of this constitution, and by its nature was drawn to what was perceived as good. Those who shared this inheritance perceived it readily in others and, according to clerical authors, were susceptible to be drawn towards them with a disinterested affection called *amicitia*. Authors composing literature for entertainment, and lyrics which proclaimed a right to a position in the ranks of the courtly and sensitive, developed phrasing and devices which realized elements of the theory in recognizable social circumstances. The intensity of feeling, the unswerving loyalty, the conception of equality – sometimes exaggerated to become the subjection of the suitor – were all represented. The refined lover was kept on the rack by inventing means by which the consummation of his desires could be delayed and the lady kept unattainable. Modes of transcendental expression were borrowed from the religious sphere, and the metaphor of service to God was complemented by that of service to a feudal lord. The *fin cuer*, bound to the object of its desire by an Aristotelian *habitus*, responded to delay by prolonged loyalty, and indeed loyalty became symptomatic of it. 'Courtly love', in the sense used by Paris, can be seen to be one specific set of circumstances selected from the conventional literary elaboration of a fundamentally psychological conception of the nature of courtliness, and of the conditioning effects of that nature on the experience of love.

NOTES

1. Paris, 'Lancelot du Lac', pp. 518–19.
2. Bédier, 'Les Fêtes de mai', p. 172.
3. Lewis, *The Allegory of Love*, p. 2.
4. Kirby, *Chaucer's Troilus*.
5. Reuters, *Friendship and Love* (p. 195), comments on the difficulty of finding anything resembling courtly love in Middle English romance before the time of Chaucer.
6. Walsh, *Andreas Capellanus on Love*, p. 1. No contemporary title for the work survives, but the commonest title in later manuscripts is *De amore*.
7. Benton, 'Clio and Venus'. See also his 'The Court of Champagne as a Literary Centre', *Speculum*, 36 (1961), 551–91.
8. LeClercq, 'L'Amour et le Mariage'. A bleaker picture is painted by Duby, *Que sait-on*.
9. The thirteenth-century poetic adaptor of the *De amore*, Drouart la Vache, records that 'j'en commencai a rire' (l. 52) on reading it. But thirteen years previously, in 1277, Bishop Stephen Tempier had publicly condemned it.
10. Brewer, 'Natural Love', p. 409.
11. Fisher, *John Gower: Moral Philosopher*, pp. 76–7.
12. Lazar, *Amour courtois et Fin'Amors*. Lazar contrasts a more hedonistic and secular conception of love in the south of France with a clerkishly moderated and moralistic one further north. He exaggerates the contrast, but is certainly justified in pointing to the rational, moralistic tone among most clerkly authors in northern France.
13. Reiss, 'Chaucer's *fyn lovynge*', p. 186.
14. Webb, 'Poem on the Deposition of Richard II', p. 412. Here it represents the relations between the kings of France and England.

15. Du Cange, *Glossarium, s.v. finus.*

16. Gilson, *Christian Philosophy,* pp. 273–9.

17. McCulloch, 'The Dying Swan'. McCulloch provides textual evidence of Gower's use of the *Trésor* in *Confessio Amantis,* IV, 104–8.

18. Michaud-Quantin, *Etudes sur le Vocabulaire,* p. 160.

19. Pickford, 'Richard de Fournival', pp. 171–2.

20. Karnein, '*Amor est Passio*', argues that *passio* in Andreas has the sense of 'sickness' in Stoic fashion, but this is probably to over-emphasize a certain clerkly distaste for passive emotions by comparison with intellectual activity.

21. Bezzola, *Origines,* I, pp. 53ff.

22. Heffernan, *Melancholy Muse,* pp. 68–73, offers the most recent account of the lovers' malady.

23. Dronke, *Rise of the European Love Lyric,* I, p. 10.

24. *Knight of the Tower,* edited by Offord, pp. 163–7.

25. For example, *Traité,* IV, 15 and also *CA,* IV, 1476, 2297; VIII, 1995ff. Honest love is strongly associated by Gower with marriage. See Bennett, 'Gower's "Honeste Love" '.

26. Benson, 'Courtly Love and Chivalry', p. 249.

Chapter 10

Courtliness and Religion

In a sermon which he wrote at the request of Hugues de Payns, Master of the Knights Templars, between 1128 and 1136, St Bernard illustrates in vigorous terms what he perceives to be the spiritual dangers which the world holds for the leisured and wealthy. Exhorting and encouraging the Templars, he contrasts the morale and conduct of these knights, who are devoted to the purposes of religion, with that of the majority of world-orientated chivalry. Not for them effeminate hair dressings, which are dangerous in battle, silken clothing, or elaborate horse-trappings. The Templars are under corporate discipline, and ascetically committed to their military purpose.

> Scacos et aleas detestantur. Mimos et magos et fabulatores, scurrilesque cantilenas, atque ludorum spectacula, tamquam vanitates et insanias falsas respuunt et abominantur. Capillos tondent, scientes, iuxta Apostulum, ignominiam esse viro, si comam nutrierit. Numquam compti, raro loti, magis autem neglecto crine hispidi, pulvere foedi, lorica et caumate fusci.
>
> (*S. Bernardi Opera*, III, 220)

> they detest chess and dice; they abhor hunting and take no pleasure, as is customary, in the silly chase of birds. They detest and abominate actors, magicians, storytellers, immodest songs and plays; these for them are vanities and follies. They cut their hair, knowing that, according to the Apostles, it is shameful for men to grow long hair. Always unkempt, rarely bathed, usually they are shaggy, dirty, dusty, and darkened by their cuirasses and by sunburn.
>
> (trans. Herlihy, *Feudalism*, p. 295)

The familiar pastimes of courtliness are the object of St Bernard's onslaught; those temptations whose attractiveness to the new knight-hood must be obliterated from their thought as they pursue a more exalted purpose, defending the faith. St Bernard is not alone in finding fault with courtliness. Indeed, it is in the denunciation of courtly ideals that we find some of the earliest evidence of its very existence, for such opposition to the values of courtliness in fact pre-dates most literature advocating its virtues, and continues to appear long after an accommodation between the two world-views had been widely accepted. Orderic Vitalis (1075–1142) parallels the opinion of St Bernard in expressing his opposition to what he considered the degeneracy of those who preferred the morally dangerous pursuits of peace to the physical perils of war.

> Ritus heroum abijciebant, hortamenta sacerdotum deridebant, barbari-cumque morem in habitu et vita tenebant. Nam capillos a vertice in frontem discriminabant, longos crines veluti mulieres nutriebant, et summopere curabant, prolixisque nimiumque strictis camisiis indui, tuni-cisque gaudebant. . . . Nocte comessationibus et potationibus, vanisque confabulationibus, aleis et tesseris, aliisque ludicris vacabant; die vere dormiebant. . . . Femineam mollitiem petulans juventus amplectitur, feminisque viri curiales in omni lascivia summopere adulantur.
>
> (Bezzola, II. 2, p. 464)

> They rejected the ways of warriors and laughed at the remonstrations of the priests. They adopted a foreign mode in dress and in way of life. For they parted their hair from the crown over the forehead, and they cherished and took the greatest care of their long tresses just like women. They delighted in excessively long and close-fitting shirts and tunics. Their nights were occupied by carousal and drunkenness, by useless gossip, by dice and other games of chance; and indeed, by day, they slept. Wanton youth adopts a feminine softness, and established courtiers exert themselves to please women by all sorts of lascivious tricks.

St Bernard's castigation of silk finery is matched by the well-known description by Geoffrey de Vigeois of the long hair and ostentatious shoes of the young, and of the trains of the dresses of fashionable women following them like snakes.[1]

These statements of disapproval are expressed in general terms, but sometimes the criticism of *curtesie* could become directed at those who were considered to be outstanding examples of courtliness, and particular individuals might find themselves the targets of clerical disapproval. William of Malmesbury directs virulent criticism against the first of the Provençal troubadours, Guillaume IX of Aquitaine, whom he seeks to patronize both morally and artistically:

> Erat tunc Willelmus comes Pictavorum fatuus et lubricus; qui postquam de Jerosolima . . . rediit, ita omne vitiorum volutabrum premebat quasi

cederet omnia fortuitu agi, non providentia regi. Nugas porro suas, falsa
quadam venustate condiens, ad facetias revocabat, audientium rictus
cachinno distendens.

(Gesta Regum, II, 510)

There lived then William, the Count of Poitou, a foolish and shifty
man, who after leaving Jerusalem ... returned to wallow in the slough of
every vice, almost as if he believed that the universe ran by chance, and
was not governed by Providence. Furthermore, spicing his petty compositions with a certain meretricious charm, he passed them off as wit,
distending the jaws of his audience with chuckling.

The further development of this passage shows William of
Malmesbury's criticism directed principally against his namesake's sexual
morality, and more particularly against his shameless publicization in
poetry of his promiscuity. William of Aquitaine is cited as a notorious
example. But, although regrettable, the open abandonment of one
individual to the eternal bonfire is not in itself sufficient reason to
explain the deep disquiet expressed so widely by monastic writers.
Dismay at sexual immorality is understandable, but why should personal
hygiene, refinement, and a love of fine things cause equal turmoil?

As we have seen in previous chapters, monastic institutions were
the channel by which Latin ideals of refinement and demeanour
(*urbanitas* and *dulcedo*), and of community (*amicitia*), were transmitted
to and developed in the medieval secular world, and it was clerks
who provided the concepts which permitted courtly psychological
analysis. It may therefore seem strange to find such virulent opposition to the world of courtliness from that quarter which had in
fact facilitated its development. For this earlier period, at least, the
answer is to be found in William of Malmesbury's words 'as if he
believed that the universe ran by chance, and was not governed by
Providence'. Behind these words lies alarm at the awareness of a
dangerous contingency: was it not possible that peacetime, leisure
and luxury might become the precursors of an alternative view of
reality to that which had hitherto informed and empowered the
Church? What alarmed these authors was that the attractions of
aesthetic values and the pleasures of social communication, the self-
absorption which characterized the courtly world, might begin to
seem to its inhabitants sufficient in themselves. Life might begin to
be lived for the present, with no regard for the distant goal of
salvation; moral values might become eclipsed by aesthetic ones,
and sensuous self-gratification might supplant intellectual direction.
The teleology of the Christian life may no longer seem so certain.

In such circumstances, the universe, lacking any ultimate purpose, would eventually be perceived as a God-less anarchy. It may well have seemed to these early critics that if courtliness spawned an influential ideology in competition with Christianity, then chaos yawned. For anyone who regarded social change in this light the secular ideology of courtliness and Christian theology must become implacably opposed.

When the Church, at the time of the millennium, had opposed secular anarchy through the *pax dei* movement, and when monastic authors had cultivated the Latin ideals of *urbanitas*, or found connections between *amicitia* and Christian charity, or when, through the Gregorian reforms, they sought to extend their reforming idealism to the outside world, they had not done so in the expectation that their ideas could have been adopted and elaborated in a purely secular context, enabling that world to seize its own moral and educational initiative. Their hope had been in the perfectibility of human nature on earth and its incorporation into a theocratic super-state united by the monastic orders, within which secular rulers governed under the guidance of the Church.[2] The frustration of this dream resulted in the monastic orders in a reaction against the secular world and a renunciation of its values. A genre of Latin literature was born which became known as the *De contemptu mundi* 'Contempt for the World' genre, from the popular title of a work by Pope Innocent III, whose official title, *De Miseria Condicionis Humane* 'Concerning the Misery of the Human Condition' was scarcely more encouraging. The purpose of the genre was to strengthen monastic zeal in pursuit of its calling by encouraging renunciation of and contempt for all those values which ordinary society esteemed highly. The world was seen as venial, corrupt, hell-bent; and the epitome of worldly values were those which were honoured among the possessors of wealth, position, and leisure, those who cultivated a manner of living based upon the refinement of personal qualities and accomplishments made possible by idleness.

Contempt for worldliness and the secular values of polite society was an initial reaction, but was not confined to any particular century. This antipathetic perspective upon courtliness, although complemented by other religious judgements, endured throughout the medieval period. The Auchinleck manuscript, produced in, or close to, London in about 1330, is a very mixed anthology consisting of tales of heroic adventure, outlines of legendary history, sentimental stories of love, a few scandalous japes, and many shorter works of piety and devotion. Among the last is the brief poem quoted below.

Where ben men biforn ous were,
Þat houndes ladden & haukes bere
& hadden feld & wode;
Þe riche leuedis in her bour,
Þat werd gold in her tresour,
Wiþ her briȝt rode?

Þai eten & dronken & made hem glade;
Wiþ joie was al her liif ylade.
Men kneled hem bifore;
Þai beren hem wel swiþe heiȝe.
Wiþ a tu[i]nkling of her eiȝe
Her soules were forlore.

Whare is þat hoppeing & þat song,
Þe trayling & þe proude gong,
Þe haukes & þe houndes?
Al þat wele is went oway;
Her joie is turned to wayleway,
To manie hard stoundes.

Dreiȝe her, man, ȝif þat þou wi[l]t
A litel pine, men þe bit.
Wiþdrawe þine aise oft.
Ȝif þe pine be vnrede,
& þou þenke of þi misdede,
It schal þe þink soft.

Ȝif þat þe fende þe foule þing
Þurth wicked rede of fals egging
Adoun þe haþ ycast,
Vp, & be gode champioun!
Stond, & falle no more adoun
For a litel blast

Take þe rode to þi staf
& þenk on him þat þeron ȝaf
His liif þat was so lef.
He it ȝaf for þe; þou ȝeld it him.
Oȝain þi fo þi staf þou nim
And wreke þe of þat þef.

Where are they who were before us, who led hounds and bore hawks,
and possessed the field and wood; the rich ladies in their bower who
wore gold in their head-dress, with their bright complexion. They ate
and drank and made merry; their life was spent in pleasure. Men knelt
before them; they conducted themselves haughtily. In a wink of their
eye their souls were damned. Where is that dancing and that song, the
trailing [dresses] and the proud youth, the hawks, and the hounds? All

that good life has vanished away, their delight is turned to cries of
'Alas', and many cruel pangs. Endure here, man, if you will a little pain
that you are allotted; curb your comfort often. If the suffering is
intense, and you think about your sins, it will seem soft to you. If that
foul creature the devil through wicked and false suggestions has cast you
down, then, up, and be a good contender! Stand, and do not fall again
from a light blow. Take the cross for your staff and think of him who
on it gave his precious life. He gave it for you; now pay him back.
Take your staff against your foe and avenge yourself on that rascal.

These stanzas are ultimately dependent upon ideals both of
courtliness and chivalry, but the perspective in which the former is
viewed is distinctly unfriendly; indeed, the values of this poem are
closer to those of the pre-courtly versions of the Vortigern story or
the strictures of St Bernard than to any which celebrate sensuous
pleasures for their own sake. Indeed, although presented as a
complete work in the Auchinleck manuscript and in MS Digby 86,
elsewhere this poem forms part of a longer work known as the
'Sayings of St Bernard', and is apparently perceived as perpetuating
his perspective on worldliness. In the Vernon manuscript, a much
edited version of it functions as the concluding summary of a
careful presentation of the popular sermon theme of the 'World,
the Flesh, and the Devil'; the three foes against which humankind
must strive.[3] As Cross has pointed out, its use of the *ubi sunt*
formula is not elegiac, but admonitory: here, the observances of
courtly life are portrayed as leading their practitioners to
destruction.[4] But, at the same time, closer attention shows the focus
of the poem to be as much consolatory as monitory. There is no
direct threat, since although to be warned by the example of the
fate of such leisured individuals of the past, the addressee of the
poem is not necessarily imagined to be one of them. Although
approving the opposition of healthy chivalric activity to courtly
indolence is a common posture among earlier clerical commentators, here this dichotomy has undergone a significant transformation.
The alternative offered to the careless enjoyment of a life of leisure
is not properly military activity, since the conception of chivalry has
been transformed. Here the addressee is exhorted to struggle against
the devil not as a chivalric knight armed with sword and shield, but
as a village *champioun* armed with a staff, a contender prepared to
resume the contest after a bad blow. It seems that the poem is
intended for a broader audience than the coterie of lords and ladies,
and the chivalric virtue which is set against courtliness is
re-conceptualized in more widely applicable terms. As in the

sermon to the Templars, combative values are preferable to those of courtliness, but the perspective has been broadened in this English verse to appeal to a much broader audience.

The theologically inspired antipathy between religious faith and the ideals of courtliness persisted among clerks and scholars throughout the medieval period, although it underwent some development in its conceptualization and expression. As we shall see in the final chapter, a Christian critique of courtliness, of its heedless extravagance and of its exclusivity, became a fundamental theme of social re-orientation in the fourteenth century, when cohorts of newly influential citizens demanded an equality of respect with inherited nobility. But even before this new social perspective had gained ground, and indeed continuing later alongside it, implacable religious-inspired antagonism to courtliness had come to be regarded as eccentric. Either it was the conscientious position of reformers and extremists, or was simply a useful rhetorical *locus* to be adopted by any clerk in an argument. However, in general, clerks and religious had quickly realized that direct confrontation between the prelates and the most influential members of polite society could serve no useful purpose, and while retaining the option of direct opposition for the purposes of theological debate and in monastic circles, accommodation with courtly values could quite quickly be made among those of less rarefied callings. In fact, the mutual adaptation of courtly and Christian values was facilitated by their largely common origins. Many values could be seen to be shared: many of the virtues of courtliness were acceptable to the Church, and vice versa. Outside the monastic life, what made this more apparent was the greater emphasis, after the turn of the thirteenth century, upon the pastoral duties of parish priests. The penitential manuals, which became widespread after the Fourth Lateran Council in 1215, directed greater attention to the analysis of human feeling and motivation in the context of moral and immoral actions. Indeed, it may be that the growing social consciousness which is apparent in the fourteenth century has its origins in the pastoral duties of parish clergy, and the social engagement of secular clerks, whose pastoral duties made them more immediately aware of circumstances concealed from those living in an enclosed monastic community. In these circumstances it became possible to see more clearly both the similarities and differences between religious and secular values.

The Middle English *Romaunt of the Rose* contains, represented as carved images on the outside of the enclosing wall of a garden, a list of vices which could not be tolerated inside such a place. This garden is best interpreted not as a garden of love, as is usually the case, but a microcosm of the world of courtliness. Within is a population of virtues personified as fashionable ladies and gentlemen. A list is given below of these vices and their opposed virtues from the *Romaunt of the Rose*, compared to a similar double list from the translation of a penitential manual, Chaucer's *Parson's Tale*.

Romaunt of the Rose		Parson's Tale	
Hate	Love	Ire	Debonairetee
Covetyse	—	Glotonye	Abstinence
Avarice	Largesse	Avarice	Pitee
Envy	Fraunchise	Envy	Charitee
Sorowe	Gladnesse	—	—
Elde	Youthe	—	—
Vilanie	Curtesye	—	—
Povert	Rychesse	—	—
Felony	—	—	—
Pope-Holy	—	—	—
—	—	Pride	Mekenesse
—	—	Lecherye	Chastitee
—	—	Accidie	Strengthe

In addition, the *Romaunt* lists *Myrthe, Idelnesse, Beaute*, and *Swete-Lokyng* as characteristic inhabitants of the garden. The presentation of virtues and vices in the *Parson's Tale* is very formal, as befits a technical treatise, and it sub-divides the head sins (*Hate* appears as a sub-head of *Ire*; *Idelnesse* under *Accidie*), matching them by the virtues which act as remedies for them. A certain degree of this matching is evident in the *Romaunt* too, but presentation in the form of a table such as that above perhaps over-emphasizes the symmetry in the actual poem. Nevertheless, there is a clear opposition between *Youthe* and *Elde*, *Avarice* and *Largesse*, *Povert* and *Richesse*. Other oppositions are inferred and alternative configurations could be argued: in particular, the positions of *Curtesye* and *Fraunchise* could easily be exchanged.

In the comparison between the conception of vices in these two works, several points stand out. First, there is general agreement between the courtly handbook and the penitential manual on the vices of *Ire* (*Hate*), *Covetyse*, *Envy* and *Avarice*. All these are vices which promote anti-social behaviour, which is equally repugnant in courtly or religious communities. The Parson condemns *Pride, Lecherye*, and *Accidie*, which receive no specific mention at this point in the

Romaunt, and the latter lists *Vilanie, Elde, Povert, Felony, Sorowe*, and *Pope-Holy*, which do not apparently concern the Parson. The coincidence between the two works is nevertheless greater than it first appears. In fact, the *Romaunt* does include Pride in another micro-allegory of the vices of love in polite society, when it appears as one of the dark arrows in Love's quiver; and later the lover is warned explicitly against the vice of *pride* (2239). *Sorowe* (*tristitia*), although not discussed in the *Parson's Tale*, is one of the traditional Christian vices allied to *accidia*, and *Pope-Holy*, the English translation of *papelardie*, is condemned in penitential manuals as the vice of hypocrisy, which is treated by the Parson. Indeed, when these adjustments have been made, the sharpest distinction between the Parson's parade of vices and that of the *Romaunt* is in the latter's disregard of Lechery, and in its elevation of a branch of *Accidie, Idelnesse*, to a virtue. In addition, whereas the *Parson's Tale* regards wealth and age as morally indifferent, the *Romaunt* treats riches and youth as desirable qualities. *Felony* and *Vilanie* are more or less ignored by the Parson, who regards the former as a psychological condition, but not specifically a sin, and like most commentators, thinks of the latter in terms of coarse speech about sexual matters, which ought by preference to be avoided. To the God of Love later in the *Romaunt* (2223–8), however, coarse speech (*vilanie*) is a serious breach of that refinement which he seeks to promote. In these fourteenth-century translations, then, there is evidently a great deal of agreement on general questions of human behaviour between the celebrated text-book of courtliness and the manual of sins. They agree on condemning hatred and anger, envy and detraction, niggardliness, and the ruthless pursuit of possessions. Less enthusiastically, they would agree on the undesirability of a morose or melancholy attitude, of coarseness in speech or demeanour, and of a hypocritically 'holier than thou' posture. Beyond this, vices and virtues become subject to divergent interpretation: what courtliness calls love might well be denounced as lechery; avarice in the *Romaunt* is countered not by Christian charity but by *largesse*, which may be motivated by *pitee*, but seeks to glorify the giver in a manner which the cleric could denounce as pride. Moreover, the *Romaunt* sets store by qualities like wealth, age, leisure, which from the point of view of the Parson are at best morally neutral. Pride is re-interpreted in the courtly poem as equivalent to *daunger*, the quality which caused ladies to refuse the attentions of even suitable suitors. Thus, although there were discrepancies, the relationship between the ideals of courtliness and those of the Christian religion was much more intertwined than the earliest opponents of courtly values were inclined to publicize.

The essential difference, however, remained: courtliness was fundamentally amoral and directed to the life and beauty of this world, whereas the purpose of religious teaching was to inculcate moral behaviour and consciousness of the promise of salvation in the next. These were facts which could never be overlooked; yet, in the minds of humbler clerical critics whose role involved closer pastoral contact with ordinary people, this theological distinction tended to be replaced by a more contingent contrast of behaviour and style of life. These latter saw pride exemplified in the ostentation of the courtly life, but also, being more immediately aware of the discrepancies between the rich and poor, viewed conspicuous consumption in more practical socio-economic terms. Thus, as we shall see in the next chapter, Langland tried to find a socially useful role for the hunter as a destroyer of vermin, the embroidering lady as the maker of vestments, and Chaucer's Parson criticizes ostentation for its economic impact on the poor.

It is probable that this detailed critique of courtliness, mounted from the perspective of pastoral experience and penitential psychology rather than the abstract viewpoint of theological condemnation, effected a steady change in the conceptions of courtliness. In the twelfth century, when Walter Map and Andreas Capellanus denied the possibility of nurture repairing defects of birth, an appeal to the insensitivity of ostentatious display which might be detrimental to the poor would have been unlikely to have been very persuasive to the reading public. By the fourteenth century, and especially in English, the public which was interested in theories of good behaviour was greatly broadened, the conception both of the state and of christendom had considerably prevailed against the community of the courtly. It was routinely argued that *gentillesse* – the inward qualities of courtliness – had its origin in specifically Christian virtues. The Auchinleck *Ubi Sunt* verses were probably intended for a monolingual English audience, interested certainly in both heroic and refined behaviour, yet able to contemplate the damnation of previous generations of ostentatious courtiers with some equanimity.

Despite the opposition which some aspects of courtliness continued to attract from the orthodox Christian perspective, in both its origin and its continued development, the ideals of courtliness were inevitably in symbiotic relationship with those of Christianity. Even alongside the early condemnation, and partly indeed provoking it, courtly theorizing owed much to religious thought and practice; but at the same time those clerics who appreciated the attractions of courtly values to secular society sought to harness them to their own purposes. An attractive alternative to outright opposition was appropriation: the sustaining myths of courtliness could be turned to the service of religion. As the accomplishments of chivalry could be directed into crusades against the heathen or the protection of the weak and the maintenance of peace at home, so the emotions arising from courtly sensitivity could be redirected back to religion, and the favoured narrative situations of courtly literature could be re-fashioned with religious reference. The apogee of this is in the French Grail romances of the later middle ages, but in the earliest text in English to mention the word *curtesie*, the *Ancrene Wisse* (*c.* 1225), the attack by the devil on the soul is already allegorized as the siege of a lady (the soul) in a castle of earth (the body). Christ, in the form of a suitor knight, offers to save her from her foe, but she treats him with *danger* until he has fought a battle to the death (the crucifixion) on her behalf.

Although it makes its earliest appearance in English in the prose *Ancrene Wisse*, the conceptualization of Christ as a knight and the lover of the soul is most fully developed in the lyric tradition. This automatically modifies the perspective on courtly ideas, since English lyrics in particular were informal literary productions rather than the lofty pronouncements of leaders of the Church. Nevertheless, lyrics were widely used in evangelical work, and indeed composed by the friars for this very purpose, in whose hands they found their way into preaching books as well as exemplary sermons.[5] As we have seen in the last chapter, when considered as a motion of the human soul, love was fundamentally distinguishable into types mainly by its objects and purposes. Both religious experience and courtly sensitivity had similar psychological roots: that same tenderness which characterized the ideal *gentil* heart was also the basis of affective piety in religion. This was exploited in numberless poems on the crucifixion, where readiness to weep at the sufferings of Christ could be seen as evidence of the possession of a good heart, of spiritual conversion or of penitence. The attractive fifteenth-century lyric 'Sodenly afraide' summarizes an entire tradition.[6] In it the author declares himself 'so harde hartid' that he may not weep. Yet, confronted by the Virgin lamenting the death of her Son, he is instructed by the refrain: 'Who cannot wepe, come lerne at me'.

Emotional sensitivity in itself was not therefore a matter of controversy between the proponents of secular and religious values, and indeed both parties esteemed it highly, but the conditions in which it was manifested could become the cause of divergence. The major potential conflict between the religious outlook and the secular was in the direction taken by the love which sprang from such sensitivity. An uncompromising and indeed unorthodox view was that love of God and love of worldly things were inevitably at odds. Most medieval Christian commentators, however, would accept the opinion of both St Augustine and St Bernard that love of worldly things represented a capacity which could mature into love of the divine.[7] The fact that the two loves enjoyed some conceptual proximity could become starkly apparent in expression, and this may take a comic turn as when one priest in the diocese of Worcester, with the singing of churchyard carollers still ringing in his ears, inadvertently opened his morning service with the words 'swete lamman dhin are ['sweet lover thy mercy']' instead of *pax vobiscum*.[8] This was a serious procedural breach, and the slip was regarded as a scandal by its chronicler, but it represents the inadvertent employment of an association whose more considered exploitation was a major feature of lyric verse. The values and procedures of secular love literature were ubiquitous in religious contexts. Nowhere is it more obviously and indeed painfully deliberate than in the love poem which the friar Thomas of Hales says was commissioned from him by 'a maid of Christ'.[9] In its focus on the transience of earthly goods, its concern with death, and its contempt for the world, this is an unusual love poem; but it nevertheless consistently presents the relation between a nun and Christ as one of human love leading on to a good marriage. Christ has all the virtues to be sought in an aristocratic lover: he is the 'treowest . . . of alle berne'; he is 'feyr & bryht on heowe, / of glede chere, of mode mylde, / of lufsum lost, of truste treowe, / freo of heorte, of wisdom wilde.' In addition, he is the 'ricchest mon of londe', so that even the king is his vassal. If the girl is willing to become this 'riche and weli' man's lady, she will be the mistress of a household whose splendour and security defy imagination, where her bower will be adorned with heavenly gold and be 'ful of fyn amur'. The choice of words archly exploits the ambivalence of the phrase *fyn amur*, drawing in a religious context on its secular associations. The tenor of this imagery is of course spiritual, illustrating the virtues proper to a nun, but the vehicle chosen to bear this instruction is very deliberately one which might appeal to a rather worldly and fashionable young woman: and the poem makes

continual reference to both the literary heroes and heroines of
courtliness – Amadas and Idoine, Tristran and Isolde, Paris and
Helen – and to an environment of emphatic sensuous richness, filled
with gem stones. The appeal here is not to a modification of
chivalric activity, as in the *Ubi Sunt* poem, but to an idealization of
the courtly and luxurious.

   The attempt to capture for religion the hearts and minds of those
whose concerns lay more readily with courtly values is everywhere
reflected in the diction of religious lyrics. Many lyrics begin with
opening lines of well-considered ambiguity. They may exploit the
device of the *reverdie*, the springtime setting in which the tender
heart is frequently affected by the song of the birds and the
flourishing of the woods and fields to thoughts of love. A Harley
lyric of the earlier fourteenth century begins:

> When y se blosmes springe
> ant here foules song,
> a suete loue-longynge
> myn herte þourhout stong,
> al for a loue newe,
> þat is so suete ant trewe,
> þat gladieþ al my song;
> ich wot al myd iwisse   'certainly'
> my ioie ant eke my blisse
> on him is al ylong.   'all depends on him'
>   (*Harley Lyrics*, ed. Brook, p. 54)

The birds, the blossoms, the love-longing felt by the poet, the
paradoxically pleasant pain of love, the statement of commitment,
all are here, catching the attention of the chance audience. It is only in
the second stanza that it becomes apparent that the poet's devotion
is not towards some lady who has captured his heart, but to Christ.
This poem is closely related to a thirteenth-century version in MS
Royal 2. F.viii, with which it shares its opening, and which ends
with words imitating a love epistle:

> Iesu, lefman swete,   'lover'
> ih sende þe þis songe
> and wel ofte ih þe grete   'I'
>   (Brown, pp. 120–2)

As in secular lyric, the contrast between the infectious joy of nature
in spring and the suffering lover's plight may also be exploited:

Somer is comen & winter gon,
þis day biginniþ to longe,
& þis foules euerichon
   Ioye hem wit songe.
So stronge kare me bint,   'binds'
al wit Ioye þat is funde
   in londe
Al for a child
þat is so milde
   of honde

                            (Brown, pp. 108–9)

Love-longing may be accompanied by the idea that the heart is set on an elevated object, which justifies the suffering felt by the tender heart:

I hafe set my herte so hye,
Me likyt no loue that lowere ys;   'No love pleases me . . .'
And alle the paynes that y may drye   'suffer'
Me thenkt hyt do me good ywys   'seem to me'
                          (Silverstein, pp. 71–2)

The friar John of Grimestone had in his Commonplace Book a lyric which offers the beauty of the Virgin as the cure for such ills (*Sche mithte my bales bete*) in words powerfully reminiscent of the secular use of the 'lady as physician' conceit. Dedication to the Virgin is naturally often expressed in terms reminiscent of that used when declaring service to an earthly mistress, and the poet begs *grace* literally from the Virgin Mary as he might metaphorically from the distant lady of his choice (Brown, p. 24). Christ is often invoked, exploiting exegesis of the Song of Songs, as the lover of the human soul. The word used in lyric diction, however, is the everyday one, *lemman*, an expression avoided by some later fourteenth-century authors as too morally suspect. But exploitation of the physical attractiveness of the Christ knight, in addition to his richness, caused no embarrassment to many lyric writers, who exploited significant contrast to emphasize his suffering at the Crucifixion:

His bodi þat wes feir & gent   'elegant'
& his neb suo scene   'face', 'bright'
Wes bi-spit & al to-rend,
His rude wes worþen grene.   'complexion was become . . .'
                             (Brown, p. 35)

From the purely theological point of view there is no reason to emphasize the physical beauty of Christ, nor is there any scriptural justification for it, but the fact that he is so often envisaged as an attractive, handsome, rich and noble lord is a measure of the extent to which those eager to reach into the values which pervaded secular society were willing to conceptualize God in terms which were immediately acceptable to their audience. Most lyrics use the familiar values and procedures of secular poetry as a means of seizing attention, then quickly develop their religious theme, but certain shorter poems, some of which may be fragmentary, and some longer ones, such as the famous *Mayden in the Mor Lay*, leave their intention unexplained. It is not easy for the modern reader (since it was not intended to be so for the original audience), to be certain whether a poem like the following brief thirteenth-century lyric refers to an earthly lady or to Christ:

> Foweles in þe frith,   'wood'
> Þe fisses in þe flod,
> And I mon waxe wod.   'mad'
> Mulch sorw I walke with
> for beste of bone and blod
>
> (Brown, p. 14)

If we consider the poem to be complete, there may be a tendency to invent a secular context for it, but there is no reason why it should not have evolved into a spring song of the Passion like that quoted above.[10] Alternatively, it may have been developed like its equally famous contemporary (quoted below) into a poem in praise of the Virgin Mary:

> Nu þis fules singet hand maket hure blisse
> and þat gres up þringet and leued þe ris;   'bough'
> of on ic wille singen þat is makeles,   'mateless/matchless'
> þe king of halle kinges to moder he hire ches. 'selected'
>
> (Brown, p. 55)

The conceptual world of these lyrics, in which courtly values and literary devices are put to religious ends, is replicated at much greater length in the fourteenth-century alliterative poem, *Pearl*. Here the author begins in the familiar teasing way. Instead of the spring, it is the autumn; he seems to be bemoaning the loss of a jewel which slipped away, rolling into a cranny in the earth. But his description, the personification and echoes in some phrases suggest the ways in which the ladies of love poetry are described:

Oute of oryent, I hardyly saye,	'safely'
Ne proued I neuer her precios pere.	'equal'
So rounde, so reken in vche araye,	'beautiful'
So smal, so smoþe her sydeȝ were,	
Quere-so-euer I jugged gemmeȝ gaye,	'wherever'
I sette hyr sengeley in synglere.	'apart as unique'

(Pearl, 3–8)

Thomas Usk, in his *Testament of Love* (ed. Skeat, *Works of Chaucer*, vii), also makes great play of his devotion to a lady called Margaret by his use of pearl imagery, but the *Pearl* poet's conceptual man-oeuvres are more subtly extended than those of his London contemporary. Here, it emerges that, although the poem does commemorate the death of a maiden, she is not the poet's lover, but his young daughter. It seems that the author is generalizing the wisdom to be gained from a tragic incident in his own experience. But the poem develops beyond the sharing of an emotional response to tragedy, and beyond the simple reconciliation with the inevitable as God's will, to a discussion of the theology of grace. It is, then, perhaps not unconnected with the ambivalence in medieval literature of the word *grace* that the author develops his own concept of *cortaysye*. Mary, as queen of *cortaysye,* heads a household in which there is no precedence (see Chapter 7): all its members are of the noblest rank, yet do not eclipse each other in esteem, and all freely acknowledge the Virgin as their leader. Echoing the teaching of St Paul in his epistles to the Romans, Corinthians and Ephesians, she likens the membership of this heavenly court to the members of the same body. The poet-dreamer recognizes the significance of the allusion and glosses the sense of the word *cortaysye* required in this context.

'Cortaysé', quod I, 'I leue,
And charyté grete, be yow among,'

(469–70)

The author makes explicit an analogy between the sense of community which unites the ideal courtly household (cf. Latini, *Trésor*, p. 212) and is expressed in ready sympathy (*pitee*), an essential of courtliness, and the charity which cements both Christendom and the court of Heaven. Still thinking in secular terms, the dreamer protests at the elevation in rank which his one-year-old daughter seems to have achieved after so short a space in the service of Christ.

But once again the reply is one which emphasizes the discrepancy between the earthly and the divine court: grace cannot be earned by length of service in the way that preferment on earth may be secured. The economics of grace are not those of the royal court, but are based upon super-abundance: even as it cannot be earned, so there is no limit to its availability.

As the re-conquest of courtliness by religious writers led to the merging of the languages and the feeling of religion and courtesy, so language with religious reference became incorporated into secular poetry from the opposed direction. When seeking for a language in which to express ultimate values, as C.S. Lewis noted, the very earliest courtly poets of love turned to the vocabularies of both feudalism and religion. So intimate is the lexical mixture that it is, in fact, a practical impossibility in most cases to state the circumstances and direction of borrowing. The words *grace*, *mercy* and *pitee*, which are exploited in courtly verse, belong as much to secular lordship as to religion, and the word *daunger* is restricted to that domain. It seems probable that those French and Provençal poems which exploited the conceit of a remote and unattainable beauty, to whom the poet owed loyalty and service as to a feudal lord, may have borrowed the vocabulary along with the analogy from the feudal world. But the fact that religious works had already employed many of these words in reference to the relationship existing between man and God opened the way for the development of an analogy between this relationship with the divine and that existing between secular lovers. In England, the development of poetry which portrays the inequality of lovers in these terms is rare and relatively late. It is present to some degree in Anglo-Norman works, but is not found in English (except in very attenuated form) before the latter half of the fourteenth century. Then, it represents a disjunction from previous English tradition and is characteristic of the French-influenced poetry of Chaucer and the London school with whom he is associated.

The analogy with divine grace to represent the relationship between the lady and her lover is only the most famous parallel between courtly and religious imagery. Other examples of the secular exploitation of religious thought and expression are common. The clerical lyric poetry sometimes sought its expression of value in the diction of verse more often written in praise of the Virgin Mary; in particular, the expressive technique of 'gemmification', the celebration of the lady's worth and beauty in terms of lists of gemstones with whose properties she may be associated. This diction occurs among the

Harley lyrics and is much favoured among aureate writers in the
fifteenth century. The Harley poem 'Annot and John' is a series of
comparisons of the lady with first precious stones, then flowers,
birds, medicinal herbs and spices, and finally exemplary figures of
legendary story. Were it not for the fact that the lady's name is
given as Annot and her relationship with John clearly stated, this
could easily be mistaken for a lyric in elevated style in praise of the
Virgin. The danger of misinterpretation is less acute in the poem
'Blow, Northerne Wind' with its more direct appreciation of the
lady's physical beauty, and her 'fyngres feyre forte folde'. Nevertheless, the following stanza, celebrating her moral qualities, would not
be out of place in one of those poems which celebrates the Virgin
in the figure of a courtly lady:

Heo is coral of godnesse,	'She'
heo is rubie of ryhtfulnesse,	'justice'
heo is cristal of clannesse,	
ant baner of bealte;	
heo is lilie of largesse,	
heo is paruenke of prouesse,	'periwinkle'
heo is solsecle of suetnesse,	'marigold'
ant ledy of lealte.	

(*Harley Lyrics*, ed. Brook, 50)

By the later fifteenth century the mutuality of language and
concepts enjoyed by the religious and secular love lyrics allowed the poet
to combine in the same poem a frank appreciation of the lady's
physical beauty with a confident prayer for Christ's approval of his
true love for her:

Iesue þat ys most of myght,
& made man aboffe all thyng
Saue my trueloue, bothe day & nyght,
& kepe hur well & yn good lykyng.

. . .

She ys the demurest þat I can see
wher-as I walke by est & weste;
noo pere she hasse yn my eye,
for off all women I loue hur beste.

hur lyppes ar lyke vnto cherye,
with tethe as whyte as whalles bone,
hur browes bente as any can be,
with eyes clere as crystall stoune.

hur fyngers be both large & longe,
with pappes rounde as any ball,
no-thyng me-thynke on hur ys wronge,
hur medyll ys bothe gaunte & small.

She hathe my harte & euer shall,
& neuer to change hur for no newe,
butt for to loue hur terrestreall,
& whyles I lyve to hur be true.

(*Secular Lyrics*, ed. Robbins, pp. 126–7)

He closes his verse epistle by sending her 'crystes dere blessyng & myne'. This is a conventional way of closing a letter, but its use confirms that the writer felt no tension between his commitment to his lady and his religious beliefs. Christ has been made the patron of true lovers. To make much of this would be contrary to the spirit which the poem represents, but it is salutary to recall how different these attitudes are from those expressed in the twelfth century. To some degree, what the earlier commentators feared has come about: religious and moral values have been subordinated to secular exigencies.[11]

As we saw earlier, the *rapprochement* between courtly values and religious instruction is a particularly close one in *Pearl*, and the parallels and distinctions are drawn with a very sure and subtle hand. In a second work, which is usually attributed to the same poet, the juxtaposition of Christian and courtly perspectives is again to be found, but the balance is somewhat different. *Sir Gawain and the Green Knight* is overtly an Arthurian romance telling of the encounter of its eponymous heroes. Nevertheless, it has a centrally Christian theme which becomes inextricably intertwined with chivalric and courtly values. Rather than theological subtleties, it is concerned more directly with life among the privileged inhabitants of this world, and becomes so involved in the niceties of courtly accomplishments and recreations that it is easy to overlook its fundamentally religious orientation. The hero is a master of courtly eloquence, spending his days in dalliance with an attractive and enticing lady; he has the accomplishments of the courtier and the trappings of knighthood. He mingles with men who are passionate about hunting, and the audience is entertained by technically correct and very up-to-date details of hunting practice and terminology. He finds lodging in a painstakingly described palace, where he enjoys rich hospitality. The poet does not decline any opportunity to describe the sensuous richness of his trappings, nor the scrupulous observance of courtly custom:

A cheyer byfore þe chemné, þer charcole brenned,
Watz grayþed for Sir Gawan grayþely with cloþez,
Whyssynes vpon queldepoyntes þat koynt wer boþe;
And þenne a meré mantyle watz on þat mon cast
Of a broun bleeaunt, enbrauded ful ryche
And fayre furred wythinne with fellez of þe best,
Alle of ermyn in erde, his hode of þe same;
And he sete in þat settel semlych ryche,
And achaufed hym chefly, and þenne his cher mended.
Sone watz telded vp a tabil on trestez ful fayre,
Clad wyth a clene cloþe þat cler quyt schewed,
Sanap, and salure, and syluerin sponez.
Þe wyȝe wesche at his wylle, and went to his mete.

(875–87)

Before the fireplace, where the charcoal was burning, a chair was pleasingly set for Gawain, with drapes and cushions with quilted coverings, both intricately worked. And then a fine mantle was placed on the man of a rich and gleaming fabric, sumptuously embroidered and well lined with fur of the best pelts, in fact entirely of ermine, and his hood to match. And he sat in that seat appropriately splendid, and swiftly warmed himself, and then his mood improved. Quickly a table was put up properly on trestles, covered with a clean cloth that looked pure white, over-cloth and salt cellar, and silver spoons. The man washed as suited him and went to his meal.

Artistic masterpiece though it is, *Sir Gawain* represents a problem which afflicts any attempt to popularize religious instruction by making it attractive through girding it in the trappings of more immediate secular interests: that is that the vehicle may obscure the tenor; the seductive representation of the secular world eclipse the religious theme. The author is content with many aspects of the courtly world, especially its manners and conversational refinement. He appreciates the subtleties of courtly discourse and, indeed, it is arguable that he puts them to work in his own interests. Rather than work in terms of sermon specifics, he seeks to encourage the interpretation of his poem by those of more sophisticated literary perception. By the interpretative collaboration of his readers, the impact of his moral and religious theme may be heightened. He emphasizes very heavily the exegesis of the pentangle on Gawain's shield, the scene on which the moral-psychological strategy of the plot depends, and the key to his deeper purpose. By its use he ensures that interpretation cannot go too far astray, but elsewhere he employs the discourses of courtesy in pursuit of his own ends.

Eloquence is turned in this poem to the purposes not of seduction, but of chastity; armour is no longer simply functional, a demonstration of force or of wealth, but is a symbol which represents the complex of virtues protecting the knight in spiritual terms. In the end, the hero of this romance, although pre-eminent among his comrades in the court, in accomplishments as in virtue, is shown to be lacking in the perfection to which the device on his shield lays claim. The poem ends somewhat enigmatically with the hero restored to a court community who have all adopted as a symbol of their unity and achievement that very green girdle which for Gawain and the attentive audience denotes the flaw which compromises his perfection. Nevertheless, the poet represents two interpretations of the girdle at this point as at once a trophy and a mark of penitence, according to the perspective of the interpreter. In *Sir Gawain and the Green Knight*, the interpenetration of courtly and religious values reaches its most complex expression, contained within the generic receptacle of the Arthurian romance, that very genre which above all acted as the propagator of the highest values of secular courtliness.

The duty placed on all good Christians of repentance for sins became a source of metaphorical inspiration nearly as productive as the doctrine of grace. The Middle English verb *repente* 'to regret (and desist from) a course of action' had a somewhat wider range of use than its modern descendant, which is more restricted to religious contexts. Nevertheless the noun *repentance* was associated with the words *shrift* ('absolution') and *penance* to describe the process of confession, forgiveness, formal penance, and sincere regret which the penitential manuals required of the sinner. The association of this with love is fully expressed in the *Romaunt of the Rose*, where the dreamer considers that the repentance of his commitment to love, which is required by Reason, would constitute disloyalty to the God of Love, and he refuses to repent (*Romaunt*, 4542–50). Chaucer's poetry is full of these courtly resolutions to love and not repent,[12] and in the *Book of the Duchess*, he exploits the analogy between the culture of refined lovers and that of the Church for purposes of courtly wit when he has the dreamer archly remark that the Black Knight has confessed his love fully, but shows none of the repentance which customarily accompanies confession.[13] The Black Knight's response is that already conventional in love poetry of this kind:

> 'Now, by my trouthe, sir,' quod I,
> 'Me thynketh ye have such a chaunce
> As shryfte wythoute repentaunce.'

'Repentaunce? Nay, fy!' quod he,
'Shulde y now repente me
To love? Nay, certes, than were I wel
Wers than was Achitofel,
Or Anthenor, so have I joye,
The traytor that betraysed Troye,
Or the false Genelloun,
He that purchased the tresoun
Of Rowland and of Olyver.'

(1112–23)

Sometimes, the connection is made simply in terms of a few words, but elsewhere it is worked out as an extensive conceit. A poem of Charles d'Orleans shows how the practices of religion could be fully exploited as the matter of courtly wit.

My gostly fadir, y me confesse,
ffirst to god and then to yow
That at a wyndow (wot ye how)
I stale a cosse of gret swetnes,   'kiss'
Which don was out avisynes;   'without premeditation'
But hit is doon, not vndoon, now –
My gostly fadir, y me confesse,
First to god and then to yow.
But y restore it shall dowtles
Ageyn, if so be that y mow;
And that, god, y make a vow,
And ellis y axe foryefnes –
My gostly fadir, y me confesse,
First to god and then to yow.

(*Secular Lyrics*, ed. Robbins, pp. 183–4)

If, for the sake of argument, we assume that this poem, like Pope's *The Rape of the Lock*, commemorates an actual event in which a lady has been offended by an unsought intimacy, then the subtlety of its strategy becomes apparent. The poem uses the phrasing of confession to create a scene where a lover acknowledges an impulsive action, not forgetting to record the sweetness of the experience, but defining it as theft. He asserts that it was without premeditation (*out avisynes*), so diminishing the transgression and flattering the lady by her implied irresistibility. Following the usual forms for absolution in cases of theft, the poet then offers to restore the stolen goods to their owner, finishing not by asking forgiveness for the original theft, but for any failure to restore the kiss. Thus, while following the outward forms of penance, the poet resolves to repeat the offence. The recipient of these verses might, of course, have been outraged by this reply to her complaint, but its witty contrivance and sheer effrontery demands instead a smile from any lady of equivalent sophistication to its author.

It is the contrivance which makes Charles's poem remarkable rather than the fundamental comparison on which it is based. By his time that comparison was commonplace,[14] and the idea of the confession of the lover had been elaborated at great length in Gower's *Confessio Amantis*. This poem, extending to more than 200,000 words, is modelled on manuals of penance and traces the lover's exchanges with the priest of love, Genius. The process commences with an account of the sins of the five senses, but quickly develops a structure in which the first six books are devoted to the traditional sequence of vices: pride, envy, ire, sloth, avarice, and gluttony, with illustrative anecdotes to elaborate each. There is no sharp distinction between Gower's treatment of Pride and those by authors with a religious motive. He divides it uncontroversially into hypocrisy, inobedience, murmur and complaint, *surquidrie* (or presumption), *avauntance* (or boasting), and vainglory, and conventionally offers humility as a remedy. All of these vices are mentioned in the *Parson's Tale* as possible sub-divisions of pride (although murmur and complaint are more fully treated there under Envy), but it is noteworthy that Gower avoids the Parson's social condemnation of ostentation and waste. Gower's account of hypocrisy follows very much what may be encountered in any discussion of the subject, including criticism of feigned devotion which hides venality, but it is also adapted to the extent that it goes on to consider the functions of hypocrisy, specifically among lovers, citing those who pretend to suffer in the cause of love and polish appealing speeches, but whose real purpose is to deceive their intended victim into showing sympathy. Similar accounts are given of the application of the other branches of pride to the particular situation of the lover.

In the seventh book, however, at the point where, according to the traditional order of treatment, we should have expected a discussion of lechery, the narrative takes an unexpected turn and undergoes a metamorphosis in genre to become a *miroir de prince*, that is, a text-book of politics, economics, and government intended for a ruler, or for any who wished to associate themselves with the skills of leadership. As with other courtly works, Gower avoids direct confrontation with the sin of lechery, preferring a perspective which considers its impact on the commonwealth. Instead of the usual account of lechery and its branches, we are told of the education of Alexander and given a sketch encyclopaedia of what it will be useful for a prince to know. Through the discussion of the subject of *Policie* is introduced the necessity to control desires and avoid lust. Lechery is exemplified by the story of a misled ruler, Tarquin, and the poem evolves into the discussion of how desires can be reconciled with reason. Love is validated by its reconciliation with reason and *honestete*:

> Forthi, my Sone, I wolde rede
> To lete al other love aweie,
> Bot if it be thurgh such a weie
> As love and reson wolde acorde.
> For elles, if that thou descorde,
> And take lust as doth a beste,
> Thi love mai noght ben honeste;
> For be no skile that I finde   'reason'
> Such lust is noght of loves kinde.
>
> (*CA*, VIII, 2020–8)

The measure of good love for Gower is its accord with decency. The sources of virtue are no longer perceived to emerge from the metaphor of the Christian sacrament of penance, but from secular and philosophical ideas of self-government and duty to the state. In Gower's poem, the symbiotic relationship between courtliness and religion has become reversed. The moral basis is now secular political theory and the metaphorical vehicle is the sacrament of confession and absolution. Unlike Charles of Orleans, Gower's morality is perfectly serious, but it is founded on philosophical humanism, on secular community rather than religion. In the imagery of repentance, a new, more reflective, courtly idealism with its roots in moral philosophy was exploiting the analogy of religious observance to present its ideals.

NOTES

1. 'Young people now wear long hair, and pointed shoes. By the fullness of the dresses which trail behind them, the women look like serpents'. Translated from Jeanroy, *Poésie lyrique*, I, p. 83.
2. Cantor, 'Western Monasticism', 47–67.
3. Howard, *Three Temptations*.
4. Cross, 'The *Sayings of St Bernard*'.

5. Wenzel, *Verses in Sermons*, pp. 61–100. On the Christ Knight motif, see Wenzel, *Preachers*, p. 234.

6. *Early English Carols*, ed. Greene, pp. 108–9.

7. St Bernard himself was accused at the Council of Sens (1140) of having written in his youth *nugis* 'trivia' and *cantiunculas mimicas et urbanos modulos*, of which he ought to be ashamed (LeClercq, *Monks and Love*, pp. 17–21).

8. *The Harley Lyrics*, ed. Brook, pp. 4–5.

9. Brown, *English Lyrics of the XIIIth Century*, pp. 68–74.

10. The difficulty of determining the intention of verses, secular or religious, is noted by Wenzel (*Preachers*, pp. 210–12). The Latin context in sermons sometimes indicates deliberate ambivalence. See also Burrow, 'Poems without Contexts'.

11. The confusion between religious modes of thought and expression and those proper to secular eroticism is startlingly demonstrated by the fragmentary Auchinleck poem 'Of a Clerk who would see the Virgin.' (Horstmann, *Altenglische Legenden*, 499–502). As a reward for dedicated service, the clerk requests and is granted a vision of the Virgin 'bodi and face, brest and swire', but has to accept the penalty of lifelong blindness in exchange.

12. It forms the refrain of the *Complaint unto Venus*, and see also *TC*, I, 392; *LGW* (F) 147.

13. Diekstra, 'Chaucer's Way', p. 224.

14. Payen, *Motif du Repentir*.

Chapter 11

Epilogue

The Auchinleck manuscript, which contains the *Ubi Sunt* poem discussed in the last chapter, is a compendium of family entertainment presumably intended for an owner among the successful London merchant class.[1] The compiler and audience of the manuscript no longer equated the use of English simply with the religious instruction of the unsophisticated, but, with William of Nassyngton, faced the fact that English was the natural language of England, and that even many gentlemen no longer spoke French. Commensurate with this awareness and cultural background, it exhibits a lively interest in English history and heroes in works such as the *Anonymous Short Metrical Chronicle* and romances about Arthur, Richard the Lionheart, Guy of Warwick, and Beues of Southampton. Although a lack of skill in reading and understanding French is foreseen in its audience, and indeed French is considered sufficiently 'foreign' to be unblushingly offered as the exotic language of early settlers in the *Short Metrical Chronicle*'s account of the foundation of England (fol. 311rb), this does not imply acceptance of cultural ignorance. Although primarily anglophone, its readership was expected to appreciate the derivation of its stories from reputable literary sources rooted in Latin tradition, and romances like *Kyng Alisaunder* make explicit reference to the dignity of their source material. Such sophistication as there is, however, mainly reflects clerkly tastes. English narrative poetry before the fifteenth century does not take courtliness as its subject, and by following French narrative plot-lines, simply reflects in an attentuated and incidental form the representation of courtliness in the French originals. The English romance genre, as represented in the Auchinleck manuscript, values true love as it values marriage, but regards military adventure more highly than either, and when, in *Beues of Hamtoun*, love becomes the spur of chivalric adventure, because the courtly world is undeveloped, the motivation of the plot remains unconvincing. It is unlikely that this omission of courtly

values from English romance was motivated by either ignorance or
the theological opposition to courtly ideas deriving from twelfth-
century antagonists, but it may well be that, at a less elevated level,
clerical opposition to pride, ostentation and lechery played a part in
limiting the development of courtly narrative in English.

A shift in attitude is detectable even in impeccably courtly
sources, which may be the response to growing criticism. The
broadening of audience for courtly narrative, which is implied in the
use of English as the language of narration, leads sometimes to an
apologetic tone in discussing the values of courtliness. Hunting came
to require defence,[2] and after the turn of the fifteenth century,
Edward, Duke of York, in the *Master of Game*, was still wryly
answering Orderic Vitalis's suspicions of the nocturnal mischief of
courtiers by his assertion that, among the leisured classes, exhausted
hunters at least slept blamelessly at night:

> than he shal goo to take þe eyre in þe euenyngis of the nyght for the
> gret hete þat he haþ had and þan he shal goo drynk and goo lye in his
> bed in faire fressh clotheʒ and shal slepe wel and stedfastly al þe nyght
> without eny evel thought of eny synne, wherfore I say þat hunters
> goon in to paradis, whan þei dey.

> (*Master of Game*, p. 8)

The idea that hunting can act as the promoter of good order and
morality as much as the occasion of heroic endeavour or fieldcraft
would seem very strange in an earlier romance. Here, earlier aristocratic
values are evidently under pressure. In the Auchinleck manuscript,
the satirical poem, *The Simonie*, echoes with a different tone the
strictures of St Bernard on worldly chivalry. The tone is scornful
rather than hortatory: knights who now show no interest in crusades
are depicted as lions in the hall, but hares in the field. They should
dress appropriately to their calling, just as friars do, yet, in fact, they
dress so eccentrically that it may be hard to distinguish a knight
from a minstrel:

> Nu ben þeih so degysed and diuerseliche idiht,
> Vnneþe may men knowe a gleman from a kniht
> Wel neih.

> (*The Simonie*, 255–7)

Earlier objections to ostentation in dress also find an echo in the
accusing words of Chaucer's Parson describing the 'outrageous array
of clothyng' adopted by some members of privileged society, which
are indicative of pride:

As to the firste synne that is in superfluitee of clothynge, which that
maketh it so deere to harm of the peple, / nat oonly the cost of enbraw-
dynge, the degyse endentynge, or barrynge, owndynge, palynge, or
bendynge, and semblable wast of clooth in vanytee, / but ther is also
the costlewe furrynge in hir gownes, so muche pownsonynge of chisel
to maken holes, so muche daggynge of sheris, / forth with the superfluitee in lengthe of the forseyde gownes trailynge in the dong and in
the myre on horse and eek on foote as wel of man as of womman that
al thilke trailynge is verraily as in effect wasted, consumed thredbare and
roten with dong rather than it is yeuen to the pouere to gret damage of
the forseide pouere folk /

(*Parson's Tale*, 417–20)

Once again, there is an interesting contrast between Geoffrey de
Vigeois's reproof of twelfth-century ladies and this fourteenth-
century one: the former frets about fashion leading to damnation;
the latter has a characteristically less transcendental aim, and is firmly
located in the world of everyday experience. Criticism of unreasonable
ostentation has been found to be justifiable on economic and social
grounds as well as purely religious ones. Waste leads to shortages,
driving up prices and causing inflation, which harms ordinary
people ('the moore that clooth is wasted the moore moot it coste
to the peple for the scarsnesse' (421)). This socially critical attitude
to courtly ostentation is repeated in a Lollard Christmas sermon.
Here such splendour is brought into explicit conflict with the
values of religion, the *ubi sunt* formula contrasting the circumstances
of the birth of Christ with that which is to be expected among
fashionable society in the late fourteenth century.

Wher weren þe grete castellis and hye toures, wiþ large halles and
longe chaumbres realli diзt wiþ doseris, costeris, and costious beddes,
and corteynes of gold and selk, able to þe birþ of so hiз an emperoure?
Where weren þoo rial ladies and worþi gentel wymmen, to be
entendaunt to þis worþi emperise, and bere hire cumpenie at þat tyme?
Wher weren þoo knyзtis and squieris to brynge seruice to þis Ladi, of
noble metes, costeli arayes, wiþ hoote spices and denteuous drynkes of
diuerse swete wynes?

(ed. Cigman, *Lollard Sermons*, p. 60)

The contrast points a lesson to rich and poor alike: for the latter to
follow the example of patient poverty offered by Christ, and for the
former to maintain charity, avoid hypocrisy, and 'to be adrad of
misvsynge of her richesse in lustis and lykyngis out of mesure'. By
the later fourteenth century, the ostentation of courtly life had

ceased to be simply the concern of those individuals whose world-liness threatened their personal salvation. Now its effects on the economy of the commonwealth were an issue. The new viewpoint and the tension between new and old values is summarized in terms of the seven capital sins in the poem *Winner and Waster* by the line 'Alle þat I wynn thurgh witt / he wastes thurgh pryde' (230). Yet, although the expression is here founded in the Christian tradition of the sins, it is clear that the values of *richesse* and *largesse* were now under scrutiny from moral viewpoints with a more secular orientation.

The newly critical secular perspective on courtliness is not restricted to non-literary sources, but is apparent too in popular romance. When compared with earlier French romance, a subtle change is apparent in the way the accomplishments of courtliness are viewed in English works. In MS Cotton Caligula A.ii, the heroine of *Emaré* has been taught courtly custom in her youth:

> Golde and sylke forto sewe,
> Amonge maydenes moo.
>
> Abro tawghte thys mayden small
> Nortur that men useden in sale,
> Whyle she was in her bowre.
> She was curtays in all thynge,
> Bothe to olde and to yynge,

(Emaré, 59–65)

Consequently, when she is shipwrecked, she can make herself useful instructing the maidens in the court of Galicia (376–84; 724–31). Her employment is sewing – one of the traditional occupations of noble-women – yet here one feels that her work has had a certain utility imposed upon it, which recalls the opinion of the *Havelok*-poet that 'it is no shame for to swinken' (800), and it is echoed in *Octavian* (1865), where Florence seems to be little more than a sewing teacher. This is a world away from the studied idleness of the elegant lady's pastimes described in the Anglo-Norman *Galeran de Bretagne* (see p. 53). Now, the splendid trappings of the courtly world are juxtaposed with the labour required to produce them. The traditional recreations of courtliness recommend themselves to Langland in terms of their practical usefulness more than their elegance. In describing ladies sewing, his diction clearly echoes the words and physical details of the earlier Anglo-Norman descriptions of aristocratic ladies, with their long fingers, sewing silks and *cendal*, but there is a new emphasis on their productivity, which now has a specific destination:

And ȝe louely ladyes with ȝoure longe fyngres,
þat ȝe han silke and sendal to sowe, whan tyme is,
Chesibles for chapelleynes cherches to honoure.

(B–text VI, 10–12)

Just as these traditional occupations of ladies have been adapted to good use, Langland also finds a place in his economy for the traditional pastimes of knights. He has no grandiose ideas about crusading conquests, but is more concerned with domestic utility. Chivalric virtues are to be turned to the physical protection of the other two estates of society, the clergy and the farmers. Their recreation is placed at the service of agriculture, as knights are enjoined to:

. . . go hunte hardiliche to hares and to foxes,
To bores and to brockes þat breketh adoun myne hegges;
And go affaite þe faucones, wilde foules to kille:
For suche cometh to my croft and croppeth my whete.

(B–text VI, 30–3)

Langland's ideal representative of knighthood is willing enough to assent to this role, even though the utilitarian nature of these instructions is evident from the disparate nature of the list of quarries assigned to him, which includes the badger but omits what was the most favoured quarry of aristocratic huntsmen, the hart. The utilitarian argument, which has survived until the present day as an apologia for foxhunting, represents a very different perspective from the passionate involvement expressed in earlier Anglo-Norman sources or more elevated English alliterative verse. These popular English works view the pastimes of courtliness, from embroidery to hunting, through the eyes not of the aristocrat but the housekeeper, the cleric, or the farmer. They have accommodated the occupations of the courtly life to the benefit of the wider community.

In the later fourteenth century not everyone sought accommodation in this way. Opposition to worldly values did not cease, and monastic contempt for secular things still found a voice. There were those, too, who still interested themselves in an exclusive and aristocratic ideal of courtliness; but in England in the fourteenth century, there was a perspective of growing influence which saw courtliness as combining a valuable refinement of behaviour with a morality based on religious teaching, free from the abstractions of theology, but accompanied by a healthy appreciation of the values of economics and politics. The views of this middle ground are represented in both popular romance and, in a more reflective and

erudite way, in the works of Chaucer, Gower, and even Thomas
Usk. All three of these authors use the word *curteisie*, but in a more
restricted way than we have encountered in earlier texts. To
designate that condition of the soul from which courtesy arises,
they prefer the word *gentillesse*, which they use more frequently.
The adjectival form, *gentil*, is especially frequent, and is used in a
very broad range of contexts, sometimes connoting no more than
vague approval, but this noun, whose most important sense is
'nobility', is used by all three in a very characteristic way to
represent the philosophical perspective on the inward nature of
individual nobility. They are not alone in this perspective, nor were
they originators of it. The word *gentil* had entered the language at
the beginning of the thirteenth century about the same time as
curteisie, and was well established in use by the beginning of the
next century. It had become a part of the diction of popular
romance in the early decades of the fourteenth century: the
Auchinleck manuscript uses it nearly a hundred and fifty times, a
third of which are in the fixed phrase *gentil kniȝt,* which is
overwhelmingly used in rhyme. Auchinleck usage points to a
continuing association with nobility of birth, recognizable in those
aspects of behaviour approved by the courtly tradition. Once or
twice it is associated with the externals of courtly behaviour:
parting, conversation and speech, hawking, and with wealth.
Generally it refers to the inward qualities. It is from the world that
demanded the writing of the Auchinleck manuscript that the
development of *gentillesse* in the works of the later, philosophical
poets springs. In his translation of Boethius, Chaucer renders
nobilitas by the word *gentillesse,* and he uses this word in the *Wife of
Bath's Tale* and elsewhere when he takes up discussion of the
Boethian topic of the true source of individual nobility. The same
perspective is adopted by both Gower and Usk, who see *gentillesse*
as deriving from individual moral virtue irrespective of the accident
of birth. In his short poem on this subject, Chaucer depicts as the
source of moral virtue the example of Christ. The acceptability of
the notion that nobility arises from Christian moral virtue was
complete for the new, wider audience for literature written in
English.[3] *Curteisie*, although by some (such as the author of *Pearl*)
still associated with these inward virtues, and still by most associated
with eloquence, mildness, and forebearance, becomes increasingly
conceptualized in the narrower sense of the courtesy books, as
'good manners', both in one's own behaviour and in relations with
others.

With a wider population laying claim to the potential for nobility, external displays of courtesy became even more essential as an acknowledgement of the validity of such claims. In May 1448 Margaret Paston reported an incident in Norwich to her husband in London. The Paston family chaplain, James Gloys, was returning home when he came face to face with one John Wymondham and two of his employees.

> And Jamys Gloys come with his hatte on his hede betwen bothe his men, as he was wont of custome to do. And whanne Gloys was ayenst Wymondham, he seid þus, 'Couere thy heed!' And Gloys seid ageyn, 'So I shall for the.' And whanne Gloys was forther passed by þe space of iij or iiij strede, Wymondham drew owt his dagger and seid, 'Shalt þow so, knaue?'

Gloys was forced to take cover in Margaret's mother's house, where he was followed by insults and a stone as big as a farthing loaf. He and Wymondham then call each other *charl* and *thef*, and when Margaret and her mother arrive on the scene, they are denounced as 'strong hores', replying with *knave* and *charl*. Much more 'large langage' was exchanged, but is not reported.[4]

Verbal clashes of this kind are frequent in guild and minor court records in which legal action is taken by litigants who feel themselves insulted by the language used to, or of, them. In the Mercers' Company records for 1468 occurs a reference to 'unfittyng and uncurtes langwage' when one John 'amonges other ungoodly wordes and unfittyng, called the said William, false . . . and the said William called the said John Carle' at which John 'with his dager brake the hed of the said William'. John was fined £26.13.4d and William 40s 'for his language'. Another entry for 1475 records that one John Shelley called his brother *fals harlott*, *knave*, and *dryvyll*, to which Thomas responded with *horeson* and *boye Shirrif* and 'more ungoodly & unconuenyent langewage'.[5] It may be assumed that some of the other unquoted but 'ungoodly' language were oaths rather than insults. Slander and insults have survived because they were the basis of the legal action, and indeed, it has been shown that the commonest insult upon which action was taken was the accusation of falsity, which impugned the integrity of the individual in the eyes of the community. Swearing and vulgar words may have been used but, since they do not form the basis of defamatory accusations, are more rarely recorded.[6]

A brief digression on linguistic vulgarity is justifiable here, but it is important to keep distinct the concept of impropriety from that of insult. Impropriety may be deplored, but it is only when it is judged to be insulting that it becomes socially disruptive. Nevertheless, a strong aversion to swearing and vulgar language is apparent in courtly doctrine from the *Roman de la Rose* onwards. The personification Reason defends direct sexual reference on grounds of the propriety of words to the objects signified, but the Lover's rejection of this argument, and preference for euphemisms, is characteristic of courtliness, at least when standing on its dignity. In fact, of course, dual standards prevailed. A posture of respectability was required in serious works, but in avowedly comic works, such as the French fabliaux, which may be written by the same authors as more reputable compositions and may share an audience with them, quite gross expression was tolerated. Such works escaped censure because they were assumed to be beneath the notice of serious-minded readers like the fifteenth-century critics of the *Roman* led by Christine de Pizan, who felt that the use of such language in a serious work formed part of an intolerable licence which detracted from its morality and decency.[7]

Morality and decency, indeed, are concepts frequently evoked in later medieval English sources on polite language. If those recording legal actions sometimes shrank from giving full accounts of bad language used, the scribe of the Hengwrt and Ellesmere manuscripts apparently agreed with the narrator of his *Merchant's Tale* (E.2363, 2378) that the use of the verb *swyven* amounted to speaking *uncurteisly*, for at the end of the line, in rhyme, he curtailed it to read *etcetera* and *swyetcetera* respectively (H.256). Various manuscripts of the *Canterbury Tales*, in reproducing the lines 'Thow seist that euery holour wol hir haue: / She may no while in chastitee abyde' (*WBProl*, 254–5) record nervous scribal variants to avoid the explicit word *holour*.[8] Such sensitivities are the cause also of the batch of euphemisms employed by the Wife of Bath – *quoniam, bele chose, instrument* – and perhaps also of the curious expression *nepergloue* in a tract on the *Fyve Wyttes* in a manuscript dated about 1400. The author complains that 'vnhoneste' speech springs from the corruption of the heart:

> For lytel reuerenceþ þey oure Lord God, þat oueral ys present, þat wol nouȝt openly in an honest mannes presence nemn his scho, bot calle it his neþergloue for a maner honeste, and wol nouȝt spare to speke in Godes presence of rebawdy and harlotry.
>
> (p. 17)

The implication that the word *scho* is one to be replaced by a euphemism, *nepergloue*, in polite company – perhaps because the former had some vulgar secondary sense – is not borne out by what dictionaries record of the use of the two words. It may rather be that the author is making the rhetorical point that it is the peculiar corruption of polite society to be willing to use foul language before God, while, intimidated by the dictates of social propriety, resorting to what he considers a ridiculous and pretentious euphemism for a perfectly ordinary object, through a fear of being judged uncultivated. The signs of sociolinguistic insecurity are unmistakable.

During the fourteenth century, the aristocratic world, reflected in the evolving conceptions of the virtues of courtliness, began to lose confidence in its independence and social autonomy. As new responsibilities and interdependencies were recognized, the old chivalric conceptions of *los* and *pris* began to fade. Instead of these heroic values, literary sources in English reflect a growing concern with the virtue of respectability, which, as we have seen, was apparent even in a hunting manual with royal connections by 1406. In middle-class circles at the turn of the fifteenth century, courtliness of language was closely bound up with what they liked to call *honeste*, that is, decency and propriety. These qualities were valued not simply for their intrinsic merit, but because they could confirm social status and ensure material success. This outlook was borrowed by Chaucer's Friar, who was quite familiar with the social circles from which it arose, and it is summed up by his slogan: 'it is nat honeste, it may noght auaunce'. Mastery of courtly skills was the key to *auauncement*, and the recognition of such *auauncement* is frequently expressed by the use of the words *worship*, *reverence*, and *honeste*. The meaning and use of these words is worth investigating at some length.

The word *honeste* was first recorded in English about 1300 and by the end of the century had become a key word in literate culture. The diversity of senses in which it is used immediately after its initial borrowing suggests the adoption of a sense range as well as a form from French. In Classical Latin *honestas* and the adjective *honestus* connoted 'good reputation, credit, respectability' or 'integrity, virtue, probity'. But the adjective could already be applied to inanimate objects in an evaluative way, and connote that which was likely to confer a good reputation. The word was associated with moral virtue in the discussion of the ideal of friendship, and Cicero used the word *honestas* in contrast with *utilitas*, making a distinction in value between those friendships which were based upon creditable motives and those which arose simply from the hope of profit. This distinction was followed by moralists in medieval Latin, so that *honestas* became part of the monastic ideal of social behaviour.

What is striking about the earliest Middle English contexts in which the word appears is the strong impression of colloquial use. There is little sense that it was felt to be foreign or to belong to a technical or literary register. The nature of its usage suggests that it must have had wide currency before it became common in English written sources. Already in the Auchinleck manuscript, less than thirty years after its first recorded use, it shows signs of having been adapted into an established technique of versification. It occurs exclusively in rhyme, and on two-thirds of these occurrences exhibits an established rhyme association with *feste*. Its senses are also extended considerably beyond the moral ones from which it may have been expected to have been borrowed. It qualifies the word *frendes*, of course, but also *drink* and *welcomynge*, and it is strongly associated with wealth (one-third of its occurrences collocate with *riche*). Christmas is said to be an *honest* time (*Richard Coer de Lion E Fragment*), not for any religious associations, but because of the leisure and feasting to be enjoyed at that season.

The sense of inner integrity, virtue, and probity, which belonged to Latin moral discourse, continues in Middle English moral writings. Most authors interpret honesty as chastity (Hoccleve, *Minor Poems*, XXI, 705, XXII, 477; Gower, *CA*, I, 475; Chaucer, *CT*, 7, *SNT*, 89) and both Chaucer's Parson and Langland (C-text, XVI, 242–4) assert that true honesty derives from religion and the example of the clergy. Gower reflects on an imagined first age in which war-making was not considered *honeste* (*CA Prol*, 216); but in a debate in *Kyng Alisaunder* (4008) a knight is declared to have acted honestly in seeking to assassinate Alexander because, in doing so, he was seeking to carry out his lord's instructions. The word *honeste*, then, participated in moral debate, implying approval of conformity to a recognized set of values. But from its earliest attestations in Middle English, *honeste* is used extensively in two other senses which reflect greater concern for worldly matters. The first is an evaluative or appreciative sense: sparrowhawks, tents, horses and, rather blatantly, the sum of one hundred pounds (*Libeaus*, 988), are declared to be *honeste*. It is not always easy to distinguish between this sense, which is purely evaluative, and the second sense which refers to whatever indicates external regard or respect: that value placed upon persons by others. Similarly, it is sometimes difficult to distinguish the precise nuance when the word is used of inanimate

things. In *St Patrick's Purgatory* the earthly paradise vacated by Adam
is described as a land filled with singing birds, and summed up:

> þat lond, þat is so honestly,
> Is ycleped paradis terestri,
> þat is in erþe here.

(1018–21)

The implication seems to be simply of a pleasant place, although
there may be associations with primal innocence. If so, this makes
an interesting contrast with Gower's application of the adjective to
the land of Egypt, whose 'honesty' consists in its example as a
model of intensive agriculture and productivity:

> And ek the lond is so honeste
> That it is plentevous and plein,
> Ther is non ydel ground in vein;

(*CA*, VII, 930–2)

Many inanimate objects or ceremonies such as welcomings or feasts
are designated *honeste* not simply for their richness, but because they
testify to the respect in which someone is held. They are *in honour
of* a recipient and their honesty may be judged by their appropriateness to his distinction. This is particularly apparent in the case of
arrangements for burial. One of the significant roles of craft guilds
was to provide adequate funeral insurance to ensure appropriate
burial for their members. The Carpenters' Guild undertakes to
provide honest burial for any member who is unfortunate enough
to require this service, and they will do so even in the case of death
outside London, within a twelve-mile radius, so long as the cause
of death is a respectable (*honeste*) one (*BLE* Guild Returns, I).

Indeed, the word *honeste* takes on a particular colouring in the
records of the London craft guilds. Their concern is with good
reputation both within a particular craft and among the townsfolk
as a whole. The *honeste* of the Faculty of Physicians is to be
defended by forbidding unqualified people to practise as physicians
or as surgeons; the Brewers' Guild demands that work on its
property be completed 'suffisauntly hably and honestly as it
belongeþ to þe werke of carpentrie'. They wanted, as modern
carpenters would understand it, 'an honest job' to the best standards
of the craft. Before Christmas 1418, the Mayor and Aldermen of
the City issued a proclamation calling upon good citizens to
celebrate the festival with a certain sobriety:

The Mair and Aldermen chargen, on þe kynges byhalf and þis Cite, þat no manere persone, of what astate degre or condicion þat euere he be, duryng þis holy tyme of Cristemes, be so hardy in eny wyse to walk by nyght in eny manere mommyng, pleyes, enterludes, or eny oþer disgisynges, with eny feynyd berdis, peyntid visers, disfourmyd or colourid visages in eny wyse, vp peyne of enprisonement of her bodyes, and makyng fyne aftir þe discrecion of þe Mair and Aldremen; Outake þat hit be leful to eche persone for to be honestly mery as he can, with-in his owne hous dwellyng. And moreouere þei charge, on þe kynges byhalf and þe Cite, þat eche honest persone, dwellyng in eny hye strete or lane of þis Citee, hang out of her hous eche night duryng þis solempne feste a lanterne with a candelle þer-in, to brenne as long as hit may endure, vp peyne to pay iiijd. to þe chaumbre at eche tyme þat hit faillith.

(*BLE* Guildhall Letterbooks, VI, 1418)

People were thus encouraged to be 'honestly mery', but uncontrolled revelry was forbidden. Such a carefully balanced attitude to celebration and good order is matched by Chaucer's Parson at the end of his onslaught on the pride of excessive display in dress and horses. His opposition to courtly ostentation is not radical or extreme, and he accepts the need for some elegance. His critical remarks, he repeats, are directed not at that modest display which is appropriate to certain occasions or social positions, but at harmful excess:

I speke this for the synne of superfluitee and nat for resonable honestetee whan resoun it requereth.

(*CT*, 12, 436)

The city council which wrote such elaborate and pretentious letters to the king (see Chapter 7) and the village priest are not opposed to social inequalities, or even the display of their trappings, but they are united in favour of order and respectability for the common good. Together, they preferred the word *profitable* to *proz*, and their notion of respectability was summed up in the word *reverence*.

The idea that, like propriety, a readiness to show respect to one's neighbour is a feature of courtesy is already stated in the description of *Vilanie* in the *Romaunt of the Rose*. She is pictured as the contrary of everything courteous, but in particular refuses to acknowledge the worth of anyone. She is utterly lacking in *reverence*; but in this passage, the key word is replaced by its synonym *worshipe*:

She semede a wikked creature
By countenaunce in portrayture;
She semed be ful dispitous
And eek ful proude and outragious.
Wel coude he peynte I vndirtake
That sich ymage coude make.
Ful foule and cherlysshe semed she
And eek vylayneus forto be
And litel coude of Norture
To worshipe any creature

(*Romaunt*, 171–80)

Like *honeste*, the word *reverence* first appeared in English in the earliest decades of the fourteenth century, but seems to have belonged at first to a more elevated register than either *honeste* or *worshipe*. It was at first used to express that sense of awe proper to the divine and to the mysteries of religion, but was soon extended to describe the attitude suitable for a subject to the king or other lord. It is used also of institutions such as womanhood, the sabbath, and so on. *Reverence* was not at first a purely secular idea, and indeed it figures in penitential lists of vices and virtues: *inreverence* is castigated by Chaucer's Parson as one of the divisions of Pride. The author of the *Weye of Paradyse* links *reverence* with the second commandment, pointing out that respect for God will restrain cursing (p. 223), and encourages servants to reprove the faults of their master mildly and *in reverence* (p. 271). Reverence is conceived of as a natural law, and a duty placed upon all creatures who conformed to natural piety. *Reverence* is due to parents from their children, and according to the *Master of Game* this is even apparent in animal species, for even wolves reverence their parents when they meet. Naturally, different species indicate their respect in different ways, but even snakes can show it in their fashion (*CA*, V, 5064). Among humans, the degree of reverence can be shown by appropriately different actions: doffing a hood to a gentleman or kneeling to an emperor (*CA*, VII, 2454). What is important is that some public display of respect is made, which reflects well on both participants in the action. This social necessity led, by the last quarter of the fourteenth century, to a semantic development in the abstract noun *reverence*, which gave rise to a count noun. On meeting, one did *a reverence*. If this gesture were omitted, it could result in trouble. It was this insult, not bad language, that sparked off the disorder in Norwich reported by Margaret Paston. It is true that in this particular case the insult was deliberate and was driven home by an explicit reference by James

Gloys to his deliberate refusal to acknowledge the offended man by removing his hat, but these events should be understood in the context of the Knight of the Tower's tale given at the beginning of Chapter 7. An act of reverence was important, and to omit it was an unspoken insult. By the close of the century, the importance of reverence could fairly be claimed to express much of the values of the prosperous urban class of the time. Chaucer's Prioress strove to be considered worthy of it, and, according to Chaucer's translation of Boethius, some people regarded the *reverence* of their neighbours as the supreme good beyond all others (III, p. 2).

But what was it that compelled the *reverence* of neighbours? In the minds of moralists there was no doubt as to the answer to the question. Chaucer, Usk, and Langland agreed that what ideally deserved *reverence* was goodness and wisdom; but they also agreed that what normally received it was wealth, position, and success. The loss of wealth brought with it loss of esteem.

> Thy selue neghebor wol thee despise
> If thow be pouere; farewel thy reuerence.
>
> (*MLProl*, 3, 116–17)

Wealth was not to be despised, of course, even by moralists, but what merited *reverence* was when that wealth was accommpanied by evident *honeste*. In a merchant society, respect of this kind was important, since credit depended on the way in which an individual's status was perceived. Chaucer's *Shipman's Tale* examines the ethics of this merchant world, where business relationships, credit, and the impression of stability are important.[9] The merchant's life is as ascetic in its way as that of a hermit: he ponders lengthily on his *nedes* and his credit standing; he does not permit himself frivolous amusements like those restrained by the proclamation of the Mayor and Aldermen:

> He neither pleyeth at the dees ne daunceth,
> But as a marchant shortly for to telle
> He let his lyf.
>
> (*CT*, 10 *ShT*, 304–6)

At home, he encourages economy and thrift. As the poem begins, a voice queries the need for display, and whether it 'causeth moore dispence / Than worth is al the cheere and reuerence' (*CT*, 10, 5–6). The doubt raised is not really a moral one, but rather whether such display is cost-effective in ensuring the respect of neighbours. Yet a merchant husband cannot afford not to invest in his wife's appearance for fear of losing his credit in society ('He moot vs clothe and he moot vs arraye / Al for his owene worship richely' (12–13)). In such a society, anxiety about receiving the *reverences* of his neighbours arises from fears not merely about social status, but also about credit rating, and it extends not just to linguistic usage but to conduct of one's life.

But satisfaction from the expressed respect of neighbours is not limited to those who need it as a confirmation of their business reputation. The *Weye of Paradys* condemns as examples of pride those who seek confirmation of their social status simply from a desire for self-glorification.

> They louen and desiren to be salued in marketes and in feyres and in other places, where as they speke with folk. They willen to be lordes and desyren to be cleped maystres and lordes.
>
> (p. 209)

Forms of address are important in confirming status. Chaucer notes the liking of guildsmen's wives for the form *dame*, and Jill Mann has pointed out that the description of the Friar in the *General Prologue* as like 'a maister or a pope' may be motivated by a prohibition placed on the use of *magister* to friars by St Francis himself.[10] Chaucer's use of *maister* as the address form by the Host to the Friar, and by various protagonists to the friar in the *Summoner's Tale* suggest that, like the hypocrites described in the *Weye of Paradys* (209) many friars had no objection to this form of address.

Clerks too derived satisfaction from the recognition implicit in this respectful mode of address. In a passage in his *Male Regle*, Hoccleve, a clerk of the Privy Seal, describing his unthrifty life as a young man about town, recalls his own vanity in being called *maister* by Thames watermen:

> And in the wyntir / for the way was deep,
> Vn-to the brigge I dressid me also,
> And ther the bootmen took vp-on me keep,
> For they my riot kneewen fern ago:
> With hem I was I-tugged to and fro,
> So wel was him / þat I with wolde fare;
> For riot paieth largely / eueremo;
> He styntith neuere / til his purs be bare.
>
> Othir than 'maistir' / callid was I neuere,
> Among this meynee, in myn audience.
> Me thoghte / I was y-maad a man for euere:
> So tikelid me þat nyce reuerence,

þat it me made larger of despense
Than þat I thoghte han been . . .

(Male Regle, Hoccleve's Works, 193–206)

The perspective of wisdom is one taught to Hoccleve by the passage
of time, and indeed one foreshadowing an account of similar practices
nearly two centuries later in Dekker's *Guls Horne-book* (1609). The
fashionable young man about London earns credit from being well
known to the boatmen, who were the taxi-drivers of the day, and
is so flattered by their recognition that he resorts to what he later
realizes was foolish largesse.

This perception of youthful vanity, aided by hindsight, represents
quite closely the unaided vision of Langland and other clerics who
regard the pursuit of *reverence* as dangerously close to the vice of pride.
Chaucer's Parson does not seek *reverence* in this way (*CT*, 1 *GP*,
527), neither, according to Langland, do holy hermits, unlike those
who hypocritically adopt the eremitical life.

> Ac ermytes þat inhabiten by the heye weye
> And in borwes among brewesteres, and beggen in churches –
> Al þat holy ermytes hatede and despisede,
> As rychesses and reuerences and ryche menne almesse,
> Thise lollares, lache-draweres, lewede ermytes
> Coueyten þe contrarye, for as coterelles they libbeth.

(C-text IX, 183–8)

The world esteems simply display and wealth, showing regard
neither for wisdom nor for noble birth when these are absent. So
people esteem the peacock not for any usefulness in eatable flesh, nor
pleasure from its song, but simply for its gorgeous plumage.

> His ledene is vnloueliche and lothliche his careyne,
> Ac for his peynted pennes þe pecok is honoured
> More þan for his fayre flesch or for his merye note.
> Riht so men reuerenceth more þe ryche for here mebles
> Then for eny kyn he come of or for his kynde wittes.

(C-text XIV, 175–9)

Langland's disgust at this misdirection of *reverence* is summed up in
his ironic picture of what he calls 'lunatik lollares', beggars and
perhaps religious fanatics of unsound mind, who through their disability
are oblivious to the demands of polite society, and in their humility
and lack of concern for worldly *reverence* come closer to the
simplicity of the Christian ideal.

And thauh a mete with the mayre ameddes þe strete,
A reuerenseth hym ryht nauht, no rather then another.
> *Neminem salutaueritis per viam.*

(C-text IX, 121–3)

Langland justifies his approval of behaviour which most would regard as uncivil by citing a passage from Luke X, which relates Christ's instructions to those he sent out in advance of his arrival in the Judaean towns. They are to go barefoot and rely on the people to provide their needs. On entering a house, they are to declare peace upon it. The connection with the behaviour of medieval friars is obvious. But in scripture the embargo on greetings along the road seems intended to concentrate the purpose of the messengers. Langland has re-interpreted the quotation to suit a special concern of his own. As he explains, he himself was considered mad or worthless when he put his precept into practice and refused to reverence those whom the world felt deserved it.

> And some lakked my lif – allowed it fewe –
> And leten me for a lorel and looth to reverencen
> Lordes or ladies or any lif ellis –
> As persons in pelure with pendaunts of silver;
> To sergeaunts ne to swiche seide noght ones,
> 'God loke yow, lordes!' – ne loutede faire.

(B-text XV, 4–9)

Professional beggars are much more socially aware. Like Hoccleve's boatmen, Langland's beggars have learned the lesson of flattering address. Pretending blindness, and simulating crippled limbs, they call for alms in a style which is calculated to match the expectations of the hypocrites mentioned in the *Weye of Paradys*:

> 'For we have no lymes to laboure with, lord, ygraced be ye!
> Ac we preie for yow, Piers, and for youre plowgh bothe,
> That God of his grace youre greyn multiplie
> And yelde yow of youre almesse that ye yyve us here;
> For we may neither swynke ne swete, swich siknesse us eyleth.'

(B-text VI, 124–8)

In recording the pleas of beggars, Langland catches a further nuance of their idiom, the courtly use of address by the plural form of the second-person pronoun. Ordinarily, he makes very little use of this, occasionally employing it as a mark of reverence for one of the personifications he encounters in his dream. However, he makes more extended and creative use of it in the court scene with the king and Lady Mede, where it reflects the pride and corruption of the court, and here in the wheedling of beggars, whose flattery functions, like that of Hoccleve's boatmen, to lubricate largesse.[11] This is the darker side of courtesy. What the author of the *Romaunt of the Rose*, or his character the God of Love, would have applauded as an *honeste* manner of greeting or a proper expression of *reverence* has become simply a mode of extortion. As the authors of idealizing works of courtliness were well aware, idealism is secondary to intention; changed intention transforms the moral status of any act.

In the world presented by Middle English popular poetry, the outline of the ideals of courtliness is recognizable, as it is also in the plots of popular romance narrative. But just as in the latter the heroes' actions may seem robbed of credible motivation, so courtliness now often consists of the outward forms, sometimes twisted to discreditable functions. The moral economy of this literature no longer derives from confidence in the superiority of noble birth and the value of beauty. Its sources are still in a conception of society, but no longer that of the noble. It is rather a conception of the commonwealth, represented in the texts we have discussed as the City of London. The unity and good order of this little state are guaranteed by conceptions of politics and government deriving from the renewed secular Latin tradition, from the pastoral role of the clergy, and from the external observances of courtesy which could be learned from courtesy books. In this society, *fin amour*, when applied to sexual relationships, had come to mean true, as much as intense, love. Significantly, Chaucer's only use of the phrase *fyn lovynge* is applied to a wife's love for her husband, and in the Auchinleck manuscript, the tale of Orpheus is no longer a tragedy but a narrative reinforcing the ideal of married love, which Gower identified as *honeste love*. *Reverence*, which according to Gower was a possible ground for love, and was the premier aspiration of this community, had come to be associated with solvency and good repute. Respectability had replaced the *los* and *pris*, and thrift the *proz*, of earlier chivalric society. Largesse and ostentation were as suspect among merchants as they were among clerics, and thrift was approved. Reformers like Langland even questioned the use of the more elegant forms of speech, and those of bookish nature sometimes supported this view by extensive Latin documentation to argue against the pretentious use of the second-person plural pronoun.[12] It seems possible that in Margaret Paston's account of James Gloys, the words 'as he was wont of custome to do' refer to a clerk's regular habit of refusing to doff his hat when meeting people in the street. If so, Gloys was of

Langland's persuasion and both were precursors of later Puritan attitudes. In these social circumstances, *vilainie*, which in earlier times had connoted all those characteristics of the churl which were repugnant to the truly *curteis*, became very much narrowed in its reference. The narrowing was closely parallel to that which had occurred with *curteisie*, so that, in everyday use in the later fourteenth century, *vilainie* often implied some blatant breach of good manners. In particular, it was often associated with coarse speech or with swearing. The fines which later medieval guilds imposed upon their members were, like those imposed in noble households, intended to help to promote good order.

During the fourteenth century, and viewed from the broader perspective which opens up with the emergence of many more works for a monolingual English audience, courtliness underwent a process of democratization. First, it had been re-interpreted to correspond more closely with the requirements of religion; now it was modified to suit the demands of an urban, commercial society. The conception of the *curteis burgeis* goes back a long way in the story of courtliness. Friendly dwarves, porters, innkeepers and town-dwellers, who are ready to offer aid and comfort to the courtly hero, are found from the twelfth century onwards. Already in *Ipomedon*, a courtly burgess appears as a credible character (333ff.) and bourgeois courtesy is encountered in English by 1330 (*Short Metrical Chronicle*, 729; *Floris and Blancheflour*, 498). But, apart from French romances such as *Perceval* and its parody, *Fergus*, where the issue of nurture and nature becomes thematic, such characters are peripheral and exceptional, indications that the virtues of courtliness may occasionally extend beyond their proper lodging in those of noble birth. By the end of the fourteenth century the courtly burgess was no longer a mere spear-bearer in an otherwise aristocratic drama, but represented the majority audience to which English literature was directed. That literature reflected his new conception of courtliness derived ultimately from monastic urbanity and chivalric values, but modified to suit his new world by an alliance between urban commerce and pastoral religion.[13] These changes transformed courtliness from an ideal appropriate to a handful of noble households into a code of behaviour appropriate to an English society which was to persist for a further five hundred years.

NOTES

1.   A similar miscellany, but with a less marked English nationalism, is MS Cotton Caligula A.ii. It contains a selection of romance, moral and religious verse, with

some historical material. The rather more sober nature of the collection is confirmed by the exclusion of comic tales and the inclusion of the courtesy text, *Urbanitatis*. Caligula A.ii comes from a similar geographical location to Auchinleck, but is more than a century later and arguably echoes the increasing sense of propriety traced in this chapter. For discussion of other fifteenth-century miscellanies from demonstrably bourgeois London backgrounds, see Boffey and Meale, 'Selecting the Text' and Thompson, 'Looking Behind the Book'.

2. Rooney, *Hunting in Middle English Literature*, pp. 39–42, 104.

3. Gray ('Chaucer and Gentilesse') gives a wide-ranging account of the *topos* that nobility does not depend on birth.

4. The historical circumstances of this clash, arising in part from competition between the Paston and Wymondham families, are discussed by Colin Richmond, 'What a Difference'.

5. Lyell and Watney, *Mercers' Company*, pp. 60–1, 85–6, 107, 112. Courteous language is seen as maintaining good relations between guilds, as well as within their ranks.

6. Lindahl, *Earnest Games*, pp. 73–84. Lindahl emphasizes that actions for slander were justified not by individual recompense obtained, but by their contribution to the maintenance of public order.

7. Muscatine, 'Courtly Literature and Vulgar Language'; Benson, 'Chaucer and Courtly Speech'. Benson summarizes: 'the history of the early development of linguistic prudery is . . . the history of courtly literature' (p. 16).

8. Half a dozen manuscripts substitute the less offensive word *harlot* for the occurrence in the *Wife of Bath's Prologue*. Euphemistic treatment is again found at *ParsT*, 857 and 877. Here the words *fooles, harlots*, and *horelis* are substituted by some scribes. On this and other similar examples, see Benson, 'Courtly Speech', pp. 26–7.

9. Scattergood, 'The Originality of the Shipman's Tale'; Cahn, 'Chaucer's Merchants and Foreign Exchange: An Introduction to Medieval Finance'.

10. Mann, *Chaucer and Medieval Estates Satire*, p. 39. The predilection for respectful greetings in the market-place is referred by the author of the *Weye of Paradys* to the pride of the scribes and Pharisees in Matthew 23, 1–12. Mann shows this passage being invoked in a tradition of satire against the friars.

11. Burnley, 'Langland's Clergial Lunatic'.

12. Finkenstaedt, *'You' and 'Thou'*; Burnley, 'Christine de Pizan and the So-called Style Clergial'.

13. The development of a 'bourgeois ethos' in later medieval English literature through the coincidence of commercial and clerical values and the sanctification of productive labour is interestingly discussed by Felicity Riddy in the case of the courtesy work, *What the Goodwife taught her Daughter*. Riddy, 'Mother Knows Best'.

References

PRIMARY SOURCES

Acts of Court of the Mercers' Company, 1453–1527, edited by Lyell, Laetitia and Frank D. Watney (Cambridge, 1936).

Albertus Magnus, *Alberti Magni Opera Omnia*, Monasterii Westfalorum in aedibus Aschendorff (Aschendorff, 1951–).

Amadas et Ydoine: roman du xiiie siècle, edited by Reinhard, John R., CFMA 51 (Paris, 1926).

Amis and Amiloun, edited by Kölbing, E., Altenglische Bibliothek 2 (Heilbronn, 1884).

Ancrene Wisse: Parts Six and Seven, edited by Shepherd, Geoffrey (London, 1959).

The Anglo-Norman Voyage of St Brendan, edited by Short, Ian and Brian Merrilees (Manchester, 1979).

An Anonymous Short English Metrical Chronicle, edited by Zettl, Ewald (London, 1935).

Aquinas, St Thomas, *Summa Theologiae*, 61 vols, edited and translated by members of the English Province of the Dominican Order (London, 1963–76).

Aristotle: Nichomachean Ethics, edited by Rackham, H., Loeb Classical Library (London, 1926).

Aristotle's De Anima in the Version of William of Moerbeke and the Commentary of St Thomas Aquinas, edited and translated by Foster OP, Kenelm and Silvester Humphries OP (London, 1951).

Aristotelis Opera cum Averrois Commentariis, Suppl. II (Venice, 1562–74; repr. Frankfurt, 1962).

The Avowing of King Arthur, edited by Dahood, Roger, Medieval Texts, vol. 10 (New York/London, 1984).

The Awntyrs off Arthure at the Terne Wathelyne: A Critical Edition, edited by Gates, Robert J. (Philadelphia, PA, 1969).

Babees Book etc, edited by Furnivall, Frederick J., EETS OS 32 (London, 1868).

Beowulf, edited by Klaeber, Fr., 3rd edn (Boston, 1950).

Blund, John, *Tractatus de anima, Iohannes Blund*, edited by Callus, D.A. and R.W. Hunt, Auctores Britannici Medii Aevi 2 (London, 1970).

A Book of London English, edited by Chambers, R.W. and Marjorie Daunt (Oxford, 1931).

Caxton's Blanchardyn and Eglantine, edited by Kellner, Leon, EETS ES 58 (London, 1890).

Caxton's Eneydos. Englisht from the French Liure de Eneydos 1483, edited by Culley, Matthew T. and F.J. Furnival, EETS ES 57 (London, 1890).

La Chanson de Roland, edited by Whitehead, F. (Oxford, 1965).

Geoffrey Chaucer: The Canterbury Tales, edited by Blake, N.F. (London, 1980).

Geoffrey Chaucer: Troilus and Criseyde, edited by B.A. Windeatt (London, 1984).

The Riverside Chaucer, edited by Benson, Larry D. (London, 1988).

A Variorum Edition of the Works of Geoffrey Chaucer, vol. 5: The Minor Poems, Part 1, edited by Pace, George B. and Alfred David (Norman, Oklahoma, 1982).

The Works of Geoffrey Chaucer, edited by Skeat, W.W., 7 vols (Oxford, 1899).

Chrestien de Troyes: Yvain (Le Chevalier au Lion), edited by Reid, T.B.W. (Manchester, 1967).

Chrétien de Troyes: Le Roman de Perceval ou Le Conte du Graal, edited by Roach, William (Genève and Paris, 1959).

Christine de Pisan. Le Livre des Fais et Bonnes Meurs du Sage Roy Charles V, edited by Solente, S., 2 vols (Paris, 1940).

Christine de Pisan: Le Livre du Corps de Policie, edited by Lucas, Robert H. (Genève, 1967).

Chronicles of the Reigns of Stephen, Henry II and Richard I, edited by Howlett, Richard, 4 vols, RS 82 (London, 1886).

The Works of Sir John Clanvowe, edited by Scattergood, V.J. (Cambridge, 1975).

Cleanness, edited by Anderson, J.J. (Manchester, 1977).

Dekker, Thomas, *The Guls Horne-booke (facsimile of the first edition)* (Menston, 1969).

'De Nobilitate Animi', edited by Colker, Marvin L., *Mediaeval Studies*, 23 (1961), 47–79.

The Divine Comedy of Dante Alighieri, edited by Sinclair, John D., 3 vols (London, 1971).

'Le Donnei des amanz', edited by Paris, Gaston, *Romania*, 25 (1896), 497–541.

The Early English Carols, edited by Greene, Richard Leighton, 2nd edn (Oxford, 1977).

English Lyrics of the XIIIth Century, edited by Brown, Carleton (Oxford, 1932).

L'Estoire des Engleis by Geffrei Gaimar, edited by Bell, Alexander, ANTS 14–16 (Oxford, 1960).

Floris and Blancheflour, edited by Taylor, A.B. (Oxford, 1927).

The Fyve Wyttes: A Late Middle English Devotional Treatise edited from BL MS Harley 2398, edited by Bremmer Jr, Rolf H. (Amsterdam, 1987).

Galeran de Bretagne: roman du xiiie siècle, edited by Foulet, Lucien and Jean Renart, CFMA 37 (Paris, 1925).

Jean Gerson: Oeuvres Complètes, edited by Glorieux, Mgr., 10 vols (Paris, 1973).

Gest Hystoriale of the Destruction of Troy, edited by Panton, G.A. and D. Donaldson, 2 vols, EETS OS 39, 56 (London, 1869–74).

Gower, John, *Mirour de l'Omme*, translated by William Burton Wilson (East Lansing, 1992).

The English Works of John Gower, edited by Macaulay, G.C., 2 vols, EETS ES 81–2 (London, 1900–1).

The Works of John Gower, edited by Macauley, G.C., 4 vols, vol. 1: The French Works (London, 1899–1902).

Robert Grosseteste, Chasteau d'amour; to which are added La vie de St Marie egyptienne and an English version of the Chasteau d'amour, edited by Cooke, M. (New York; repr. 1967).

Guillaume le Clerc, The Romance of Fergus, edited by Owen, D.D.R., Arthurian Literature VIII (Woodbridge, 1989).

The Harley Lyrics: The Middle English Lyrics of MS. Harley 2253, edited by Brook, G.L., 3rd edn (Manchester, 1964).

Hauelok, edited by Smithers, G.V. (Oxford, 1987).

Historia Britonum: 3 The Vatican Recension, edited by Dumville, David N. (Cambridge, 1985).

Historia Regum Britannie of Geoffrey of Monmouth: I Bern, Burgerbibliothek, MS. 568, edited by Wright, Neil (Cambridge, 1984).

Hoccleve's Works: The Minor Poems, edited by Furnivall, F.J. and I. Gollancz, EETS ES 61, 73 (revised Jerome Mitchell and I.A. Doyle, 1970).

The Holy Bible, by John Wycliffe and his Followers, edited by Forshall, J. and Sir F. Madden (Oxford, 1850).

Huarte de San Juan, Juan, *Examen de ingenios or, The Tryal of Wits*, translated by Mr Bellamy (London, 1678).

Ipomedon: Poème de Hue de Rotelande, edited by Holden, A.J. (Paris, 1979).

Kyng Alisaunder, edited by Smithers, G.V., 2 vols, EETS OS 227, 237 (London, 1952–57).

The Works of Lactantius, edited by Fletcher, William, 2 vols (1886).

Laȝamon: Brut, edited by Brook, G.L. and R.F. Leslie, 2 vols, EETS OS 250 & 277 (London, 1963–78).

Li Livres dou Tresor de Brunetto Latini, edited by Carmody, Francis J. (Berkeley and Los Angeles, 1948).

Lollard Sermons, edited by Gloria Cigman, EETS OS 294 (Oxford, 1989).

Lotario de Segni (Pope Innocent III): De Miseria Condicionis Humane, edited by Lewis, Robert E., The Chaucer Library (Athens, 1978).

Lydgate's Fall of Princes, edited by Bergen, Henry, 4 vols (Washington, 1923–27).

Lydgate's Troy Book, edited by Bergen, Henry, 3 vols, EETS ES 97, 103, 106 (1906–10).

The Lyfe of Ipomydon. Vol. 1: Text and Introduction, edited by Ikegami, Tadahiro, vol. 21 (Tokyo, 1983).

Oeuvres de Guillaume de Machaut, edited by Hoeppfner, E., SATF (Paris, 1908–21).

Malmesbury, William of, *Gesta Regum*, 2 vols, RS (London, 1889).

Malory: Works, edited by Vinaver, Eugène, 2nd edn (London, 1977).

Sir Thomas Malory: The Morte Darthur. Parts Seven and Eight, edited by Brewer, D.S. (London, 1968).

Marie de France: Lais, edited by Ewert, Alfred, Blackwell's French Texts (Oxford, 1976).

The Master of Game by Edward, Second Duke of York, edited by Baillie-Grohman, Wm A. and F. (London, 1904).

The Middle English 'Weye of Paradys', edited by Diekstra, F.N.M. (Leiden, 1991).

Monmouth, Geoffrey of, *The History of the Kings of Britain*, translated by Lewis Thorpe (Harmondsworth, 1966).

Minor Poems of the Vernon Manuscript, edited by C. Horstmann, EETS OS 98 (1892).

Der mittelenglische vers-roman über Richard Löwenherz, edited by Brunner, K., Wiener beiträge zur englischen Philologie 42 (Vienna, 1913).

Das Moralium Dogma Philosophorum des Guillaume de Conches, edited by Holmberg, J. (Uppsala, 1929).

Morte Arthur: A Critical Edition, edited by Hamel, Mary (New York, 1984).

Mum and the Sothsegger, edited by Day, M. and R. Steele, EETS OS 199 (1936).

Nims, Margaret F., *The Poetria Nova of Geoffrey of Vinsauf* (Toronto, 1967).

Of Arthour and of Merlin, edited by Macrae-Gibson, O.D., 2 vols, EETS OS 268, 279 (London, 1973–79).

On the Properties of Things: John Trevisa's Translation of Bartholomaeus Anglicus De Proprietatibus Rerum, edited by Seymour, M.C., 3 vols (Oxford, 1975–88).

The Owl and the Nightingale, edited by Stanley, E.G. (London and Edinburgh, 1960).

Parisiana Poetria of John of Garland, edited by Lawler, Traugott (New Haven and London, 1974).

The Parlement of the Thre Ages, edited by Offord, M.Y., EETS OS 246 (London, 1959).

Patience, edited by Anderson, J.J. (Manchester, 1969).

Pearl, edited by Gordon, E.V. (Oxford, 1953).

The Peterborough Chronicle, edited by Clark, Cecily, 2nd edn (Oxford, 1970).

Piers Plowman: The B Version, edited by Kane, George and E. Talbot Donaldson (London, 1975; rev. 1988).

Promptorium Parvulorum: The First English–Latin Dictionary, edited by Mayhew, A.L., EETS ES 102 (London, 1908).

Rhetorica ad Herennium: Ad C. Herennium Libri VI de ratione dicendi (M. Tulli Ciceronis ad Herennium Libri VI), edited by Caplan, H., Loeb Classical Library (London, 1954).

Le Roman de Brut de Wace, edited by Arnold, Ivor, 2 vols, SATF 72 (Paris, 1938–40).

Le Roman de Toute Chevalerie, edited by Foster, B., 3 vols, ANTS 29–31 (London, 1976).

The Romance of Horn, edited by Pope, Mildred K. and T.B.W. Reid, 2 vols, ANTS 9, 10 (Oxford, 1955).

The Romance of Sir Beues of Hamtoun, edited by Kölbing, Eugen, 3 vols, EETS ES 46, 48, 65 (London, 1885–94).

The Romance of Tristran by Beroul, edited by Ewert, A. (Oxford, 1963).

Rotuli Parliamentorum ut et petitiones et placita in Parliamento, 7 vols (London, 1783–1832).

S. Bernardi Opera, edited by LeClercq, J. and H.M. Rochais, 8 vols, vol. 3: Tractatus et Opuscula (Rome, 1957–77).

Sancti Thomae Aquinatis, In Aristotelis Librum de Anima Commentarium, edited by Pirotta OP, P.F. Angeli M. (Turin, 1959).

Secretum Secretorum, edited by Manzalaoui, M.A., EETS OS 276 (London, 1977).

Secular Lyrics of the XIVth and XVth Centuries, edited by Robbins, Rossell Hope, 2nd edn (Oxford, 1954).

Seven Sages of Rome, edited by Brunner, Karl, EETS OS 191 (London, 1933).

Simplicii Commentarii in Libros De Anima Aristotelis Quos Ioannes Faseolus Patauinus ex graecis latinos fecit (Venice, 1543).

Oeuvres de Simund de Freine, edited by Matzke, John E., SATF 47 (Paris, 1909).

Sir Gawain and the Green Knight, edited by Tolkien, J.R.R. and E.V. Gordon, and revised by Norman Davis, 2nd edn (Oxford, 1967).

St Modwenna, edited by Baker, A.T. and Alexander Bell, Anglo-Norman Texts, 7 (Oxford, 1947).

St Patrick's Purgatory, edited by Easting, Robert, EETS OS 298 (London, 1991).

Steenberghen, Fernand van, 'Un commentaire semi-Averroiste du Traité de l'Âme', in *Trois commentaires anonymes sur le Traité de l'Âme d'Aristote*, edited by Gide, M., F. van Steenberghen, and B. Bazán, Philosophes médiévaux 11 (Louvain and Paris, 1971).

The Story of England by Robert Manning of Brunne, edited by Furnivall, F.J., 2 vols, RS (London, 1887).

Thomas of Britain: Tristran, edited by Gregory, Stewart, Garland Library of Medieval Literature, vol. 78 (New York/London, 1991).

Thomasset, Claude Alexandre, *Placides et Timéo ou Li secrés as philosophes* (Geneva, 1980).

Timaeus, a Calcidio translatus commentarioque instructus, edited by Waszink, J.H., Corpus Platonicum Medii Aevi, Plato Latinus 4 (London, 1962).

Un Traité de l'Amour du xiie siècle, edited by Davy, M.-M. (Paris, 1932).

The fragments du Tristan de Thomas, edited by Wind, B.H. (Leiden, 1950).

La Vie Seint Edmund Le Rei. Poème Anglo-Normand de xiie siècle par Denis Piramus, edited by Kjellman, Hilding (Gothenburg, 1935), Slatkine Reprints (Genève, 1974).

Vinsauf, Geoffrey de, *Documentum de Modo et Arte Dictandi et Versificandi*, translated by Roger P. Parr (Milwaukee, 1968).

Volume of Vocabularies, edited by Wright, T., vol. I (London, 1857).

Walter Map: De Nugis Curialium. Courtiers' Trifles, edited and translated by James, M.R., revised by C.N.C. Brooke and R.B. Mynors (Oxford, 1983).

The Wanderer, edited by Dunning, T.P. and A.J. Bliss (London, 1969).

The Wars of Alexander, edited by Duggan, Hoyt N. and Thorlac Turville-Petre, EETS SS 10 (Oxford, 1989).

Webb, J., 'Jean Créton: Poem on the Deposition of Richard II (1399)', *Archaeologia*, 20 (1814), 295–423.

William Caxton: The Book of the Knight of the Tower, edited by Offord, M.Y., EETS SS 2 (London, 1971).

William of Palerne: An Alliterative Romance, edited by Bunt, G.H.V. (Groningen, 1985).

Ywain and Gawain, edited by Friedman, A.B. and N.T. Harrington, EETS OS 254 (London, 1964).

SECONDARY SOURCES

Bachrach, Bernard S., 'Charles Martel, Mounted Shock Combat, The Stirrup, and Feudalism', *Studies in Medieval and Renaissance History*, 7 (1970), 47–75.

Barnes, Geraldine, *Counsel and Strategy in Middle English Romance* (Cambridge, 1993).

Baugh, A.C., 'The Date of Walter of Bibbesworth's Traité', in *Festschrift für Walter Fischer*, edited by H. Oppel (Heidelberg, 1959), pp. 21–33.

Bédier, Joseph, 'Les Fêtes de mai et les commencements de la poésie lyrique au Moyen Âge', *Revue des deux mondes* (mai 1896).

Bédier, Joseph, *Les Legendes épiques: Recherches sur la formation des chansons de geste*, 2nd edn, 4 vols (Paris, 1914–21).

Bennett, J.A.W., 'Gower's "Honeste Love"', in *Patterns of Love and Courtesy*, edited by John Lawlor (London, 1966), pp. 107–21.

Benson, L.D., 'Courtly Love and Chivalry in the Later Middle Ages', in *Fifteenth Century Studies: Recent Essays*, edited by R.F. Yeager (Hamden, Connecticut, 1984), pp. 237–57.

Benson, Larry, 'Chaucer and Courtly Speech', in *Genres, Themes, and Images in English Literature*, edited by Piero Boitani and Anna Torti (Tübingen, 1988), pp. 11–30.

Benton, John, 'The Court of Champagne as a Literary Centre', *Speculum*, 36 (1961), 551–91.

Benton, John, 'Clio and Venus: An Historical View of Courtly Love', in *The Meaning of Courtly Love*, edited by F.X. Newman (Albany, NY, 1968), pp. 19–42.

Bezzola, Reto R., *Les Origines et la Formation de la Littérature Courtoise en Occident (500–1200)*, 6 vols (Paris, 1958–).

Bloch, Marc, *Feudal Society*, trans. L.A. Manyon, 2nd edn, 2 vols (London, 1962).

Boase, Roger, *The Origin and Meaning of Courtly Love: A Critical Study of European Scholarship* (Manchester, 1977).

Boffey, Julia, *Manuscripts of English Courtly Love Lyrics in the Later Middle Ages* (Cambridge, 1985).

Boffey, Julia and Carol M. Meale, 'Selecting the Text: Rawlinson C.86 and some other Books for London Readers', in *Regionalism in Late Medieval Manuscripts and Texts*, edited by Felicity Riddy (Cambridge, 1991), pp. 143–69.

Bornstein, D., 'Chaucer's Tale of Melibee as an Example of "Style Clergial" ', *Chaucer Review*, 12 (1978), 236–54.

Bornstein, Diane, 'French Influence on Fifteenth-century English Prose as Exemplified by the Translation of Christine de Pisan's *Livre du corps de policie*', *Mediaeval Studies*, 39 (1977), 369–86.

Brault, Gerard J., *The Song of Roland: An Analytical Edition*, 2 vols (University Park and London, 1978).

Brewer, D.S., 'Natural Love in the Parlement of Foules', *Essays in Criticism*, 5 (1955), 407–13.

Brewer, D.S., 'The Ideal of Feminine Beauty in Medieval Literature, especially the Harley Lyrics, Chaucer, and some Elizabethans', *Modern Language Review*, 50 (1955), 257–69.

Brewer, D.S., *Tradition and Innovation in Chaucer* (London, 1982).

Brewer, D.S., 'Honour in Chaucer' in *Tradition and Innovation in Chaucer* (1982), pp. 89–109.

Britnell, R.H., *The Commercialisation of English Society, 1000–1500* (Cambridge, 1993).

Bruyne, Edgar de, *Études d'Esthétique Médiévale*, 3 vols (Bruges, 1946; repr. Genève, 1975).

Burnley, David, 'Langland's Clergial Lunatic', in *Langland, the Mystics and the Medieval English Religious Tradition: Essays in Honour of S.S. Hussey*, edited by Helen Phillips (Cambridge, 1990), pp. 31–8.

Burnley, J.D., 'The 'Roman de Horn': Its Hero and Its Ethos', *French Studies*, 32 (1978), 385–97.

Burnley, J.D., *Chaucer's Language and the Philosophers' Tradition* (Cambridge, 1979).

Burnley, J.D., 'Fine Amor: Its Meaning and Context', *Review of English Studies*, ns 31 (1980), 129–48.

Burnley, J.D., 'Criseyde's Heart and the Weakness of Women: An Essay in Lexical Interpretation', *Studia Neophilologica*, 54 (1982), 25–38.

Burnley, J.D., 'Courtly Speech in Chaucer', *Poetica*, 24 (1986), 16–38.

Burnley, J.D., 'Curial Prose in England', *Speculum*, 61 (1986), 593–614.

Burnley, J.D., 'Christine de Pizan and the So-called Style Clergial', *Modern Language Review*, 81 (1986), 1–6.

Burnley, J.D., 'Comforting the Troops: An Epic Moment in Popular Romance', in *Romance in Medieval England*, edited by Maldwyn Mills, Jennifer Fellows, and Carole M. Meale (Cambridge, 1991), pp. 175–86.

Burnley, J.D., 'Style, Meaning and Communication in *Sir Gawain and the Green Knight*', *Poetica*, 42 (1995), 23–37.

Burrow, J.A., 'Poems without Contexts: The Rawlinson Lyrics', in *Essays on Medieval Literature* (Oxford, 1984), pp. 1–26.

Cahn, Kenneth S., 'Chaucer's Merchants and Foreign Exchange: An Introduction to Medieval Finance', *Studies in the Age of Chaucer*, 2 (1980), 81–119.

Cantor, Norman F., 'The Crisis of Western Monasticism', *American Historical Review*, 66 (1960), 47–67.

Carruthers, Mary J., *The Book of Memory: A Study in Medieval Culture* (Cambridge, 1990).

Chibnall, Marjorie, *The World of Orderic Vitalis* (Oxford, 1984).

Chronicles of the Reigns of Stephen, Henry II and Richard I, edited by Richard Howlett, 4 vols., RS 82 (London, 1886).

Chydenius, J., 'Symbolism of Love in Mediaeval Thought', *Commentationes Litterarum Humanarum*, 44 (1970), 1–68.

Clanchy, M.T., *From Memory to Written Record: England 1066–1307* (London, 1979).

Colby, Alice M. *The Portrait in Twelfth-Century French Literature: An Example of the Stylistic Originality of Chrétien de Troyes* (Geneva, 1965).

Colker, Marvin L., 'De Nobilitate Animi', *Mediaeval Studies*, 23 (1961), 47–79.

Collins, Marie, 'Feminine Response to Masculine Attractiveness in Middle English Literature', *Essays & Studies* (1985), 12–28.

Contamine, Philippe, *War in the Middle Ages* (Oxford, 1984).

Crane, Susan, *Insular Romance: Politics, Faith, and Culture in Anglo-Norman and Middle English Literature* (Berkeley, Los Angeles and London, 1986).

Creytens, R., 'Le Manuel de conversation de Philippe de Ferrare, O.P. (†1350), *Liber de introductione loquendi*', *Archivum Fratrorum Praedicatorum*, 16 (1946), 107–35.

Cross, J.E., 'The *Sayings of St Bernard* and *Ubi Sount Qui ante nos Fuerount*', *Review of English Studies*, ns 9 (1958), 1–7.

Cross, Tom Peete, 'The Celtic Element in the Lays of Lanval and Graelent', *Modern Philology*, 12 (1915), 585–644.

Curry, Walter Clyde, *The Middle English Ideal of Personal Beauty; as found in the Metrical Romances, Chronicles, and Legends of the XIII, XIV, and XV Centuries* (Baltimore, Maryland, 1916/1970).

Curtius, E.R., *European Literature and the Latin Middle Ages*, trans. Willard R. Trask (New York, 1953).

Diekstra, F.N.M., 'Chaucer's Way with His Sources: Accident into Substance and Substance into Accident', *English Studies*, 62 (1981), 215–36.

Dobson, E.J., *The Origins of Ancrene Wisse* (Oxford, 1976).

Donaldson, E. Talbot, 'The Myth of Courtly Love', in *Speaking of Chaucer* (London, 1970), pp. 154–63.

Doyle, A.I., 'English Books In and Out of Court from Edward III to Henry VII', in *English Court Culture in the Later Middle Ages*, edited by V.J. Scattergood and J.W. Sherborne (London, 1983), pp. 163–81.

Dronke, Peter, *Medieval Latin and the Rise of the European Love Lyric*, 2nd edn, 2 vols (Cambridge, 1968).

Du Cange, C. du F., *Glossarium Mediae et Infimae Latinitas* (Niort and London, 1884–87).

Duby, Georges, *The Chivalrous Society*, trans. Cynthia Postan (London, 1977).

Duby, Georges, *Medieval Marriage. Two Models from Twelfth-century France*, trans. Elborg Forster (Baltimore, Maryland, 1978).

Duby, Georges, *Que sait-on de l'amour en France au xiie siècle?* (Oxford, 1983).

Duby, Georges, *Love and Marriage in the Middle Ages* (Cambridge, 1994).

Dumville, David N., *Histories and Pseudo-histories of the Insular Middle Ages* (Aldershot, 1990).

Elliott, R.W.V., *Chaucer's English* (London, 1974).

Faral, Edmond, *Les Arts Poétiques du XIIe et du XIIIe siècle* (Paris, 1924).

Faral, Edmond, *La Légende Arthurienne*, 3 vols (Paris, 1929).

Fellows, Jennifer, Rosalind Field, Gillian Rogers, and Judith Weiss, eds, *Romance Reading on the Book: Essays in Medieval Narrative presented to Maldwyn Mills* (Cardiff, 1996).

Ferrante, J.M. and G.D. Economou, *In Pursuit of Perfection. Courtly Love in Medieval Literature* (Port Washington, NY, 1975).

Field, Rosalind, 'Ipomedon to Ipomadon A: Two Views of Courtliness', in *The Medieval Translator: The Theory and Practice of Translation in the Middle Ages*, edited by Roger Ellis (Cambridge, 1989), pp. 135–41.

Finkenstaedt, T., *'You' and 'Thou': Studien zur Anrede im Englischen* (Berlin, 1963).

Fisher, John H., *John Gower: Moral Philosopher and Friend of Chaucer* (London, 1965).

Frappier, Jean, 'Vues sur les conceptions courtoises dans la littératures d'oc et d'oil au xiie siècle', *Cahiers de Civilisation médiévale*, 2 (1959), 135–56.

Frappier, Jean, 'Sur un procès fait à l'amour courtois', *Romania*, 93 (1972), 145–93.

Frappier, Jean, *Amour Courtois et Table Ronde* (Geneva, 1973).

Gallo, Ernest, 'Matthew of Vendôme: Introductory Treatise on the Art of Poetry', *Proceedings of the American Philosophical Society*, 118, no. 1 (1974), 51–92.

Ganshof, F.L., *Feudalism*, trans. Philip Grierson, 3rd edn (London, 1964).

Gilson, E., *The Christian Philosophy of St Thomas Aquinas*, trans. L.K. Shook (New York and Toronto, 1956).

Gravdal, Kathryn, *Vilain and Courtois: Transgressive Parody in French Literature of the Twelfth and Thirteenth Centuries* (Lincoln, Nebraska, 1989).

Gray, Douglas, 'Chaucer and Gentilesse', in *One Hundred Years of English Studies in Dutch Universities*, edited by E.S. Kooper, G.H.V. Bunt, J.L. Mackenzie, and D.R.M. Wilkinson (Amsterdam, 1987), pp. 1–27.

Green, Richard Firth, *Poets and Princepleasers: Literature and the English Court in the Late Middle Ages* (Toronto/Buffalo/London, 1980).

Guddat-Figge, Gisela, *Catalogue of Manuscripts containing Middle English Romances* (Munich, 1976).

Gunn, Alan, *The Mirror of Love* (Lubbock, Texas, 1952).

Hands, Rachel, ed., *English Hawking and Hunting in The Boke of St Albans* (London, 1975).

Heffernan, Carol Falvo, *The Melancholy Muse. Chaucer, Shakespeare and Early Medicine* (Pittsburgh, Penn., 1995).

Herlihy, David, ed., *The History of Feudalism* (Newark, NJ and Brighton, 1979).

Hicks, Eric, *Le Débat sur le Roman de la Rose*, Bibliothèque du xve siècle 43 (Paris, 1977).

Hilton, Rodney, *English and French Towns in Feudal Society: A Comparative Study* (Cambridge, 1992).

Hines, John, *The Fabliau in English* (London, 1993).

Horstmann, C., *Altenglische Legenden, Neue Folge* (Heilbronn, 1884).

Howard, Donald R., *The Three Temptations: Medieval Man in Search of the World* (Princeton, NJ, 1966).

Hunt, Tony, 'The Emergence of the Knight in France and England, 1000–1200', *Forum for Modern Language Studies*, 17 (1981), 93–114.

Jaeger, Stephen C., *The Origins of Courtliness: Civilizing Trends and the Formation of Courtly Ideals, 939–1210* (Philadelphia, 1985).

Jeanroy, Alfred, *La Poésie lyrique des Troubadours* (Toulouse, 1934).

Jones, G.F., *The Ethos of the Song of Roland* (Baltimore, Maryland, 1963).

Karnein, Alfred, '*Amor est Passio* – A Definition of Courtly Love?', in *Court and Poet. Selected Proceedings of the Third Congress of the International Courtly Literature Society (Liverpool 1980)*, edited by G.S. Burgess and Alan Deyermond (Liverpool, 1981), pp. 215–21.

Kelly, H.A., *Love and Marriage in the Age of Chaucer* (Ithaca, NY, 1975).

Kibbee, Douglas A., *For to Speke Frenche Trewely. The French Language in England, 1000–1600: Its Status, Description and Instruction*, Amsterdam Studies in the Theory and History of Linguistic Science 60 (Amsterdam/Philadelphia, 1991).

Kirby, Thomas A., *Chaucer's Troilus: A Study in Courtly Love*, Louisiana State University Studies 39 (Baton Rouge, 1940).

Lawlor, J., ed., *Patterns of Love and Courtesy: Essays in Memory of C.S. Lewis* (London, 1966).

Lazar, Moshé, *Amour courtois et Fin'Amors dans la Littérature du xiie siècle* (Paris, 1964).

LeClercq, Jean, *Monks and Love in Twelfth-century France* (Oxford, 1979).

LeClercq, Jean, 'L'Amour et le Mariage vus par des Clercs et des Religieux, specialement au xiie siècle', in *Love and Marriage in the Twelfth Century*, edited by Willy van Hoecke and Andries Welkenhuysen (Leuven, 1981), pp. 102–15.

Legge, M. Dominica, 'William of Kingsmill – A Fifteenth-century Teacher of French in Oxford', in *Studies in French Language and Literature presented to M.K. Pope* (Manchester, 1939), pp. 241–6.

Legge, M. Dominica, *Anglo-Norman Literature and its Background* (Oxford, 1963).

Lewis, C.S., *The Allegory of Love* (Oxford, 1936).

Lindahl, C., *Earnest Games: Folkloric Patterns in the Canterbury Tales* (Bloomington and Indianapolis, 1987).

McCulloch, Florence, 'The Dying Swan: A Misunderstanding', *Modern Language Notes*, 74 (1959), 289–92.

Mann, J., *Chaucer and Medieval Estates Satire* (London, 1973).

Mathew, Gervase, 'Ideals of Knighthood in Late Fourteenth-century England', in *Studies in Medieval History presented to Frederick Maurice Powicke*, edited by R.W. Hunt, W.A. Pantin, and R.W. Southern (Oxford, 1948), pp. 354–62 .

Mathew, Gervase, *The Court of Richard II* (London, 1968).

Meale, Carol M., 'The Compiler at Work: John Colyns and BL MS Harley 2252', in *Manuscripts and Readers in Fifteenth-century England*, edited by Derek Pearsall (Cambridge, 1983), pp. 82–103.

Mellinkoff, Ruth, *Outcasts: Signs of Otherness in Northern European Art of the Late Middle Ages*, 2 vols (Berkeley, Los Angeles and Oxford, 1993).

Meyer, P., 'Les Manuscrits français de Cambridge', *Romania*, 32 (1903), 18–120.

Michaud-Quantin, P., *Etudes sur le Vocabulaire philosophique du Moyen Age* (Rome, 1970).

Mills, Maldwyn, Jennifer Fellows, and Carol M. Meale, eds, *Romance in Medieval England* (Cambridge, 1991).

Muscatine, C., 'Courtly Literature and Vulgar Language', in *Court and Poet: Selected Proceedings of the Third Congress of the International Courtly Literature Society (Liverpool, 1980)*, edited by G.S. Burgess and Alan Deyermond (Liverpool, 1981), pp. 1–19.

Newman, F.X., ed., *The Meaning of Courtly Love* (Albany, NY, 1968).

Newman, William R., *The Summa Perfectionis of Pseudo-Geber. A Critical Edition, Translation and Study*, vol. 35 (Leiden, 1991).

Nicholls, J.W., *The Matter of Courtesy. Medieval Courtesy Books and the Gawain-Poet* (Woodbridge, 1985).

O'Donoghue, Bernard, *The Courtly Love Tradition* (Manchester, 1982).

Olson, Glending, *Literature as Recreation in the Later Middle Ages* (Ithaca, NY and London, 1982).

Orme, Nicholas, 'The Education of the Courtier', in *English Court Culture in the Later Middle Ages*, edited by V.J. Scattergood and J.W. Sherborne (London, 1983), pp. 64–85.

Paris, Gaston, 'Lancelot du Lac: Le Conte de la Charette', *Romania*, 12 (1883), 459–534.

Payen, Jean-Charles, *Le Motif du Repentir dans la Littérature Française Médiévale (des Origines à 1230)* (Genève, 1967).

Pearsall, Derek, *Old and Middle English Poetry*, The Routledge History of English Poetry, vol. I (London, 1977).

Pearsall, Derek, 'The Franklin's Tale, Line 1469: Forms of Address in Chaucer', *Studies in the Age of Chaucer*, 17 (1995), 69–78.

Pensom, Roger, 'The Lexical Field of "Fiers" in Old French', *Archivum Linguisticum*, ns 1 (1970), 49–66.

Peristiany, J.G., ed., *Honour and Shame. The Values of Mediterranean Society* (London, 1965).

Pickford, Cedric E., 'The *Roman de la Rose* and a Treatise attributed to Richard de Fournival: Two Manuscripts in the John Rylands Library', *Bulletin of the John Rylands Library*, 34 (1951–52), 333–65.

Press, A.R., 'The Precocious Courtesy of Geoffrey Gaimar', in *Court and Poet: Selected Proceedings of the Third Congress of the International Courtly Literature Society (Liverpool 1980)*, edited by G.S. Burgess and Alan Deyermond (Liverpool, 1981), pp. 267–76.

Ramage, Edwin S., *Urbanitas: Ancient Sophistication and Refinement* (Norman, Oklahoma, 1973).

Reiss, Edmund, 'Chaucer's *fyn lovynge* and the Late Medieval Sense of *fine amor*', in *Medieval Studies in Honor of Lillian Herlands Hornstein*, edited by Jess B. Bessinger, Jr, and Robert R. Raymo (New York, 1976), pp. 181–91.

Reiss, Edmund, ' "Fin" Amors: Its History and Meaning in Medieval Literature', *Medieval and Renaissance Studies*, 8 (1979), 74–99.

Reuters, Anna Hubertine, *Friendship and Love in the Middle English Metrical Romances* (Frankfurt, 1991).

Richardson, Helen G., 'Business Training in Medieval Oxford', *American Historical Review*, 46 (1941), 259–80.

Richmond, Colin, 'What a Difference a Manuscript Makes: John Wyndham of Felbrigg, Norfolk (d. 1475)', in *Regionalism in Late Medieval Manuscripts and Texts*, edited by Felicity Riddy (Cambridge, 1991), pp. 129–41.

Richter, M., *Sprache und Gesellschaft im Mittelalter: Untersuchungen zur mündliches Kommunikation in England von der Mitte des elften bis zum Beginn des vierzehnten Jahrhunderts* (Stuttgart, 1979).

Riddy, Felicity, 'Mother Knows Best: Reading Social Change in a Courtesy Text', *Speculum* 71 (1996), 66–86.

Robertson, D.W., *A Preface to Chaucer: Studies in Medieval Perspectives* (Princeton, NJ, 1962).

Robertson, D.W., 'Courtly Love as an Impediment to the Understanding of Medieval Literary Texts', in *The Meaning of Courtly Love*, edited by F.X. Newman (Albany, NY, 1968), pp. 1–18.

Rockinger, Ludwig, *Briefsteller und Formelbucher des 11. bis 14. Jahrhunderts*, Quellen und Erorterung zur Bayerischen Geschichte, Alte Folge 9 (Aalen, 1969).

Rooney, Anne, *Hunting in Middle English Literature* (Cambridge, 1993).

Rothwell, W., 'The Teaching of French in Medieval England', *Modern Language Review*, 63 (1968), 37–46.

Rothwell, W., 'The Role of French in Thirteenth-century England', *Bulletin of the John Rylands Library*, 58 (1975), 445–66.

Salter, Elizabeth, *Fourteenth-Century English Poetry: Contexts and Readings* (Oxford, 1983).

Sayles, G.O., *The Medieval Foundations of England*, 2nd edn (London, 1964).

Scaglione, Aldo, *Knights at Court: Courtliness, Chivalry and Courtesy from Ottonian Germany to the Italian Renaissance* (Berkeley/Los Angeles/Oxford, 1991).

Scattergood, V.J., 'The Originality of the Shipman's Tale', *Chaucer Review*, 11 (1977), 210–31.

Scattergood, V.J., 'Literary Culture at the Court of Richard II', in *English Court Culture in the Later Middle Ages*, edited by V.J. Scattergood and J.W. Sherborne (London, 1983), pp. 29–43.

Scattergood, V.J. and Sherborne, J.W., eds, *English Court Culture in the Later Middle Ages* (London, 1983).

Schaar, Claes, *The Golden Mirror: Studies in Chaucer's Descriptive Technique and Its Literary Background* (Lund, 1967 repr.).

Silverstein, Theodore, *Medieval English Lyrics,* York Medieval Texts (London, 1971).

Smith, Nathaniel B. and Joseph T. Snow, *The Expansion and Transformations of Courtly Literature* (Athens, GA, 1980).

Specht, Henrik, *Poetry and the Iconography of the Peasant: The Attitude to the Peasant in Late Medieval English Literature and in Contemporary Calendar Illustration* (Copenhagen, 1983).

Specht, Henrik, 'The Beautiful, the Handsome, and the Ugly: Some Aspects of the Art of Character Portrayal in Medieval Literature', *Studia Neophilologica*, 56 (1984), 129-46.

Stemmler, Theo, '"My Fair Lady": Parody in Fifteenth-century English Lyrics', in *Medieval Studies Conference, Aachen 1983*, edited by Wolf-Dietrich Bald and Horst Weinstock (Frankfurt, 1983), pp. 205–13.

Stevens, John, *Medieval Romance: Themes and Approaches* (London, 1973).

Tatlock, J.S.P., *The Legendary History of Britain: Geoffrey of Monmouth's Historia Regum Britanniae and its Early Vernacular Versions* (Berkeley, 1950).

Thompson, John J., 'Looking Behind the Book: MS Cotton Caligula A. ii, part 1, and the Experience of its Texts', in *Romance Reading on the Book: Essays in Medieval Narrative presented to Maldwyn Mills*, edited by Jennifer Fellows et al. (Cardiff, 1996), pp. 171–87.

Turville-Petre, Thorlac, 'Humphrey de Bohun and *William of Palerne*', *Neuphilologische Mitteilungen*, 75 (1974), 250–2.

Urquhart, Elizabeth, 'Fifteenth-century Literary Culture, with particular reference to the Patterns of Patronage, focussing on the Patronage of the Stafford Family during the Fifteenth Century' (Unpublished PhD thesis, Sheffield University, 1985).

Walsh, P.G., *Andreas Capellanus on Love* (London, 1982).

Wenzel, Siegfried, *Verses in Sermons: Fasciculus Morum and its Middle English Poems*, Medieval Academy of America Publications 87 (Cambridge, Mass., 1978).

Wenzel, Siegfried, *Preachers, Poets, and the Early English Lyric* (Princeton, NJ, 1986).

White Jr, Lynn, *Medieval Technology and Social Change* (Oxford, 1962).

Whiting, Bartlett Jere and Helen Wescott Whiting, *Proverbs, Sentences, and Proverbial Phrases from English Writings mostly before 1500* (Cambridge, Mass., 1968).

Wilson, D.M., *The Bayeux Tapestry* (London, 1985).

Wimsatt, James I., *Chaucer and the Poems of 'Ch', in University of Pennsylvania MS French 15* (Cambridge, 1982).

Wormald, F., 'Style and Design', in *The Bayeux Tapestry*, edited by Sir Frank Stenton (London, 1965), pp. 25–36.

Yates, Frances A., *The Art of Memory* (London, 1966).

Index

gentillesse, 53, 94, 140–1, 185, 206
Geoffrey de Vigeois, 177
Geoffrey of Monmouth, 15, 122, 126
Geoffrey of Vinsauf, 37
Gest Hystoriale of the Destruction of Troye, 161
Gower, 101, 122, 141
    Balades, 152–3, 160, 172
    Confessio Amantis, 101, 114, 115, 198–9, 211
    Mirour del Omme, 154, 158, 167
    Traitié, 150, 172
Granson, Oton de, 124
Grosseteste, Robert, 155
Guillaume de Lorris, 53, 73, 77, 110
Guillaume IX of Aquitaine, 177
Guy of Warwick, 158

habitus, 165–6, 174
Harley lyrics, 122, 188, 193
Harold, 2, 25
Havelok, 5, 61, 204
hawking, 10, 13, 25, 31
Hengest, 15–18, 137
Henry I, x, 126
Henry II, 11, 61, 96, 102, 124, 126
Henry IV, 94, 132
Heremod, 9
Hereward the Wake, 32
Hippocrates, 95
hired, 23
Hoccleve, 122, 145, 215–16
honeste, 199, 209ff.
Horace, 102, 145
household, 5, 6, 14, 23–4, 34, 59, 79, 95, 129, 187, 191
Huarte, *Examen de Ingenios*, 82, 90
hunting, 13, 25, 31, 54, 106, 205
    manuals, 129, 132ff.
    terminology, 133–4, 194

imaginacioun, 82–3, 98n
Isidore of Seville, 91

Jean de Meun, 107
John of Garlande, 120n

John of Grimestone, 189
John of Hoveden, 157
Jones, G.F., 8
joy (and pity), 9, 66, 80, 159
judicium dei, 20
juvenes, 5

knighthood, 3, 6, 176–7, 194, 205
Kyng Alisaunder, 28, 137, 201
Kyngesmylle, William, 120n

Lactantius, 74n
largesse, 33, 64, 71–3, 75n, 151, 184, 204, 216
Laȝamon, *Brut*, 137–40
Lewis, C.S., 23, 149, 162, 192
Life of St Modwenna, 76
lineage, 7
love-sickness, 169–71
loyalty (*leal, loialte*), 8, 13n
Lydgate, 93, 111, 122, 127, 171

Machaut, Guillaume de, 92, 171
Malory, Sir Thomas, 80, 106, 134
Mann, Jill, 215
Map, Walter, x, 61, 73, 96, 102, 185
mareschal, 6, 21n
    marshal of the hall, 130–1, 135
Marie de Champagne, 150
Marie de France, 20, 33, 43–5, 51, 74, 122, 125–6
    Eliduc, 74
    Lanval, 20, 33, 42–3, 58, 72
Master of Game, 77, 132–4, 202, 213
mastiffs, 76, 97–8n
Matthew of Vendôme, 38
Maxims, xi, 14
mestre, 6, 11, 29, 34, 95, 107, 141
mesure, 64, 68–71, 75n, 80
Morte Arthur, 23
Mum and the Sothsegger, 96

Nennius, 15, 139
Nero, 96
nightingale, 77